Indian People and Society

The Imperial Archives

FROM DISCOVERY TO THE CIVILISATIONAL MISSION: ENGLISH WRITINGS ON INDIA

Volume 2

Indian People and Society

Editor

Pramod K. Nayar

B L O O M S B U R Y

NEW DELHI • LONDON • OXFORD • NEW YORK • SYDNEY

BLOOMSBURY INDIA
Bloomsbury Publishing India Pvt. Ltd
Second Floor, LSC Building No. 4, DDA Complex, Pocket C – 6 & 7,
Vasant Kunj, New Delhi, 110070

BLOOMSBURY, BLOOMSBURY ACADEMIC INDIA and the Diana logo are trademarks of Bloomsbury Publishing Plc

First published in India 2022
This edition published 2022

Bloomsbury Academic
An imprint of Bloomsbury Publishing Plc

ISBN: HB: 978-93-54356-61-2; ePDF: 978-93-54356-66-7
2 4 6 8 10 9 7 5 3 1

Printed & bound in India by Replika Press Pvt. Ltd.

CONTENTS

PREFATORY NOTE

The archival texts have been retained in their original font, style and content in order to clearly show the environment of the time when these documents were produced. It is important to show in a book such as this the views held at that time and the profound effect they had on society. We acknowledge that several of the texts are derogatory about Indians, women and communities of different religious faiths like many hundreds of other colonial-era-based works. While these are clearly unacceptable to us today, we have not attempted to change any wording or redact the texts so that the contemporary reader may experience the rhetoric, attitude and ideologies that so clearly marked the Raj. In places, where the text had been smudged and rendered impossible to read, that specific segment has been deleted.

We would like to make clear that these are not the views held by the editor or Bloomsbury India and do not reflect our mission and values which are clearly stated on our website (https://www.bloomsbury.com/in/connect/about-us/missions-and-values/)

GENERAL INTRODUCTION: ARCHIVE AND EMPIRE

That the British writings on India occupy over several miles of shelf space in the British Library, London, is an apocryphal tale, but one which *may* have substance, given that there was no aspect of the subcontinent that did not pique the curiosity of the British or generate some document or the other.

In his *The Imperial Archive: Knowledge and the Fantasy of Empire* (1993), Thomas Richards demonstrated how the documentation (the subject of considerable work, notably in Bernard Cohn and others) and archivisation not only produced knowledge about the colonies but were also instrumental in generating the fantasy of absolute control. And yet, it is never easy to read these records produced by a diverse set of English, Irish and Scottish missionaries, administrators, men of leisure, nurses, teachers, wives and/or sisters of the men who occupied official posts in the colony, soldiers, mercenaries and others—many of whom, for many reasons, had their own dynamics and tensions with the *English*.

Several approaches to the imperial record exist, and this introductory chapter sets out some of them.[1] In the process, it also flags what the archive does in terms of the imperial structure and processes.[2]

The Power of the Archive

The archive is not a mere compilation of what John Malcolm (1823) advised his officers on the right approach to the native officers, or what Thomas Williamson (1808) described as the potential for the hunt in India. The archive is not a passive reflection of imperial power—it constitutes and constructs it. As diverse commentators—such as Cohn's work on the 'survey modality' (1997) and C.A. Bayly's *Empire and Information* (1999)—have pointed out, the Empire ran on information,

[1] I use the term 'imperial archive' throughout to refer to the corpus of published material across genres, as diverse as maps, geographical accounts, census reports, travelogues, administrative reports, ecclesiastical documents.

[2] These volumes work only with the print archive of British India, although a vast archive of visual material also exists, and has been the subject of significant studies. See, for example, Guégan (2011), Chaudhury (2012), Pinney (2014), Dohman (2017) on colonial photography, and Tobin (1999), De Silva (2011), Eaton (2013), among others, on colonial/imperial art and paintings.

and information-gathering constituted not just an act of power but was a *constituent* of the power structure. It classified, organised and legislated on the subject peoples, through the census, the geographies and anthropological studies. In the process, it defined who is counted as a subject/citizen. For instance, writing about the Todas or the Gonds, and then examining the numbers of Muslim students in schools, both the educationist and the statesman were constructing model imperial citizens who would benefit, resist or accept from 'modern' education. In other words, the imperial archive on education was not merely advocating 'modern' education: it was constructing *educate-able* citizens from among their colonial subjects while abandoning the others. Thus, archivisation and informatisation were ultimately about the power wielded over the identity-making and rights of the subjects.[3]

Relatedly, the archive and the documentation also made the subjects *visible to themselves*. With 'modern' education, for instance, the Indian colonial subject in school or college came to identify themselves in particular ways. They learnt what it means to be a good citizen, to be modern, to develop and demand certain skills, etc. They recognised their location on the civilisational scale in the books they read and assimilated (*primitive* and *non-modern* as opposed to the modern European). In an argument that resonates with my claims above, Antoinette Burton and Isabel Hofmeyr write about the power of the English book:

> The embodiment of English manly authority, the book was not simply 'a surrogate Englishman in his highest and most perfect state,' it was the very emblem of imperial sovereignty—with the rigorous spine a testimony to its singularity, its probity, its titular power … books impressed themselves in the everyday lives of imperial subjects, manifesting the formal values of an elite or bourgeois self and modeling in their material form the coherence and commanding presence of British imperial power itself. (2014: 1–2)

The colonial subjects were told, through these English books, what kind of spiritual and moral training was required for them to 'improve'.

[3] It must be noted that it was not only the human subjects in the colony that became objects and subjects of the imperial archive. Fauna and flora, climate, landscape and topography—indeed the natural world in its entirety—were also archived. For studies, see Edney (1997) and Damodaran et al. (2015), among others.

As A.H. Benton of the Indian Civil Service wrote in *Indian Moral Instruction and Caste Problems*:

> [The Indian] People are on the whole kindly, docile, alert, keen-spirited, high and low, one of the best-mannered peoples in the world, and they would appear to offer a very promising field for right spiritual treatment. (1917: 92)

The education archive, and especially its insistence on moral training and moral apprenticeship of the subjects as a *preliminary* to training for political citizenship, was built on the

> founding assumption … that the native readership of English texts, and the recipients of English education, were amenable to their teachings, which led them to abandon their traditional manners and disciplines. This necessitated a solid moral training to make them good citizens. (Nayar 2020: 142)

The archive also, frequently, captures the rift and fracture within the colonial subject's responses to, say, Western/English education. See, for instance, Syed Mahmood's anguish about the Indian Muslim's refusal to accept this education:

> Such feelings of aversion towards English education entertained by the Mahomedans … stand in sharp contrast to the attitude of the Hindu community.… This difference in the sentiments of the two communities towards English education, is the real key to the reasons of the vast disparity of progress of English education which the two nationalities have respectively made. The effects of this disparity have been most baneful to the interests of British India in general, and to the Mahomedan community in particular. (1895: 23)

In time, the colonial subject, convinced of the 'truth' in the power of the Englishman's word or photographic record, not only accepted the arguments about their inferiority but also welcomed the interventions in the form of the civilisational mission of the Empire. The archive had, therefore, produced the *willing* colonial subject.

In particular cases, such as Thuggee, the archive enabled the colonial structures of law enforcement and the judiciary to enact legislation and, in the process, demonise specific cultural practices. Examining the Thuggee archive, Alexander Macfie writes:

> [W]hereas Sleeman and his colleagues tended to define the activities of the thugs in terms of wickedness, murder, deceit, cowardice and criminality, the thugs themselves tended to evaluate them in terms of courage, enterprise, bravery, daring, cunning, adventure and martial

> skill ... in terms usually associated by both the British and the Indians with the heroic values of war. (2008: 396)

The Archive, the Coloniser, the Colonised and Cultural Exchanges

Shifting focus, Antoinette Burton has demonstrated how the imperial archive also fed into the coloniser's psyche, imagination and political imagination. A pithy summary of how the imperial corpus fuelled, inspired and controlled the social imaginary, policies, attitudes and responses of the Britons in the nineteenth century is available in Burton's *Empire in Question*. Victorian culture, writes Burton,

> as a racialized landscape shaped by decades, if not centuries, of colonial peoples, goods, and ideas coursing through its highways and byways ... as always already imperial not just implicitly but as part of a pedagogical meta-narrative about the relationship of modernity to the world-historical phenomenon of colonialism in world history.... (2011: 2–3)

Burton proposes that English 'sensibility' was shaped by Britain's imperial role and character, and its concomitant racialised hierarchies—thus makes the production and consumption of texts (and commodities) about and from the colonised peripheries central to the making of Britain itself (also see Hall 2002).

The archive also instantiates, other than the racialised power binaries (white/black, coloniser/colonised), cross-cultural *influences* and *exchanges*. Contacts across races, ethnic groups and the coloniser–colonised divide were frequent through the colonial period.

The English language took into itself words from their colonial subjects. They also sought to document the grammars of the languages of the subcontinent for their own officers and staff. As a consequence, a vibrant field of cultural exchanges opened up in the languages, with Indian pandits and English philologists and grammarians collaborating. The imperial archive in this domain shows mutual influences of English on Indian languages and vice versa (including Sanskrit [Naregal 2001]) but also the *organisation* of knowledge around the latter (Lelyveld 1993; Rao 2004; Mir 2010; Auer 2014).[4] Scholars—the famous 'Orientalists'—translated texts from, say, Sanskrit into English. Organisations and societies, such as the Asiatic Society, the

[4] A detailed annotated bibliography on these and other aspects of English colonial discourse on India can be found in Nayar 2021.

Zoological Survey of India, the Archaeological Survey of India, were spaces through which the English statesman, *memsahib* and trader encountered Indian temples, art, food practices, superstitions, systems of healing, among others.

English literary texts, as numerous commentators have shown (Leask 1993; Teltscher 1997), began to introduce Indian 'themes' and motifs, whether the *sati* or the wealth of the country's landscape. This field of literary studies was one of contestation and adaptation (Vishwanathan 1990). Be that as it may, the circulation of the English novel in nineteenth-century India catered to the Indian audience attuned to the melodramatic and informed their own creative work (Joshi 2003). Other commentators like Harish Trivedi (1993) have noted how English literature was received in India and the transactional nature of this reception.

Local experts, *writers* and translators were an integral component of the East India Company and the British government. Even account and trade books were produced through a collaborative project (Ogborn 2007). In other domains, such as translations, Indian scholars like Kasinatha Bhattacharya enabled the work of Charles Wilkins (Davis 2015).

Manners, protocols of civic interaction and norms of social, interracial interaction were also sites where cultural exchange and mutual influence were visible. Even the idea of 'civility', as Anindyo Roy has argued, was treated by the native—and projected as such by *English* textbooks and teachers—as markers of 'modern progress and mobility' (Roy 2005: 11). Therefore, both English and Indian commentators (Webb 1915; El Edroos 1922) produced advice and courtesy books for Indians and Englishmen in India (Nayar 2016, 'Civil Modernity'). These contained suggestions like:

> Members of each class, without entering into political or official discussions and avoiding personal remarks, may have much pleasant intercourse by asking about and describing the manners and customs peculiar to each other's nationality, or about their art, music, poetry and literature.... Talk about sport is most suitable at club. (El Edroos: 89)

The Archive and the Global

Another approach to the imperial archive chooses to see the archive as instantiating not just the sensibilities, attitudes and modes of the British coloniser and the subcontinent's colonised, but as enabling *global and globalising imperial networks.* That is, the archive is seen as embodying not just the binary of an imperial 'centre' and 'periphery' (the colony), but a vast network of global connections. We see this interpretation in the work of John Darwin.

In *The Empire Project: The Rise and Fall of the British World-System, 1830–1970* (2009), Darwin shows how the 'interdependence' of various regions and colonies shaped the British Empire in four specific domains. First, there is the military interdependence of various geopolitical regions:

> the most obvious forms of such inter-dependence were naval and military.... British ability to provide naval protection or to send reinforcements to the scene of a conflict would have been very limited without the resources the imperial system supplied. It was strategic control of the Cape Colony (whose economic value was derisory before 1870) that secured the naval gateway to Asia from European waters. The prime function of Egypt, occupied by the British in 1882, was to preserve British use of the Suez Canal and protect the 'Clapham Junction' of imperial communications. Malta, Aden, Ceylon, Singapore, Hong Kong, Esquimalt (on Vancouver Island), the Falklands and Halifax, Nova Scotia, formed the network of bases from which the Royal Navy patrolled the world's sea-lanes. India played several roles in the British world-system, but perhaps its critical function was to be the main base from which British interests in Asia could be advanced and defended. Indian soldiers and a British garrison paid for by Indian revenues were the 'strategic reserve' of the British system in Asia. Because India played this role, other British possessions and spheres east and south of Suez were largely exempted from the costs of defence—a fact of crucial importance to their economic viability. (3–4)

Then there is the commercial interdependence and linkages:

> Both colonial territories and 'informal' colonies had to compete for investment and credits from London to expand their economies ... with the grand exception of the United States (which had received one-fifth of British foreign investment by 1913), British capital was shuttled by the City of London between the various sectors of its commercial empire (a vast global realm among whose key provinces were Canada, Argentina, India, Australia, Southern Africa, China and the Middle East), employing a calculus of prospective return and speculative gain. (4)

The third domain of such connections would be the demographic interdependence:

> Although two-thirds of British migrants went to the United States up until 1900, almost all the rest were distributed between the four main settlement zones of Canada, Australia, New Zealand and South Africa. Indeed, their economic development was usually seen as being closely dependent upon drawing labour and skills from the British supply.... Between 1834 and 1937, India exported some 30 million people to other British possessions as indentured labour, and perhaps one-fifth remained as permanent settlers. In the tropical empire (which British migrants avoided) they supplied much of the labour and business expertise to promote commercial expansion. (4–5)

Finally,

> the spheres of British expansion were progressively linked by a complex system of communication. From the 1840s onwards, this was provided by subsidised mail services, telegraph wires, undersea cables, an expanding rail network, fast passenger steamers and (in the twentieth century) imperial air routes. (5)

In consonance with the work of Darwin, other commentators have mapped these global connections and interdependencies of the British Empire. Thus, Tony Ballantyne, Jonathan Hyslop, among others, in their contributions to the *New Imperial Histories Reader*, map racial imaginings and knowledge formations, working-class presences across the Empire, from India to Australia and Southern Africa. The migration of people and goods in the 1850–1914 period, argue Gary Magee and Andrew Thompson in *Empire and Globalisation: Networks of People, Goods and Capital in the British World, c. 1850–1914* (2010), was instrumental in the making of an international economy. This, of course, put tremendous pressure on the colonised peoples but also made '"transnationalism"—living in and identifying with more than one country or place—a normal way of life for many British people in the half-century before 1914' (5); an argument that resonates with that of Antoinette Burton about Victorian England cited earlier.

Alan Lester's work in the field of imperial humanitarianism and the 'civilisational mission' has made similar connections to argue for a trans-imperial history. Through the late eighteenth and the nineteenth centuries, notes Alan Lester, we can discern the rise of a 'moral geography of the globe', where the Europeans felt responsible for 'distant strangers' (2000: 278). Thus, imperialism intersected with, fed into and drew from humanitarian ideologies and thought in *different* parts of the world/Empire. Subsequently, Lester et al.'s work focused on not 'national boundaries' (Britain's) but on 'transnational and trans-imperial connections' (2020: 2). They argue that 'the principles of freedom, civilisation and liberalism that motivated them were dissolved in a solution of violent racism through which British power was applied' in *various* colonies and geographical locations (2). Through a reading of three years—1838, 1857 and 1879—and the archive of Victorian imperialist statesmen and legal luminaries like James Stephen, Lester et al. demonstrate the linkage and common foundations (ideological, racism, etc.):

> [T]he ending of slavery and the rise of free trade doctrine, repeated Indian famines and the Uprising of 1857, the First and Second Afghan Wars, the First and Second Opium Wars, the Great Xhosa Cattle Killing and the Anglo-Zulu War, mass emigration from the British Isles, the self-governance of settler colonies in North America, Australasia and southern Africa and the devastation of Indigenous societies. (11)[5]

The Archive in 'New Imperial Histories'

The modes through which the archive has been read and employed have come in for criticism in the *new imperial history* turn. Nicholas Dirks summarises the problem with the slide between the production of the imperial archive and the production of the historical events within imperialism. Dirks writes:

> Begins the histories behind and beneath the production of the kinds of primary sources that have represented colonial knowledge even as they have been used to determine and justify colonial policy. The archive has enshrined, in [Michel] Foucault's sense, this raw material

[5] Philippa Levine and John Marriott in their Introduction to the massive *The Ashgate Research Companion to Modern Imperial Histories* (2012) argue that for many commentators, such as C.A. Bayly, 'modernity' in Europe itself is a consequence of its imperial actions—'The putative simultaneity of Europe's imperial ascent, globalisation and the birth of the modern world has led many to see an intimate interconnectedness.' (2)

However the trouble with this reading is, they note, 'that not only did Europe (or the west if we include the Americas) continue to display significant characteristics that might be regarded as pre-modern, but many of the features identified as modern were to be found equally in societies beyond and often unconnected to Europe.' (2)

> for subsequent historical representation. In the Indian case, the archive is both the precipitate of the history of conquest and rule and the basis on which that history has been written by colonial administrators. (2010: 95)

This 'colonial history' most notably in the 'Cambridge School' of historians, argues Dirks reading the archive of John Seeley and others, was in fact 'colonial fiction', which forwarded the idea that 'Indian politics emerged as a direct reflex of administrative initiatives set in motion by colonial rule' (95). Dirks continues:

> [such colonial histories argued] that local elites, the very groups that had been the collaborators for British rule, turned nationalist—in the context of participation in the progressively enlarged electoral arenas of provincial and municipal politics—when they realized that more of the pie could be obtained through autonomous political institutions than through colonial ones.... (95)

This meant

> [The Cambridge School] proved its arguments by using colonial sources—frequently police records and confidential files—that documented the spurious activities of nationalist figures in what was a large-scale colonial effort to track, contain, and debunk the very politics that sought to overthrow colonial rule. (96)

More recent readings have shown how colonial and imperial legacies and their discursive remains, even in the postcolonial era, turn to and retain its ideologies and representational modes. Nadine Attewell writes in *Better Britons*:

> [in] the afterlife of empire insofar as the projects of nation building with which it is concerned ... sexual reproduction [is the] key to, and a potent figure for, the (re)constitution of the national body after the 'end' of empire. (2014: 6)

This implies that the archive and the historical record—even as we debate what counts as the historical record—is very much an active constituent of the present postcolonial thought and actions as well.

*

The volumes here are only a small sample of the imperial archive. The range and depth of the archive are impossible to encapsulate in a few volumes. While I have made attempts elsewhere to capture some of this variety (Nayar 2007; 2009; 2013; 2016 [*Siege and Prison Writings*]; 2017; 2019), much more is required and possible. For example, the visual archive of the Empire, with its modalities and aesthetic grammars of 'composing' the subcontinent, whether in photography or painting (some of which may be found in Archer 1972), requires much more presence in the form of collections.

The present volumes focus on select aspects of the imperial archive: the accounts of 'discovery' and exploration—flora and fauna, geography, climate—the people of the subcontinent, English domesticity and social life in the subcontinent, the wars and skirmishes—including the *Mutiny* of 1857–1858—and the *civilisational mission.* It excludes legal documents and the many Acts and laws enacted by the British government.

Volume I consists of documents that deal with England's *discovery* of India, its exploration and mapping of the Indian land. This volume includes material as diverse as the letter from India of Thomas Stephens, often called 'the first Englishman in India', chorographic and cartographic accounts from geographical, meteorological, archaeological surveys that the various organisations and societies established for the purpose produced.

Volume II includes English studies of Indian languages and the social order. Ethnographic surveys of the subcontinent's people and cultural practices were published from the late eighteenth century. Practices like female infanticide, sati and thugee, seen as emblematic of the 'barbarous' Oriental, received special attention in the documentation. The characteristics of various tribes and ethnic group were also mapped in considerable detail.

Volume III shifts the focus entirely to the English home and social life. The documents include advice on gardening—an integral part of the English home—and on housekeeping. In the latter, the English were given instructions on how to monitor the domestic economy and manage the servants. Advice manuals on hunting and field sports were also published. Given the interracial dynamics at work, officers were issued manuals on etiquette and behaviour. Accounts of hill-stations and camps, and the social life in the Presidencies make up the rest of the volume.

Volume IV is a collection of accounts of a very different British life in India: as prisoners, under siege and in conditions of war. Starting with the notorious *Black Hole* of Calcutta to the 1857 *Mutiny*, the English wrote about being assailed, besieged and tormented in their war journals and prison accounts. These documented physical and emotional suffering, the losses of families and lives, even as they strove to depict British grit and determination.

Volume V documents England's *civilisational mission*. These documents offer a glimpse into British opinions and strategies on diverse subjects. It includes Macaulay's (in)famous Minute of 1835, accounts of medical missionary activities, views on establishing missionary activities and the British views on women's education.

Works Cited

Archer, Mildred. *Company Drawings in the India Office Library.* London: HMSO, 1972.

Attewell, Nadine. *Better Britons: Reproduction, National Identity, and the Afterlife of Empire.* Toronto: University of Toronto Press, 2014.

Auer, Blain. 'Early Modern Persian, Urdu, and English Historiography and the Imagination of Islamic India under British Rule', *Études de Lettres* 2–3 (2014): 199–206.

Bayly, C.A. *Empire and Information: Intelligence-Gathering and Social Communication in India.* Cambridge: Cambridge University Press, 1999.

Benton, A.H. *Indian Moral Instruction and Caste Problems: Solutions.* London: Longmans, Green and Co., 1917.

Burton, Antoinette and Isabel Hofmeyr. 'Introduction. The Spine of Empire? Books and the Making of an Imperial Commons'. In *Ten Books that Shaped the British Empire: Creating an Imperial Commons*, edited by Antoinette Burton and Isabel Hofmeyr. Durham and London: Duke University Press, 2014.

Burton, Antoinette. *Empire in Question: Reading, Writing, and Teaching British Imperialism.* Durham and London: Duke University Press, 2011.

Chaudhury, Zahid R. *Afterimage of Empire: Photography in Nineteenth-Century India.* Minneapolis: University of Minnesota Press, 2012.

Cohn, Bernard S. *Colonialism and Its Forms of Knowledge: The British in India.* New Delhi: Oxford University Press, 1997.

Damodaran, Vinita, Anna Winterbottom and Alan Lester, eds. *The East India Company and the Natural World.* London: Palgrave Macmillan, 2015.

Darwin, John. *The Empire Project: The Rise and Fall of the British World-System, 1830–1970.* Cambridge: Cambridge University Press, 2009.

Davis, Richard. 'Wilkins, Kasinatha, Hastings, and the First English *Bhagavad Gītā*', *International Journal of Hindu Studies* 19, no. 1–2 (2015): 39–57.

De Silva, Prasannajit. 'Representing Home Life Abroad: British Domestic Life in Early Nineteenth-Century India', *Visual Culture in Britain* 12, no. 3 (2011): 313–331.

Dirks, Nicholas B. 'Coda: The Burden of the Past.' In *The New Imperial Histories Reader*, edited by Stephen Howe, 92–105. Oxford: Routledge, 2010.

Dohman, Renata, ed. *Empire and Art: British India*. Manchester, UK: Manchester University Press, 2017.

Eaton, Natasha. *Colour, Art and Empire: Visual Culture and the Nomadism of Representation*. London: I.B. Tauris, 2013.

Edney, Matthew. *Mapping an Empire: The Geographical Construction of British India, 1753–1843*. Chicago: University of Chicago Press, 1997.

El Edroos, Aboobaker. *Modern Indian Etiquette: Of Mixed Society, Describing Ancient Social Usages and Important Indian Manners and Customs, Aiming at Social Amity Between Indians and Non-Indians*. Surat: H.R. Scott at the Mission Press, 1922.

Guégan, Xavier. 'Visualizing Alienation: Symbolism and Duality in Samuel Bourne's Photographs of British India', *Visual Culture in Britain* 12 no. 3 (2011): 349–365.

Hall, Catherine. *Civilising Subjects: Colony and Metropole in the English Imagination, 1830–1867*. Chicago: University of Chicago Press, 2002.

Joshi, Priya. *In Another Country: Colonialism, Culture, and the English Novel in India*. Oxford: Oxford University Press, 2003.

Leask, Nigel. *British Romantic Writers and the East: Anxieties of Empire*. Cambridge: Cambridge University Press, 1993.

Lelyveld, David. 'The Fate of Hindustani: Colonial Knowledge and the Project of a National Language'. In *Orientalism and the Postcolonial Predicament: Perspectives on South Asia*, edited by Carol Breckenridge and Peter van der Veer, 189–214. Philadelphia: University of Pennsylvania Press, 1993.

Lester, Alan, Kate Boehme and Peter Mitchell. *Ruling the World: Freedom, Civilisation and Liberalism in the Nineteenth-Century British Empire*. Cambridge: Cambridge University Press, 2021.

Lester, Alan. 'Obtaining the "due observance of justice": The geographies of colonial humanitarianism', *Environment and Planning D Society and Space* 20, no. 3 (2000): 277–293.

Levine, Philippa and John Marriott, eds. *The Ashgate Research Companion to Modern Imperial Histories*. London: Ashgate, 2016.

Macfie, Alexander Lyon. 'Thuggee: An Orientalist Construction?' *Rethinking History* 12, no. 3 (2008): 383–397.

Magee, Gary and Andrew Thompson. *Empire and Globalisation: Networks of People, Goods and Capital in the British World, c. 1850–1914*. Cambridge: Cambridge University Press, 2010.

Mahmood, Syed. *History of English Education in India, Its Rise, Development, Progress, Present Condition and Prospects. Being a Narrative of the Various Phases of Educational Policy and Measures Adopted under the British Rule from Its Beginning to the Present Period (1781 to 1893)*. Aligarh: M.A-O. College, 1895.

Malcolm, John. 'Notes of Instructions to Assistants and Officers Acting under the Orders of Major-General Sir John Malcolm, GCB.' In *A Memoir of*

Central India: Including Malwa, and Adjoining Provinces, Vol. 2, edited by John Malcolm. London: Kingsbury, Parbury and Allen, 1823.
Mir, Farina. *The Social Space of Language: Vernacular Culture in British Colonial Punjab*. Berkeley: University of California Press, 2010.
Naregal, Veena. *Language Politics, Elites, and the Public Sphere: Western India under Colonialism*. New Delhi: Permanent Black, 2001.
Nayar, Pramod K. 'English Discourse and India'. *Oxford Bibliographies Online*. New York: Oxford University Press, 2021, https://www.oxfordbibliographies.com/view/document/obo-9780190221911/obo-9780190221911-0114.xml.
______. 'Civil Modernity: The Management of Manners and Polite Imperial Relations in India, 1880–1930', *South Asia: Journal of South Asian Studies* 39, no. 4 (2016): 740–757.
______. 'Moral Readership and Political Apprenticeship: Commentaries on English Education in India, 1875–1930'. In *The Edinburgh History of Reading. Vol. IV. Subversive Readers*, edited by Jonathan Rose, 138–161. UK: Edinburgh University Press, 2020.
______. *Colonial Education and India*, 5 vols. London: Routledge, 2019.
______. *Days of the Raj: Life and Leisure in British India*. New Delhi: Penguin, 2009.
______. *English Siege and Prison Writings: From the 'Black Hole' to the 'Mutiny'*. London: Routledge, 2016.
______. *Indian Travel Writing, 1830–1947*. 1830–1947, 5 vols.
______. *The Penguin 1857 Reader*. New Delhi: Penguin, 2007.
______. *Women in Colonial India: Historical Documents and Sources*, 5 vols. London: Routledge, 2013.
Ogborn, Miles. *Indian Ink: Script and Print in the Making of the English East India Company*. Chicago and London: Chicago University Press, 2007.
Orsini, Francesca. *The Hindi Public Sphere: Language and Literature in the Age of Nationalism*. Oxford: Oxford University Press, 2010.
Pinney, Christopher. 'Sepia Mutiny: Colonial Photography and Its Others in India.' In *Feeling Photography*, edited by Elspeth Brown and Thy Phu, 71–92. Durham, NC: Duke University Press, 2014.
Rao, Velcheru Narayana. 'Print and Prose: Pundits, *Karanams*, and the East India Company in the Making of Modern Telugu'. In *India's Literary History: Essays on the Nineteenth Century*, edited by Stuart Blackburn and Vasudha Dalmia, 146–166. New Delhi: Permanent Black, 2004.
Richards, Thomas. *The Imperial Archive: Knowledge and the Fantasy of Empire*. London: Verso, 1993.
Roy, Anindyo. *Civility and Empire: Literature and Culture in British India, 1822–1922*. London: Routledge, 2005.
Teltscher, Kate. *India Inscribed: European and English Writing on India, 1600–1800*. Delhi: Oxford University Press, 1997.

Tobin, Beth Fowkes. *Picturing Imperial Power: Colonial Subjects in Eighteenth-Century British Painting*. Durham, NC: Duke University Press, 1999, 110–138.

Trivedi, Harish. *Colonial Transactions: English Literature and India*. Calcutta: Papyrus, 1993.

Viswanathan, Gauri. *Masks of Conquest: English Literary Studies and India*. London: Faber & Faber, 1990.

Webb, William Trego. *English Etiquette for Indian Gentlemen*. 5th ed. 1895. Calcutta: S.K. Lahiri, 1915.

Williamson, Thomas. *Oriental Field Sports*. London: W. Bulmer, 1808.

INTRODUCTION

The landscape provided, understandably, endless prospects of the survey and the map. But the British were also keen on documenting the people. In the studies generated for 400 years, the British documented castes, religions, education, economies, professions, cultural practices, states of health and sickness, and other domains. With projects like the Census and the *People of India*, the land's inhabitants were classified and, eventually, also typecast—the 'evil' Brahmin, the 'poor' *sati*, the 'murderous' *thug* emerged from and contributed to the colonial discourse about the native/colonised.

The archive was also added to other domains. The languages of the subcontinent were of perpetual interest to the British statesman, grammarian and the curious officer in the Company. The codification, translation and documentation of languages, the preparation of dictionaries and guidebooks for the British officer proceeded, with its 'orientalist' agenda but also as a mode of knowledge gathering and production.

Thomas Roe's extended stay in the court of Jahangir as documented in his account offers his perspective on cultural exchanges with the Mughals, including the *darbar*, the customs officials and the ceremonies that attend these settings. Rivers's account of the *todas* provides numerous ethnographic details, whereas the *Census of India* and Risley's *The People of India* did so for the entire subcontinent. These texts eventually became authoritative interpretations for statesmen, policy makers and even the general public back in Britain, when consumed at Royal Society gatherings and in the form of reviews in periodicals. Then there are texts from Fanny Parkes, John Fryer, John Kaye and W.H. Sleeman, which focus on specific events, regions and people. This could be in the form of a travelogue (Parkes and Fryer), or in the form of a report-cum-memoir (Sleeman and Kaye), covering subjects that fascinated the British: female infanticide, thugee and *sati*. The Indian languages produced works like Gilchrist's excerpted here, paving the way for the Linguistic Survey of India later. The grand spectacle of the 'imperial assemblage' created to reinforce racial and administrative hierarchies while also co-opting the native rulers and princes into the Raj finds its document in the Talboys Wheeler excerpt.

Colonial discourse, as several of the documents show, emphasized British spectacle as a contrast to Indian ruins, presenting the British as saviours, conservationists, and protectors—whether from predatory animals or bandits.

ACKNOWLEDGEMENTS

The Raj has been a perennial favourite when it comes to research and writing, and I cannot remember a year when I did *not* do some 'Raj work'.

Chandra Sekhar of Bloomsbury was very receptive to the project idea, and has been incisive and encouraging when it came to subjects like the volumes' organisation, content and final form—to him, this project owes much.

I express my thanks to journals and anthologies, and their editors and reviewers whose comments have enabled me to sharpen my thoughts on the Raj-topic-of-the-moment. Among journals, I acknowledge: *South Asia, South Asian Review, Anglo-Saxonica* and *Asiatic*. Among the anthologies, I acknowledge *Ireland's Imperial Connections*; *The Edinburgh History of Reading*; *The English Renaissance, Orientalism, and the Idea of Asia*; *Cultural Histories of India*. To Debra Johanyak and Walter S. Lim, Rita Banerjee, Daniel Roberts and Jonathan Wright, Mary Hammond and Jonathan Rose, editors of these fabulous anthologies, many thanks for your invitation to contribute and the work you put into the volumes of which I am now a part.

To Kate Teltscher, whose work *India Inscribed* showed me where to go way back in the mid-1990s, I owe an intellectual debt of enormous proportions.

I am also grateful to publishers and editors at Penguin, Bloomsbury, Palgrave-Macmillan, Edinburgh University Press, Orient BlackSwan, Wiley-Blackwell and Routledge for their comments, suggestions and, above all, interest in this area and my contributions to it.

To Soma Ghosh, Librarian (English) at the Salar Jung Museum, Hyderabad, and her constant efforts, all undertaken with cheer and grace, to obtain materials when I have worked there, immeasurable gratitude.

Many books germinate in conversations with Anna Kurian, who is always enthusiastic about any Raj-work I do, especially if they are multivolume projects. For the constant-traveller role that you assay with such commitment, solidarity and affection, it is my privilege, Anna, to acknowledge you.

Thank you, Molly ('Chechu'), for enquiring lovingly about her 'little one'.

Nandana Dutta has been unceasing in her interest in my work, and her always gentle and loving urging to think in certain ways, even as she tries to catch up with her reading of what I publish. To your attention, insights and perspicacity, Nandana—much, much gratitude.

Professor K. Narayana Chandran established, for some of us willing ones, the standards in academic scholarship and publishing—that he sustains these standards even now, after four decades, is nothing short of the marvellous. To KNC's indomitable spirit of inquiry and work ethic, and showing us the way to do things, I am very grateful.

Friends who drop in 'WhatsAppingly', regularly, to check on me—Neelu, Bhalla, Ajeet, Kulsoom, Om, Archana, Ashish, Krishna Ram, Sai Jawahar, Savita, Vaishali, Soma and Zahid—thank you.

To Nandini, Pranav, my parents and parents-in-law, I owe unquantifiable gratitude, for never complaining at the volume of work I take on, my frequently distracted state of being and, more importantly, for creating an extraordinarily supportive environment.

And thank you, Shubha, for obtaining, wizard-like, essays and journal articles in minutes, and for your enthusiasm for my work.

To the works of P.G. Wodehouse, Agatha Christie, Stephen King, the comics around Batman—my regular reading—many of which unwittingly capture the horror, the abyss and the comedy of academia, I can never express enough gratitude.

It is a pleasure to thank Atul Nair who compiled many of the materials meticulously.

I am grateful to the Institution of Eminence (IoE) project's Professional Development Fund.

Thomas Roe

***The Embassy of Sir Thomas Roe to India, 1615–19, as Narrated in his Journal and Correspondence*, edited by William Foster. London: Oxford University Press, Humphrey Milford, 1926.**

January 10.—I went to Court at 4 in the euening to the *Durbar*,[1] which is the Place wher the. Mogull sitts out daylie, to entertayne strangers, to receiue petitions and presents, to giue Commandes, to see, and to bee seene. To digresse a little from my reception, and declare the Customes of the Court, will enlighten the future discourse. The king hath no man but Eunuchs that Comes within the lodgings or retyring roomes of his house: His weomen watch within, and guard him with manly weapons. They doe Justice on vpon another for offences. He comes every Morning to a wyndow called the *Jarruco*[2] looking into a playne before his gate, and showes him selfe to the Common People. At noone hee returns thither and sitts some howers to see the fight of Eliphants and willd beasts; vnder him within a rayle attend the men of rancke; from whence hee retiers to sleepe among his woemen. At after-noone he returnes to the *Durbar* before mentioned. At 8 after supper he Comes downe to the *Gazelcan*,[3] a faire Court, wher in the middest is a Throune erected of free stone

[1] In Mr. Douglas's *Bombay and Western India* (i, p. 305) is given a coloured drawing from an old painting at Jaipur which, in the author's opinion, represents the Emperor Jahángír giving audience to Sir Thomas Roe. Such an interpretation, however, appears exceedingly doubtful, for the figure pointed out as Roe is not only very unlike him in appearance, but occupies quite a subordinate position in the picture. Moreover, the costume and weapons are native, whereas we know from Terry (p. 218) that Roe and his suite wore always English dress. "For my Lord Ambassadour and his Company, we all kept to our English habits, made as light and coole as possibly we could have them; His wayters in Red Taffata cloakes, guarded with green Taffata, which they alwayes wore when they went abroad with him; myself in a long black Cassock." We must therefore take leave to doubt the correctness of the ascription, especially as no such claim was put forward when the picture was first brought to notice in the *Journal of Indian Art*, No. 25 (1889).

[2] The *Jharukhá*, or "interview-window," which Roe describes at greater length later. The royal headquarters were at the fort, now called the Magazine, on the city side of which there is a window answering to Roe's description (*Rajputana Gazetteer*, ii, p. 123).

[3] *Ghuzl-khána*, "bath-room," hence "private apartment" (privy chamber).

wherein he sitts, but some tymes below in a Chayre; to which are none admitted but of great qualetye, and few of these without leaue; wher he discourses of all matters with much Affabilitye.[1] Ther is noe busines done with him Concerning the state, gouerment, disposition of warr or peace, but at one of these two last Places, wher it is publiquely propounded, and resolued, and soe registred,[2] which if it were woorth the Curiositye might bee seene for two shillings, but the Common basse people knew as much as the Councell, and the Newes euery day is the kings new resolutions tossed and censured by euery rascall. This Course is vnchangeable, except sicknes or drinck preuent yt; which must be known, for as all his Subjects

[1] Compare Terry's account (p. 389):—

"First, early in the morning, at that very time the Sun begins to appear above the Horizon, He appears unto his people in a place very like unto one of our Balconies, made in his houses or Pavilions for his morning appearance, directly opposite to the East, about seven or eight foot high from the ground; against which time a very great number of his people, especially of the greater sort, who desire as often as they can to appear in his eye, assemble there together, to give him the *Salam*, or good morning, crying all out, as soon as they see their King, with a loud voice, *Padsha Salamet*, which signifies, *live O great King*, or *O great King, health and life*. . . . At noon he shows himself in another place like the former, on the South-side; and a little before Sun-set, in a like place, on the West-side of his house or Tent; but as soon as the Sun forsakes the Hemisphear, he leaves his people, ushered in and out with Drums and Winde instruments, and the peoples acclamations. . . . And between seven and nine of the clock at night, he sits within his House or Tent more privately, in a spacious place called his *Goozalcan*, or bathing house, made bright like day by abundance of lights; and here the King sits mounted upon a stately Throne; where his Nobles, and such as are favoured by him, stand about him; others find admittance to, but by special leave from his Guard, who cause every one that enters that place to breath upon them, and if they imagine that any have drunk wine, they keep him out."

"At this time my Lord Ambassadour made his usual addresses to him, and I often waited on him thither, and it was a good time to do business with that King, who then was for the most part very pleasant, and full of talk unto those who were round him, and so continued till he fell asleep (oft times by drinking), and then all assembled immediately quitted the place, besides those who were his trusted servants, who by turns watched his Person."

[2] See Blochmann's *Áin-i-Akbari*, i, p. 258.

are slaues, so is he in a kynd of reciprocall bondage, for he is tyed to obserue these howres and Customes so precisely that if hee were vnseene one day and noe sufficient reason rendred the people would mutinie; two dayes noe reason can excuse, but that he must consent to open his doores and bee seene by some to satisfye others.[1] On Tuesday at the *Jarruco* he sitts in Judgment, neuer refusing the poorest mans Complaynt, where hee heares with Patience both parts: and some tymes sees with too much delight in blood the execution done by his Eliphants. *Illi meruere: sed quid tu vt adesses?*[2]

At the *Durbar* I was led right before him, at the enterance of an outward rayle, where mett mee two Principall Noble slaues to conduct mee nearer. I had required before my going leaue to vse the Customes of my Country, which was freely granted, soe that I would performe them Punctually. When I entred within the first rayle I made a reuerance; entering in the inward rayle a Nother; and when I came vnder the king a theird. The Place is a great Court, whither resort all sorts of people. The king sitts in a little Gallery ouer head; Ambassidors, the great men and strangers of qualety within the inmost rayle vnder him, raysed from the ground, Couered with Canopyes of veluet and silke, vnder foote layd with good Carpetts; the Meaner men representing gentry within the first rayle, the people without in a base Court, but soe that all may see the king. This sitting out hath soe much affinitye with a Theatre—the manner of the king in his gallery; The great men lifted on a stage as actors; the vulgar below gazing on—that an easy description will informe of the place and

---

[1] Cp. *Bernier's Travels* (Constable's edn.), pp. 265-6. An admirable description of the Mogul court and system of government will be found in Mr. Stanley Lane-Poole's *Life of Aurangzib.*

[2] This may be freely rendered: "Doubtless they have merited their punishment; but why should you be present?"

fashion. The king preuented my dull enterpreter, bidding me welcome as to the brother of my Master. I deliuered his Majesties lettre translated; and after my Commission, wheron hee looked Curiously; after, my presents, which were well receiued. He asked some questions, and with a seeming Care of my health, offering me his Phisitions, and aduising mee to keepe my house till I had recouered strength; and if in the interim I needed anything I should freely send to him, and obteyne my desiers. He dismissed me with more fauour and outward grace (if by the Christians I were not flattered) then euer was showed to any Ambassador, cyther of the Turke or Persian, or other whatsoeuer.[1]

January 12.—Hee sent a gentellman for my Commission to show his queene the seale, which he kept one night, and returned yt with such care that the bringer durst not deliuer it but to my owne handes.[2]

January 14.—I sent to the Prince Sultan Coronne, his third sonne by byrth but first in fauour, that I determined to visitt him, not doubting he would vse me with due respect; for I was enformed he was enemy to all Christians and therfore feared some affront. He answered I should be welcome, and receiue the same Content I had from his father. Hee is lord of Suratt, our cheefe residence, and his fauour important for us.

January 15-21.—These dayes I stirred not abroad, the

---

[1] Some additional details of Roe's presentation will be found in his letters on pp. 110 and 118. His commission and King James's letter are printed in Appendix B.

[2] This incident (omitted by Purchas) is significant. Probably Núr Mahál had expressed a doubt whether Roe were really a properly accredited ambassador, or (like his predecessors) a mere emissary of the merchants.

It is scarcely necessary to recall the romantic story of Núr Mahál (better known by her later title of Núr Jahán)—her marriage to Shír Afgan, his assassination, and her subsequent union with the emperor, who had already been attracted to her before her first marriage. At this period her influence over her husband was so unbounded that she practically ruled the empire, and Roe soon found out the error he had made in not seeking to conciliate her and her partisans.

offer; professing to be ignorant of anything past, but what hee had receiued by Asaph Chan[1] deliuered by mee; especially of any Command to dismisse us,[2] which the Gouernor had falsly Coyned and for which he should dearly answer. Soe he dismissed mee full of hope to rectifye the decayed estate of our reputation, with promise of a *firmaen* for Suratt effectually.

January 24.—I went to the *Durbar* to visitt the King, who, seeing mee afarr off, beckned with his hand, giuing signe I should not staye the Cerimony of Asking leaue but Come vp to him; where hee appoynted me a place aboue all other men, which I after thought fitt to mayntayne.[3] I gaue him a small present,[4] it beeing the Custome when any body hath busines to giue somewhat, and those that cannot come neare to speake send in or hould up their guift, which hee eccepts, bee it but a *rupie*, and demands their bussines. The same course hee held with

---

[1] Mírza Abul Hasan, better known by his title of Ásaf Khán. He held a strong position at court, as son of the prime minister, elder brother of Núr Mahál, and father of Prince Khurram's favourite wife, Mumtáz Mahál. When the prince came to the throne as Sháh Jahán, Ásaf Khán was advanced to high dignities; and he died (November, 1641) in possession of great wealth. His eldest son was Sháista Khán, who, as Governor of Bengal, came into collision with the English settlers at Húglí.

[2] See pp. 74, 79. After Roe's departure the Governor had forced the General and others to give an undertaking in writing "for clearing the Cuntry after the expiration of one yeare to come, sayeing it was the great Mugolls pleasure to be soe ordred; yett not anye wayes denying vs free trade, but enioyned vs not to make any residence of aboad longer then our shipps were theare" (Peyton's Journal, f. 34).

[3] The exact position of each dignitary was minutely regulated (See *Áín-i-Akbari*, i, p. 160).

[4] A "clock and two other trifles" (*Letter to E. I. Co.*, January 25, 1615-16; reproduced in part at p. 118).

None of the presents given to the Mogul by Roe from time to time has been traced in after years. Mr. Keene, in 1874, exhibited to the Archæological Society of Agra an English striking watch, found in a well in the Fort there, which from its date (1614) he considered was probably one of the novelties brought by Roe for the emperor; but this, though not impossible, is only a conjecture.

mee. Having looked Curiously and asked many questions of my present, he demanded what I required of him. I answered: Justice: That, on the assurance of his Majesties *Firmaen* sent into England, the king my Master had not only giuen leaue to many of his subjects to come a dangerous voyadge with their goodes, but had sent mee to Congratulate the amytye so happely begunne betweene two soe mighty Nations, and to Confirme the same: But that I found the English seated at Amadauas[1] enjured by the Gouernor in their Persons and goodes, fined, exacted upon, & kept as prisoners: that at euerie Towne new Customes were taken of our goodes passing to the Port, contrarie to all Iustice and the former Articles of trade.[2] To which hee answered hee was sorry: it should be amended; and presently gaue order for two *firmanes* very effectually according to my desire to be signed, one to the Gouernor of Amadavaz to restore mony exacted from Master Kerridge,[3] and to vse the English with all fauour. The

---

[1] Ahmadábád.

[2] Roe had consulted Ásaf Khán, who had "encouraged him to complayne," that particular city "beeing absolute under the King."

[3] Thomas Kerridge, who in the following month (February 18, 1616) was chosen agent at Surat in succession to Aldworth. He had gone out with Best in 1612, and had spent some time at the Mogul court after the death of Canning. On Edwards' arrival, Kerridge moved down to Ahmadábád to provide indigo for the lading of the fleet. His letters from that city, and later from Surat, will be found in Brit. Mus. *Addl. MS.* 9366. As will be seen, his imperious temper led to much friction between him and Roe, and though the latter acknowledged his opponent to be "quick and sufficient," he held that he had "too much heate and opinion of abilitye."

Kerridge was back in England by June, 1622, but in January, 1624, he was reappointed agent at Surat. He reached his post in October, and remained until 1628. After his return he was elected a "Committee" of the Company, and served almost continually till 1648. In 1646 he was nominated for the post of Deputy-Governor, but was not elected. In 1654-55 he took part in the management of the United Joint Stock; and this is the last trace we have of him.

The wrongs complained of in the text are detailed in Kerridge's letters mentioned above. At Ahmadábád, a dispute with a native merchant over some indigo led to their broker being beaten and imprisoned. Kerridge himself was beaten; and in addition was

other to release all Customes required on any pretence on the way, or if any had beene taken to repay it; of his owne accord wishing mee that, if these gaue not speedy remedy, I should renew my Complaynt against the disobeyour, and hee should be sent for to answere there. And soe hee dismissed mee.

January 25-30.—I Made my dispatches for England, and wrote earnestly to the factory at Suratt for a Particular of the Gouernors debts, exactions and Iniuryes;[1] and solicited the *firmaens* Promised, of which the Prince sent by his officers one for Suratt, but withall Articles for mee to signe very dishonorable, wherin among others it was required that I should firme a Peace and safe Conduct to the Portugalles shippes and frigotts to Come safely to Suratt, without any accord, promise or Counter securytye of Peace on their Partes; which I vtterly refused, but made offer that for the Princes sake I was Content to giue the Viceroy of Goa 6 Monthes liberty to enter into leauge, and to open the Portes. But the present writing was required to be sealed; wherby, besydes the folly and dishonor, they might vnder coullor of Frendship haue rode amonge our fleete with boates laden with fire woorkes to haue taken aduantage. So, as I absolutely rejected the Motion, I was answered I should then haue no *firmaen* for Suratt. Soe it rested two dayes. I, supposinge the fault only in the Princes officers, sent to Asaph Chan, to complayne of the vnequalle demandes of Sultan Carronne and that the *firmaen* promised beeing sealed was deteyned from mee, Contrarye to all the Prinnces faire woordes and

fined on the pretext that he had defrauded the governor of the estate of Aldworth, who was alleged to have died in the town and to have been carried forth by the English to escape the confiscation of his goods. When the English merchandise was ready to start for Surat the governor demanded four per cent. duty, though at last he accepted one and a half per cent., and a bribe of a hundred rupees.

[1] This had been asked for by the Prince at the late interview.

September 20.—In the Morning the Generall dispatched Bidolf ashoare with a lettre signed by the Generall to the Gouernor of Suratt, to signifie my arriuall; the Coppie I keepe in my boock.[1] At two a Clocke wee weighed, having sounded the barr 3 foote at lowe water, and with the last quarter ebb stood back two mile to the edge of the barr, and some what nearer the land, and Came to Anchor at 5 fadom and a halfe at Lowe water, bringing the lowe smooth poynte with the two highe Palmeto trees S. by E. and the Northwardmost land showeing like an Island N.N.E.

September 21.—The Generall sent ashoare, but had no returne. The *Expedition* gott over the Barr.[2]

September 22.—A Messenger came from the Gouernor of Suratt with answer of the lettre, a Complement that I should be welcome, and if I would dessigne the daye he would send 30 horse for my traine, and his Commanders to meette me, and in all things studdie to giue me that Contentment his power or the means of the Place did affoord; and if the Merchants could find a howse emptie, he would Command it for me. But because hee offered me none, I sent to take one.

September 23.—I sent ashoare about my house, and with a Complement to the Gouernor this Message, that, vnder-

[1] See folio 56 of the MS. It announces that in consequence of the friendly reception of former messengers and the agreement made with Captain Best, the King of England, "for the better establishment and Confirmation of the said happy amytie and loue" has sent a "nobleman of his Court and Chamber, with letters of Credence and rich Presents . . . . authorised with full Commission vnder the Great Seale of England and firma of his Majestie as his Ambassador as well to Congratulate the said mighty King the Great Mogull as to propound, treate, and conclude of sundry Matters of Consequence;" and it gives notice that the envoy proposes to land and repair to some town of rest (having been long at sea) until the pleasure of the Emperor is known as to his journey to the Court.

[2] "Soe that I could comaund boeth sea and land round me with my ordnance, by which meanes our boates going and retoarning from the shoare weare secured from pilfering vessells & friggottes, which otherwise would haue intercepted them, as in former voyadges" (Peyton's Journal, p. 29).

standing the Custome of the Kings officers to search euerie thing that came ashoare, euen to the Pocketts of mens Cloathes on their backs, for Custome, I, beeing an Ambassador from a Mightie King, did expect to haue all things appertayninnge to myselfe and my Followers free by priuiledg; giuinge him the woord of one of my qualetye that there should not be landed vnder that protection one penny woorth of Marchandize, and that if any such affront were offered me, I would returne to the shipes, vntill I had order from the King his Master.

This day I dispatched a lettre to Master Edwardes at Adiumere the Mogulles Court, which the Generall signed with me, the Coppie whereof I keepe.[1]

September 24.—Answer was returned that it was the Custome of this Cuntrie that nothing could passe but by the Custome house, and thear to be searched; but, because they would doe me as much fauour as they could answere, the Gouernor would send an officer to the waterside to take note of those things belonging to me and seale them, and they should goe without stopp to my house, wher the Customer should Come and visitt them, but not in the nature of a search, but only to be able to answere they had seene what I landed; for myselfe and my followers, they should be free from all offer of affront. After some dispute with the Messenger, I yeeilded to yt, and returned answer that on the morow, the 25, I would land my Chests and on the 26 come ashoare in expectation of the horses and Company offered and the Honorable reception promised by the Gouernor.

September 25.—I landed my Chests and prouitions, with directions to suffer them to be sealed, but not opened; and to deliuer them at my house and to prepare yt next day. This day came a handsome frigatt from Cambaya with a

[1] See f. 56 of the MS. It announces Roe's arrival and directs Edwards to acquaint the King therewith.

principall Seruant of the Gouernors aboord the Generall, and with Complements of Frendship and desire of trade to theyr towne as a head City. He gaue the Generall a Present of sweetmeates and some fewe stuffs in the Name of the Gouernor, and desiring to buy some varietyes or toyes for theyr Master, especially enquiring for English Swyne for the Mogull, in which beast hee takes infinite delight, having had two from one ship the last yeare; telling the Generall he should find the new Gouernor of Suratt a Clowne and a frend of our enemyes, but that if wee would make our residence at Cambaya we should receiue notable Content. The Generall tould them ther was an Embassador sent by the king of England, that was the next Morning to land, a man of qualetye: and vntill he sawe what reception he should fynd, and how theyr busines stood with the factory, with the Principalls wher-off he had not spoken, he could resolue nothing; but in other Complements gaue them Content. At this name of an Ambassador they laughd one vpon another; it beeing become ridiculous, so many hauing assumed that title, and not performed the offices; and though the Generall did endeauour to make them better vnderstand yt, they would not, and so did neuer offer to uisitt me. Besides, when the Generall dealt with the *Makadow*[1] of Swally (a frend to the English) that they must not esteeme me in the qualetye of my forerunners, with all the right he Could doe to honor his Majestie, yet he when he was ashore answered he could not tell, nor any else, but that I might be an Imposture as well as the rest; and this was dayley objected unto vs, euen from the Cheefe of Suratt. I mention these only to lett the Company vnderstand how meanly an Embassador was esteemed at my landing; how they subiected them-selues to all searches and barbarous Customes, and became

---

[1] Hindustani *mokuddum*, from the Arabic *mukaddam*, a head-man.

sutors to the Gouernors and great men, who, as appears by the discourse Following, sufficiently vnderstand the rights belonging to that qualetye; and that therefore, if it seeme to any that shall heare of my first carriadge that I was eyther too stiff, to Punctuall, too high, or to Prodigall, lett them Consider I was to repayre a ruynd house and to make streight that which was crooked. If I had beene the first that euer landed vnder that title, I would haue done noe less; and I best know that see yt, these men triumph ouer such as yeeld, and are humble enough when they are held vp. The Kings Honor was engaged more deepely then I did expect, and I was resolued eyther to rectifye all or lay my life and fortune both in the ground.

September 26.—A sine beeing made from land that the Suratts were come ready to receiue me, I landed, accompanyed with the Generall and the Captaines and the Principall Merchannts; The Generall having first sent 100 shott by Captaine Harris to make me a Court of Guard, and the shippes in their best Equipage giuing me their ordinance as I passed; with his trumpetts and Musique ahead my boate in the best manner he Could, which I only signify for acknowledgment vnto him.[1] At my landing the cheefe officers of Suratt with about 30 Companions wer sitting vnder an open Tent vpon good Carpetts, in graue order. Comming almost to them and they not rising, I stayd and sent them woord I would not come farthur if they satte still; whervpon they all rose, and I entered the tent and went streight vp and tooke my place in the middest of them, turning my face toward the Generall

---

[1] "The Lorde Ambassador landed, being accompanied by the generall, captains, and merchants of the fleet (on shoare), for his Lordshipps better grace; alsoe fower score menn in armes with shott and pyke redye ordred vpon the sand in rancks against his landing for guard, and 48 peeces great ordnance discharged from our fleete; this daye our shipps were all hansomlye fitted with their waistclothies, ensignes, flagges, pendentes and streamers" (Peyton's Journal, p. 29).

and the English, who stood right before vs. They by an enterpreter bade me welcome with a long Complement, which was payd in the same mettle. And I added to yt that the Kings Majestie hauing receiued assurance from the great Mogull of the good affection borne to his Majestie and our Nation, and vnder Confidence of the *firma*[1] sent by Captain Best, to receiue his Ambassador in the behalfe of the Merchants trading in his Dominions, had sent me with full commission as his Ambassador, as well to congratulate the happy frendship begunn betweene too soe Mighty Princes and their subiects, as also to assure a readines in the Kings Majestie on his part to Continew the same inviolably; and to propound vnto the great Mogull many other matters of great Consequence both for the maynten-ance and securitye of the leauge already treated on, and for the Mutuall good of the Subiects of both the kings: That I did receiue yt as an assurance of the good affection of the Great Mogull and off his Commanders and ministers in these parts that they did soe much Honor the King my Master to meete me in so respectiue manner, and furnishe mee with horses to theyre towne, for which I gaue them thancks, and did not doubt that my Comming would proue beneficiall and acceptable to them: and that I was ready to take horse and accompany them to Suratt to repose my selfe vntill I could be prepared to aduance toward the Court. Then they begann a new tune, that I would be pleasd to be Content that all my Company might be searched, according to the Custome of the Cuntrye. I replyed it was strange to me to heare any motion from them contrary to the promise of the Gouernor, whervpon only I sett my foote ashore: That I was the Ambassador of a Mightie and free Prince: that I would neuer dishonnor my

[1] This word is familiar as signifying an order, patent, or passport (Pers. *farmán*). As noted in Yule and Burnell's *Hobson-Jobson*, Roe sometimes writes it *firma*, as if suggestive of the Italian for "signature".

Master so much, whose Person I bare, as to subiect myselfe to so much slauery: I would engage my Honor (which I esteemed as my life) that no follower of myne had the worth of a *Pice*[1] of trade or Marchandice: and that in Europe and most Parts of Asia all Ambassadors and theyr traynes were so far priuiledged as not to be subiect to Common and barbarous vsage: that seeing I found so little assurance in that woord which had drawne me ashoare, I would retyre to the shipes, to attend the Mogulles pleasure: for that I could not answere it with my head to loose the right and freedome due to the Embassador of a Christian king. They answered it was also more then the Gouernor could avow to let them passe vnsearched: it was a great curtesy don to my person, and sufficient acknowledgment of me, all others pretending my place having neuer had so much honor:[2] that it was absolutely the Custome of this Cuntrie, and they Could not breake it. I replyed: I had thought that they had vnderstood that free kyngs and theyre Ambassadors had beene aboue ordinary customes; which since they would not take notice off, I would not perswade them to breake theyrs, and I was resolued I would not dishonor my selfe; but I would send to the Great Mogull and attend his Majesties answere: that I hoped they had come to entertayne and honor me, not to enslaue and entangle me with barbarous Customes. And so after much dispute I turnd about and departed to our boates. Then by the mediation of messengers they offered that I should choose to my self [illegible] persons, whom I would, that in honor of me should goe free; and that they only would for a Cerimony sake lay theyr handes about the rest, not as to search but to embrace them. So I landed

[1] A copper coin of the value of about one-third of a penny.

[2] Edwards and his company had had to submit to this indignity the previous year, being "verie familyarlye searched all of vs to the bottom of our pocketts, and nearer too, modestlie to speake yt" (Dodsworth's MS. narrative.—I.O. Records).

againe and repeating the offer by my interpreter, that I was content they should lay theyr handes vpon my seruants, not with intent to search but to embrace, calling to wittnes the Generall, what were my Conditions, they intend not to search but to embrace. They desired me not to take yt in ill part that they did not yeild in all my desire; that they would signifie to the great Mogull I would not yeild to that Custome they Claymed, and that they did it in Honor there, that they might send before to the officers of Suratt that all Ceremonyes were ended; because, if the Gouernor should insist vpon yt when I came to Suratt, it would be more dishonor to returne or suffer it publiquely, and that this would preuent farther question. Whervpon I called five of my Company to stand behynd me, expecting what they would doe to the rest. But seeing them stand still I asked if all were done, that wee might goe to horse. They answered they were ready. Soe taking leaue of the Generall and all the rest, Accompanied with Master Boughton, Master Barkeley[1] and four other Merchants, I tooke horse with all my followers; the Surattes keeping me Company. When I was about halfe way they sent to me that I would call three or four of the better sort to ryde with me, and that they would follow in order, and that after them my men might Come in ranke, pretending to enter the Towne in this fashion. I, doubting nothing, appoynted yt soe, and called three or four to me, and one of the Principall of them to ride with me, euery man obseruinge this order, at some distance betweene me and the Surattes, and betweene the Surattes and my seruants. They were about 50 horse and 200 foote, and all my Company were 23. On the Suddeyne, I being before, they stayd, and vnder pretence of drinck called my men, who

---

[1] George Berkeley, afterwards President at Bantam, where he died in March, 1617. His travels in Eastern Europe are chronicled in Purchas's third volume (pp. 625, 631).

wisely came, and beeing among them, they tooke houlde of their horses and offered by force to search them. Master Wallis breaking out came vp after me, and tould me this treachery; wheron I turnd my horse, and with all speed rode backe to them, I confess too angry. When I came vp, I layd my hand on my swoord, and my men breake throwgh and came about me. Then I asked what they entended by soe base treachery: I was free landed, and I would die soe, and if any of them durst touch any belonging to me, I bade him speake and shew himselfe. Then they desired me not to take yt in ill part: it was done in frendship. I called for a Case of Pistolls and, hanging them at my saddle, I replyed those were my Frendes, in them I would trust: that they had dealt treacherously with me, and soe I did esteeme them. They desiered me to goe on: that all was mistaken I answered I would returne to the shipes but that they would basely suppose it to bee feare: therfore I would goe on to seeke Justice; but tould them they should not mingle with my trayne: I tooke them for enemyes to the King my Master, that soe sought my dishonor; but that eyther they or I would goe before and the other follow, for if any came among myne they should expect the entertaynment of one that was highly offended. It were much vanety to say in what a feare the best of them were, beeing so many; but the truth is not ashamed. So we rode on, in seuerall troupes, they before. On the way they stayd all in a shade, and called to me as I passed, but I did not looke towards them. Then they sent after, desiring me to eate a Plantine, which I refused, with answer: vntill I had satisfaction for the affront done my seruants, I would not receiue any thing as Curtesye. They replyed they had searched None, and did mean only to excecute the Ceremony agreed on at the Tent, without farther purpose of Injurye. So I tooke this for answere and left them at theyr refreshing, till I came to the water syde ouer against the Towne. But noe boates would Carrie me vntill they arriued. At last they Came, and with many good woordes, did assure me they had no purpose to Injure mee; that they only entended to doe what I yeeilded too, there in priuat, that they might certifie all was finished, least the officers of the Custome howse (that knew no Ciuility) should stay me at the enterance of the Towne; and perswaded me to be yet Content withall. I answered I was euer equall with my woorde, and that though they had taught me to breake my woord, it was a lesson I scornd to learne: but I would bee a wittnes of theyr fashion, least they vnder Coulor of Ceremony did vse villany. Soe I entered a boate with the Officers and called five to mee, Master Boughton, my Chaplain, and three seruants, who Came in free. The rest stood to enter after this Ceremony of embracing. The first that Came they playnly, insteed of embracing, offered to feele his Pocketts without; whereat I rose and sayd I would not endure yt; and in extreame Cholar telling them it was a Custome to be vsd to rouges and theeues and not to free men: I was resolued not to returne to my Cuntry with shame; I would rather dye there with Honor. Wheruppon they lett all of them Come to me without more woordes; and smiling desired me to be appeased, seeing I was satisfied in all. So soone as I was putt off they tempted me a New (knowing I could not now goe back): I must goe see the Gouernor, before I went to my house. I anwered I was weary and vnfitt for visitation. They tould me it was the Custome and I could not refuse yt. Then I saw how euery way they besett me. I sayd playnly I would not nor could be Compelled: that in all their dealinges ther was new falshood, I was resolued: They could not but vnder trust haue cercumvented me: That I durst not answere visiting the Gouernor vntill he had visitted mee: that I doubted not he, beeing borne a

Persian, vnderstood the right due vnto mee : if not, yet I would rather returne then loose it. In this dispute we arriued att the stayres to enter the Towne, whereas the Gouernors brother with many attendants to Conduct me to the Castle. But, after some few woordes betweene them, he bad me welcome, and desiered me to take my rest in my howse this night: that to morrow would be fitter for Ceremony. I gladly and shortly accepted yt, and tooke horse, the sackbotts of the Towne goeing before and many following me. I gott my house, resoluing it should be my Castle. But, Comming in, I found, Contrary to all faith, that my necessaries sent before were kept at the Custome house, and would not be deliuered without search. Whereupon I sent to the Gouernor that it was strange to me to receiue soe many discourtesyes after his woord Past, but that I doubted not he would vpon better aduise giue me Content the next day, it beeing to late at Present : I only desired my bed and such provisions as I could not want.[1] Which was granted, and a message withall that on the Morrow I should receiue the rest without delay. Soe I was satisfyed with hope, and ended a wearisome day.[2]

---

[1] *I.e.* could not do without. Mun (*England's Treasure by Forraign Trade*) advises that, in selling goods to foreign nations, special profit should be made out of those " which they cannot want."

[2] Terry (p. 173) mentions an incident of this day to which Roe makes no allusion. It may be quoted as an example of the disorderliness amongst the English subordinates which was a constant cause of friction with the authorities at almost every port frequented by the Company's ships.

" When my Lord Ambassadour at first arrived at Surat, it so was, that an English Cook he carried with him, the very first day of his comming thither, found a way to an Armenian Christians house, who sold wine in that place, they call Armenian wine. . . . . The Cook had his head quickly over-freighted with it, and then staggering homeward, in his way met the Governors Brother of Surat, as he was riding to his house ; the Cook made a stand, staying himself up upon his sword and scabbard, and cry'd out to the Governours Brother : *Now thou heathen dog.* He not understanding his foul language replyed civilly in his own : *Ca-ca-ta* [*kyá kahtá*], which signifies : What sayest thou? The Cook answered him with

September 27.—I sent to the Custome house for my stuff, but it was refused me, except I would concent it should be opened there. I answered I would neuer agree to any condition Contrary to the priuiledge I claymed as my right and Contrary to that conclusion I made before my landing: I was a stranger to such doublings: but that I was resolued to lett them rott there, and not be further behoulding to him, but would dispatch a messenger to the Great Mogull of the faythlesse dealing and barbarous vsage of me, beeing Ambassador to a mightie King in leauge with him, and come a far Journy vpon his royall woord: and that they should farther forbeare to putt new deuices vpon me: I would not be wrought on vpon any pretence. Hee sent me woord I should take my Course. Within an hower he sent me a Messenger to perswade me to come visitt him, and that then he would bring me to my house & do me all Honor, and all my desires should be fullfilled. I replyed it was too late to offer me Curtesyes, especially vnder pretence of dishonoring my Master: That it was the Custome of Europe to visitt those of my qualety first, and that I durst not breake yt in penaltye of my head, haveinge expresse Command from my Master to Mayntayne the Honor of a free king, and to visitt none but such as first did that respect due to his Majestie: and that therfore I would neuer doe yt. He returned me answere it was the Custome of this Cuntry that all Embassadors did first Come to the Gouernors, and that he was seruant to a Great King

---

his sword and scabbard, with which he stroock at him, but was immediatly seised on by his followers, and by them disarm'd and carried to Prison. The Ambassadour had present intelligence of the misbehaviour of his drunken servant, and immediatly sent word unto the Governours Brother that he was not come thither to patronize any disorderly person, and therefore desir'd him to do with him what he pleased; upon which he presently sent him home, not doing him the least hurt. But before I leave this storie, it will not be amiss to enquire who was the *Heathen dog* at this time, whether the debaucht drunken Cook who call'd himself a Christian, or that sober and temperate Mahometan who was thus affronted."

as well as I: that no man could be a better man than he, exept he were made so by his Master: That all other that pretended to be embassadors before me did not only come, but sue to the Gouernors, had their personns and goodes publiquely searched, which had not beene done to me, nor should not be offered to the prouisions remayning if I would see him: And that hee was no way inferior to any former Gouernor. I replyed: for the Customes of Embassadors to visitt Gouernors I did know the Contrary by the Persian; and that I did beleeue he did neuer receiue any at this Port, nor euer from a Christian King; and hee beeing Gouernor for the Prince (as yet a subject) I could not thinck he wronged himselfe to visitt me that did represent the Person of a King: But my businesse here was not to dispute titles: I was not sent to him, and therefore would not see him: for the prescedentes of former men, they were noe rules to me that was a full Ambassador, and they, though sent by the king, yet were but Agents to prepare my way and to negotiate in the behalfe of the Honourable Company: But because I did desire to giue him all reasonable satisfaction, if he would Honor my Master so much as to see me and giue me welcome, I would showe him my Commission vnder the great seale of England, and his Master's *firma* conditioning to recieue an Ambassador with all due respect, which I had in keeping, and vnder Confidence wheroff the King had sent me, wherby he might receiue assurance it was no disparagement to him; and the next day I would visitt him in requitall, which I could Alsoe hardly answere, before I had presented my selfe before his Master: But if hee were not purposed, I would not perswade him to breake his pretended Custome, and desiered him not to expect that I would disobey and dishonor my Master: but leauing Ceremonyes apart, I did looke for, according to his promise, my prouisions detayned in the Custome house. Then hee sent me answere he would not nor durst see me first, but that, if I would Come to him, he would Come forth of his house and receiue me in the place of Audience: if not, I must be contented to haue my Chests searched. I answered: I card not for them: the breach of his woord was enough: but to visitt him in his Place of audience was a proposition most obsurd: it was as much as I would doe to his Master. But because these Ceremonyes should not hinder our businesse, I said if he would meete me in an indifferent Place a horsebacke, when neyther might be before other, I would Condescend, and soe neyther of us should wronge his Master, though in that he brake all rule of Curtesie: if not I desired him to trouble me with no more Articles: I was resolued to keepe my howse and expect his Masters answer to the affrontes done to me. Thus we wore out the day and yt rested. Wherupon hee Commanded none in the Towne to sell vs anything but victualles, and imprisoned some that did; Master Barkley and the Merchantes, thincking this night to returne to the shipes, could not be suffered, nor any from them to Come to vs. This made me somewhat Iealous of treachery, but breake not my sleepe.

September 28.—In the Morning the Merchants went to Aske leaue to depart; beeing warned by me to make no motion concerning me, but to gett aboord and I would trye it out with him. But they were delayed till after dinner, basely begging of Presents that he did expect, and withall sayd: your Embassador lookes I should visitt him; what Iewell or diamond will he giue me? and so, only provoking guifts, dismised them. After noone they sollicited him againe, and in answere of his desire of presents sayd the first sent him, beeing small, was only at their first arriuall: but that there was entended a better present for him, but it was kept vntill they saw what entertaynment he would giue the Kings Ambassador, and Could not be

January 10.—I went to Court at 4 in the euening to the *Durbar*,[1] which is the Place wher the. Mogull sitts out daylie, to entertayne strangers, to receiue petitions and presents, to giue Commandes, to see, and to bee seene. To digresse a little from my reception, and declare the Customes of the Court, will enlighten the future discourse. The king hath no man but Eunuchs that Comes within the lodgings or retyring roomes of his house : His weomen watch within, and guard him with manly weapons. They doe Justice on vpon another for offences. He comes every Morning to a wyndow called the *Jarruco*[2] looking into a playne before his gate, and showes him selfe to the Common People. At noone hee returns thither and sitts some howers to see the fight of Eliphants and willd beasts; vnder him within a rayle attend the men of rancke; from whence hee retiers to sleepe among his woemen. At after-noone he returnes to the *Durbar* before mentioned. At 8 after supper he Comes downe to the *Gazelcan*,[3] a faire Court, wher in the middest is a Throune erected of free stone

[1] In Mr. Douglas's *Bombay and Western India* (i, p. 305) is given a coloured drawing from an old painting at Jaipur which, in the author's opinion, represents the Emperor Jahángír giving audience to Sir Thomas Roe. Such an interpretation, however, appears exceedingly doubtful, for the figure pointed out as Roe is not only very unlike him in appearance, but occupies quite a subordinate position in the picture. Moreover, the costume and weapons are native, whereas we know from Terry (p. 218) that Roe and his suite wore always English dress. "For my Lord Ambassadour and his Company, we all kept to our English habits, made as light and coole as possibly we could have them ; His wayters in Red Taffata cloakes, guarded with green Taffata, which they alwayes wore when they went abroad with him ; myself in a long black Cassock." We must therefore take leave to doubt the correctness of the ascription, especially as no such claim was put forward when the picture was first brought to notice in the *Journal of Indian Art*, No. 25 (1889).

[2] The *Jharukhá*, or "interview-window," which Roe describes at greater length later. The royal headquarters were at the fort, now called the Magazine, on the city side of which there is a window answering to Roe's description (*Rajputana Gazetteer*, ii, p. 123).

[3] *Ghuzl-khána*, "bath-room," hence "private apartment" (privy chamber).

wherein he sitts, but some tymes below in a Chayre; to which are none admitted but of great qualetye, and few of these without leaue; wher he discourses of all matters with much Affabilitye.[1] Ther is noe busines done with him Concerning the state, gouerment, disposition of warr or peace, but at one of these two last Places, wher it is publiquely propounded, and resolued, and soe registred,[2] which if it were woorth the Curiositye might bee seene for two shillings, but the Common basse people knew as much as the Councell, and the Newes euery day is the kings new resolutions tossed and censured by euery rascall. This Course is vnchangeable, except sicknes or drinck preuent yt; which must be known, for as all his Subjects

[1] Compare Terry's account (p. 389):—

"First, early in the morning, at that very time the Sun begins to appear above the Horizon, He appears unto his people in a place very like unto one of our Balconies, made in his houses or Pavilions for his morning appearance, directly opposite to the East, about seven or eight foot high from the ground; against which time a very great number of his people, especially of the greater sort, who desire as often as they can to appear in his eye, assemble there together, to give him the *Salam*, or good morning, crying all out, as soon as they see their King, with a loud voice, *Padsha Salamet*, which signifies, *live O great King*, or *O great King, health and life*. . . . At noon he shows himself in another place like the former, on the South-side; and a little before Sun-set, in a like place, on the West-side of his house or Tent; but as soon as the Sun forsakes the Hemisphear, he leaves his people, ushered in and out with Drums and Winde instruments, and the peoples acclamations. . . . And between seven and nine of the clock at night, he sits within his House or Tent more privately, in a spacious place called his *Goozalcan*, or bathing house, made bright like day by abundance of lights; and here the King sits mounted upon a stately Throne; where his Nobles, and such as are favoured by him, stand about him; others find admittance to, but by special leave from his Guard, who cause every one that enters that place to breath upon them, and if they imagine that any have drunk wine, they keep him out."

"At this time my Lord Ambassadour made his usual addresses to him, and I often waited on him thither, and it was a good time to do business with that King, who then was for the most part very pleasant, and full of talk unto those who were round him, and so continued till he fell asleep (oft times by drinking), and then all assembled immediately quitted the place, besides those who were his trusted servants, who by turns watched his Person."

[2] See Blochmann's *Áín-i-Akbari*, i, p. 258.

are slaues, so is he in a kynd of reciprocall bondage, for he is tyed to obserue these howres and Customes so precisely that if hee were vnseene one day and noe sufficient reason rendred the people would mutinie; two dayes noe reason can excuse, but that he must consent to open his doores and bee seene by some to satisfye others.[1] On Tuesday at the *Jarruco* he sitts in Judgment, neuer refusing the poorest mans Complaynt, where hee heares with Patience both parts: and some tymes sees with too much delight in blood the execution done by his Eliphants. *Illi meruere : sed quid tu vt adesses ?*[2]

At the *Durbar* I was led right before him, at the enterance of an outward rayle, where mett mee two Principall Noble slaues to conduct mee nearer. I had required before my going leaue to vse the Customes of my Country, which was freely granted, soe that I would performe them Punctually. When I entred within the first rayle I made a reuerance; entering in the inward rayle a Nother; and when I came vnder the king a theird. The Place is a great Court, whither resort all sorts of people. The king sitts in a little Gallery ouer head; Ambassidors, the great men and strangers of qualety within the inmost rayle vnder him, raysed from the ground, Couered with Canopyes of veluet and silke, vnder foote layd with good Carpetts; the Meaner men representing gentry within the first rayle, the people without in a base Court, but soe that all may see the king. This sitting out hath soe much affinitye with a Theatre—the manner of the king in his gallery; The great men lifted on a stage as actors; the vulgar below gazing on—that an easy description will informe of the place and

---

[1] Cp. *Bernier's Travels* (Constable's edn.), pp. 265-6. An admirable description of the Mogul court and system of government will be found in Mr. Stanley Lane-Poole's *Life of Aurangzib.*

[2] This may be freely rendered: "Doubtless they have merited their punishment; but why should you be present?"

fashion. The king preuented my dull enterpreter, bidding me welcome as to the brother of my Master. I deliuered his Majesties lettre translated; and after my Commission, wheron hee looked Curiously; after, my presents, which were well receiued. He asked some questions, and with a seeming Care of my health, offering me his Phisitions, and aduising mee to keepe my house till I had recouered strength; and if in the interim I needed anything I should freely send to him, and obteyne my desiers. He dismissed me with more fauour and outward grace (if by the Christians I were not flattered) then euer was showed to any Ambassador, eyther of the Turke or Persian, or other whatsoeuer.[1]

January 12.—Hee sent a gentellman for my Commission to show his queene the seale, which he kept one night, and returned yt with such care that the bringer durst not deliuer it but to my owne handes.[2]

January 14.—I sent to the Prince Sultan Coronne, his third sonne by byrth but first in fauour, that I determined to visitt him, not doubting he would vse me with due respect; for I was enformed he was enemy to all Christians and therfore feared some affront. He answered I should be welcome, and receiue the same Content I had from his father. Hee is lord of Suratt, our cheefe residence, and his fauour important for us.

January 15-21.—These dayes I stirred not abroad, the

---

[1] Some additional details of Roe's presentation will be found in his letters on pp. 110 and 118. His commission and King James's letter are printed in Appendix B.

[2] This incident (omitted by Purchas) is significant. Probably Núr Mahál had expressed a doubt whether Roe were really a properly accredited ambassador, or (like his predecessors) a mere emissary of the merchants.

It is scarcely necessary to recall the romantic story of Núr Mahál (better known by her later title of Núr Jahán)—her marriage to Shír Afgan, his assassination, and her subsequent union with the emperor, who had already been attracted to her before her first marriage. At this period her influence over her husband was so unbounded that she practically ruled the empire, and Roe soon found out the error he had made in not seeking to conciliate her and her partisans.

offer; professing to be ignorant of anything past, but what hee had receiued by Asaph Chan[1] deliuered by mee; especially of any Command to dismisse us,[2] which the Gouernor had falsly Coyned and for which he should dearly answer. Soe he dismissed mee full of hope to rectifye the decayed estate of our reputation, with promise of a *firmaen* for Suratt effectually.

January 24.—I went to the *Durbar* to visitt the King, who, seeing mee afarr off, becknead with his hand, giuing signe I should not staye the Cerimony of Asking leaue but Come vp to him; where hee appoynted me a place aboue all other men, which I after thought fitt to mayntayne.[3] I gaue him a small present,[4] it beeing the Custome when any body hath busines to giue somewhat, and those that cannot come neare to speake send in or hould up their guift, which hee ecceps, bee it but a *rupie*, and demands their bussines. The same course hee held with

---

[1] Mírza Abul Hasan, better known by his title of Ásaf Khán. He held a strong position at court, as son of the prime minister, elder brother of Núr Mahál, and father of Prince Khurram's favourite wife, Mumtáz Mahál. When the prince came to the throne as Sháh Jahán, Ásaf Khán was advanced to high dignities; and he died (November, 1641) in possession of great wealth. His eldest son was Sháista Khán, who, as Governor of Bengal, came into collision with the English settlers at Húglí.

[2] See pp. 74, 79. After Roe's departure the Governor had forced the General and others to give an undertaking in writing "for clearing the Cuntry after the expiration of one yeare to come, sayeing it was the great Mugolls pleasure to be soe ordred; yett not anye wayes denying vs free trade, but enioyned vs not to make any residence of aboad longer then our shipps were theare" (Peyton's Journal, f. 34).

[3] The exact position of each dignitary was minutely regulated (See *Áín-i-Akbari*, i, p. 160).

[4] A "clock and two other trifles" (*Letter to E. I. Co.*, January 25, 1615-16; reproduced in part at p. 118).

None of the presents given to the Mogul by Roe from time to time has been traced in after years. Mr. Keene, in 1874, exhibited to the Archæological Society of Agra an English striking watch, found in a well in the Fort there, which from its date (1614) he considered was probably one of the novelties brought by Roe for the emperor; but this, though not impossible, is only a conjecture.

mee. Having looked Curiously and asked many questions of my present, he demanded what I required of him I answered: Justice: That, on the assurance of his Majesties *Firmaen* sent into England, the king my Master had not only giuen leaue to many of his subjects to come a dangerous voyadge with their goodes, but had sent mee to Congratulate the amytye so happely begunne betweene two soe mighty Nations, and to Confirme the same: But that I found the English seated at Amadauas[1] enjured by the Gouernor in their Persons and goodes, fined, exacted upon, & kept as prisoners: that at eueric Towne new Customes were taken of our goodes passing to the Port, contrarie to all Iustice and the former Articles of trade.[2] To which hee answered hee was sorry: it should be amended; and presently gaue order for two *firmanes* very effectually according to my desire to be signed, one to the Gouernor of Amadavaz to restore mony exacted from Master Kerridge,[3] and to vse the English with all fauour. The

[1] Ahmadábád.

[2] Roe had consulted Ásaf Khán, who had "encouraged him to complayne," that particular city "beeing absolute under the King."

[3] Thomas Kerridge, who in the following month (February 18, 1616) was chosen agent at Surat in succession to Aldworth. He had gone out with Best in 1612, and had spent some time at the Mogul court after the death of Canning. On Edwards' arrival, Kerridge moved down to Ahmadábád to provide indigo for the lading of the fleet. His letters from that city, and later from Surat, will be found in Brit. Mus. *Addl. MS.* 9366. As will be seen, his imperious temper led to much friction between him and Roe, and though the latter acknowledged his opponent to be "quick and sufficient," he held that he had "too much heate and opinion of abilitye."

Kerridge was back in England by June, 1622, but in January, 1624, he was reappointed agent at Surat. He reached his post in October, and remained until 1628. After his return he was elected a "Committee" of the Company, and served almost continually till 1648. In 1646 he was nominated for the post of Deputy-Governor, but was not elected. In 1654-55 he took part in the management of the United Joint Stock; and this is the last trace we have of him.

The wrongs complained of in the text are detailed in Kerridge's letters mentioned above. At Ahmadábád, a dispute with a native merchant over some indigo led to their broker being beaten and imprisoned. Kerridge himself was beaten; and in addition was

other to release all Customes required on any pretence on the way, or if any had beene taken to repay it; of his owne accord wishing mee that, if these gaue not speedy remedy, I should renew my Complaynt against the disobeyour, and hee should be sent for to answere there. And soe hee dismissed mee.

January 25-30.—I Made my dispatches for England, and wrote earnestly to the factory at Suratt for a Particular of the Gouernors debts, exactions and Iniuryes;[1] and solicited the *firmaens* Promised, of which the Prince sent by his officers one for Suratt, but withall Articles for mee to signe very dishonorable, wherin among others it was required that I should firme a Peace and safe Conduct to the Portugalles shippes and frigotts to Come safely to Suratt, without any accord, promise or Counter securytye of Peace on their Partes; which I vtterly refused, but made offer that for the Princes sake I was Content to giue the Viceroy of Goa 6 Monthes liberty to enter into leauge, and to open the Portes. But the present writing was required to be sealed; wherby, besydes the folly and dishonor, they might vnder coullor of Frendship haue rode amonge our fleete with boates laden with fire woorkes to haue taken aduantage. So, as I absolutely rejected the Motion, I was answered I should then haue no *firmaen* for Suratt. Soe it rested two dayes. I, supposinge the fault only in the Princes officers, sent to Asaph Chan, to complayne of the vnequalle demandes of Sultan Carronne and that the *firmaen* promised beeing sealed was deteyned from mee, Contrarye to all the Prinnces faire woordes and

fined on the pretext that he had defrauded the governor of the estate of Aldworth, who was alleged to have died in the town and to have been carried forth by the English to escape the confiscation of his goods. When the English merchandise was ready to start for Surat the governor demanded four per cent. duty, though at last he accepted one and a half per cent., and a bribe of a hundred rupees.

[1] This had been asked for by the Prince at the late interview.

John Fryer

[On fakirs] *A New Account of East-India and Persia*. London: R.I. Chiswell, 1698.

a-day, and expound the *Alchoran* once a-week, and that on *Friday*, which day they are not to lye with their Women, ſetting it apart for the Service of God.

The *Xeriff* their High-Prieſt.

Here is a *Xeriff*, who is as it were their Primate, under him the *Cazys*, or Judges, are the next, then the Inferior Clergy, as the *Mullahs*, and *Scribes*, or Teachers of Youth in the *Arabick* Tongue.

Extravagancies of the *Fakiers* or Holy Men.

With theſe, by the favour of the preſent *Mogul*, who lived long in that Order, till he came to the Throne, muſt be numbred the *Fakiers* or Holy Men, abſtracted from the World, and reſigned to God, for the Word will bear that Interpretation; on this Pretence are committed ſundry Extravagancies, as putting themſelves on voluntary Penances. Here is one that has vowed to hang by the Heels, till he get Money enough to build a *Moſch* to *Mahomet*, that he may be held a Saint. Another ſhall travel the Country with an Horn blowed afore him, and an Ox it may be to carry him and his Baggage, beſides one to wait on him with a Peacock's Tail; whilſt he rattles a great Iron Chain fettered to his Foot, as big as thoſe Elephants are Foot-locked with, ſome two yards in length, every Link thicker than a Man's Thumb, and a Palm in length; his ſhaking this ſpeaks his Neceſſity, which the poor *Gentiles* dare not deny to relieve; for if they do, he accuſes them to the *Cazy*, who deſires no better opportunity to fleece them: For they will not ſtick to ſwear they blaſphemed *Mahomet*, for which there is no evaſion but to depoſit, or be cut, and made a *Moor*.

They make every place their home, and all their own.

Moſt of theſe are Vagabonds, and are the Peſt of the Nation they live in; ſome of them live in Gardens and retired Places in the Fields, in the ſame manner as the *Seers* of old, and the Children of the Prophets did: Their Habit is the main thing that ſignalizes them more than their Virtue; they profeſs Poverty, but make all things their own where they come; all the heat of the Day they idle it under ſome ſhady Tree, at night they come in Troops, armed with a great Pole, a *Mirchal* or Peacock's Tail, and a Wallet; more like Plunderers than Beggers; they go into the Market, or to the Shopkeepers, and force an Alms, none of them returning without his ſhare: Some of them paſs the bounds of a modeſt Requeſt, and bawl out in the open Streets for an Hundred *Rupees*, and nothing leſs will ſatisfy theſe.

How clad.

They are cloathed with a ragged Mantle, which ſerves them alſo for a Matraſs, for which purpoſe ſome have Lyons, Tygres or Leopards Skins to lay under them: The Civileſt of them wear Fleſh-coloured Veſts, ſomewhat like our Brick-makers Frocks, and almoſt of that Colour. The Merchants, as their Adventures return, are bountiful towards them, by which means ſome of them thrive upon it.

They are become formidable.

Theſe Field Conventiclers at the hours of Devotion beat a Drum, from them called the *Fakiers* Drum; here are of theſe Strolers about this City enough to make an Army, that they are almoſt become formidable to the Citizens; nor is the Governour powerful enough to correct their Inſolencies. For lately ſetting on a Nobleman of the *Moors*, when his Kindred came to demand Juſtice, they unanimouſly aroſe

Letter II.

rose in defence of the Aggressor, and rescued him from his deserved Punishment.

The Governor not able to quell them.

For all the Governor comes to his Seat attended every Morning with 300 Foot with Fire-Arms, Three Elephants in their Cloathing (which is here also a principal Mark of the Greatness of these Men in place, the more Elephants they keep, they are looked on as more Honourable) Forty Horses mounted, Four and twenty Banners of State; besides a large Retinue of the *Cazy's*, who is always present to assist him in Law Points. Moreover he has Loud Trumpets made as big, and like our *Stentoro-Phonica*, or speaking Trumpet, with Thundring Kettle-Drums; yet neither the Formality of this Appearance, nor regard due to his Office, is terrible enough to prevail with these to submit to resign the Caitiff, and hardly is his whole Force able to keep them from bare-faced Rebellion.

The Villany of the Governor's Servants had a Tragical Event.

But though these Outlaws (for as such they ought to be look'd on, while they disown all Subjection) behave themselves thus, the poor Inhabitants that work for their Bread, are under severer Restraints; for the Governor's Servants being upheld by as uncontrouled Licentiousness, on pretence of pressing the Craftsmen from their daily Labour into the Governor's Service, extort continued Fees from them, or else they are sure to be set on work, without any thing for their Pains: Which was but even now made a Publick Grievance, by the Resistance of a sturdy *Patan*, (who is sprung from a Warlike People, of whom it is said, They never draw their Swords, but Blood must follow): And thus it happen'd; The *Patan* having employ'd a Taylor at his house, one of the Governor's Men seized him for his Master's Service; but the *Patan* rushing in to release him, the Soldier ran a young Brother of the *Patan's* through, naked and unconcerned in the Scuffle; which so enraged the *Patan*, that forcing the Sword out of the hand of this inhuman Butcher, he kill'd him and two more that came to his Rescue; and going into his house, slew his own Wife, and Sister, and a little Son of his own, that they might not fall a Sacrifice to the Governor's Rage: The wretched Taylor, animated by the Example of the *Patan* (tho but coolly), had murder'd his Wife had she not fled; but laying hold on his Old Father and Mother, he dispatched them; and bolting forth into the Street, set upon what Governor's Men he and the *Patan* could meet: Tidings whereof striking the Governor's Ears, he came with all his Power to beset the exasperated and desperate Men; but though a Thousand Men were up in Arms, and gazing upon the *Patan* standing with his Sword in his hand at the Entrance of the House, none durst venture to apprehend him; till his Fury abating, and Promises given by a Great Man, of Favour if he resigned; he attending to his Parley, in the mean while two Men with Guns from atop of the House discharged on him, and wounded him and the Taylor mortally, but not before they had carried this false Great Man with some of his Attendants along with them out of the World: So that these Curs set to keep the Sheep, are the first that worry them.

Lest therefore all Shew of Justice should be banished, now and then, when they have not Mony to buy it off, or the Emperor be inform-

informed, ſome Exemplary Puniſhments are inflicted: Some Inſtances whereof I ſhall relate.

Chap. I.

Some exemplary Puniſhments.

The one was of an *Armenian*, *Chawbucked* through the City for ſelling of Wine. The other was of a Goldſmith who had coined Copper *Rupees*; firſt they ſhaved his Head and Beard, as our Countrymen do Bayliffs when they preſume to Arreſt in Priviledg'd Places; then putting a Fool's Cap on his Head, they ſet him on an Aſs, with his Face to the Tail, which is led by an *Holencore*, and one of their Drums is beat before him, which is an Affront of the higheſt degree; thus they lead him up and down the City, where the Boys and Soldiers treat him but ſcurvily, pelting him all the way he paſſes: Being brought back to Priſon, they cut off his Hand, and let him lye during the Governor's Pleaſure. The Third was of a Pack of Thieves that had infeſted the Roads a long time, and after ſome whiles Impriſonment the *Banyans* proffered Money for their Redemption; but the *Great Mogul* ſending an Expreſs, they were led to Execution; They were Fifteen, all of a Gang, who uſed to lurk under Hedges in narrow Lanes, and as they found opportunity, by a Device of a Weight tied to a Cotton Bowſtring made of Guts, (with which they tew Cotton) of ſome length, they uſed to throw it upon Paſſengers ſo, that winding it about their Necks, they pulled them from their Beaſts, and dragging them upon the Ground ſtrangled them, and poſſeſſed themſelves of what they had: One of theſe was an Old Man with his two Sons, the youngeſt not fourteen. This being their Practice, they were ſentenced, according to *Lex Talionis*, to be hang'd; wherefore being delivered to the *Catwal*, or Sheriff's Men, they led them two Miles with Ropes about their Necks to ſome wild Date-Trees: In their way thither they were chearful, and went ſinging, and ſmoaking Tobacco, the *Banyans* giving them Sweetmeats, they being as jolly as if going to a Wedding; and the Young Lad now ready to be tied up, boaſted, That though he were not Fourteen Years of Age, he had killed his Fifteen Men; wherefore the Old Man, as he had been a Leader of theſe Two, was firſt made an Example for his Villany, and then the two Striplings were advanced, as all the reſt were, half a Foot from the Ground; and then cutting their Legs off that the Blood might flow from them, they left them miſerable Spectacles, hanging till they dropped of their own accord.

Delinquents of another kind.

The following Delinquents being of another kind, we ſhall ſee how they fare: The one was of a Rich Merchant of the *Moors* killing his Wife, and a Child he had by her of Three Years old, upon taking her with her Paramour in Adultery; for which Crime a Pecuniary Mulct excuſed him: The other was a Boy's ſticking a *Sodomitiſh Moor* to the Heart with his own *Catarre*, while he attempted upon his Body; which Fact was ſo far from being accuſed as a Fault, that the Boy came off with Commendation; though there is nothing more frequently committed among them, than the unnatural Sin of Buggery.

The Crime of growing rich.

There is another thing above all the reſt an unpardonable Offence; for a *Banyan* or Rich Broker to grow Wealthy without Protection of ſome Great Perſon; for it is ſo mighty a Diſquiet to the Governor,

O that

Henry Colebrooke

'On the Sanscrit and Prakrit Languages'.

Asiatic Researches 7 (1803).

VII.

ON THE

SANSCRIT AND PRÁCRIT LANGUAGES.

By H. T. Colebrooke, Esq.

In a treatise on rhetorick, compiled for the use of Mánicya Chandra, *Rájá* of *Tirabhucti* or *Tirhút*, a brief enumeration of languages, used by *Hindu* poets, is quoted from two writers on the art of poetry. The following is a literal translation of both passages.

" Sanscrïta, *Prácrïta*, *Paiśáchí* and *Mágad'hí*, are in short the four paths of poetry. The Gods, &c. speak *Sanscrïta*; benevolent genii, *Prácrïta*; wicked demons, *Paiśáchí*; and men of low tribes and the rest, *Mágad'hí*. But sages deem *Sanscrïta* the chief of these four languages. It is used three ways; in prose, in verse, and in a mixture of both."

" Language, again, the virtuous have declared to be fourfold, Sanscrïta [or the polished dialect,] *Prácrïta* [or the vulgar dialect], *Apabhranśa* [or jargon], and *Miśra* [or mixed]. *Sanscrïta* is the speech of the celestials, framed in grammatical institutes; *Prácrïta* is similar to it, but manifold as a provincial dialect, and otherwise; and those languages which are ungrammatical, are spoken in their respective districts."

The *Paiśáchí* seems to be gibberish, which dramatick poets make the demons speak, when they bring these fantastic beings on the stage. The mixture of languages, noticed in the second quotation, is that which is employed in dramas, as is expressly said by the same author in a subsequent verse. It is not then a compound language, but a mixt dialogue, in which different persons of the drama employ different idioms. Both the passages above quoted are therefore easily reconciled. They in fact notice only three tongues. 1. *Sanscrĭt*, a polished dialect, the inflections of which, with all its numerous anomalies, are taught in grammatical institutes. This the dramatic poets put into the mouths of Gods and of Holy personages. 2. *Prácrĭt*, consisting of provincial dialects, which are less refined, and have a more imperfect grammar. In dramas it is spoken by women, benevolent genii, &c. 3. *Mágad'hí*, or *Apabhrans'a*, a jargon destitute of regular grammar. It is used by the vulgar, and varies in different districts: the poets accordingly introduce into the dialogue of plays a provincial jargon spoken by the lowest persons of the drama *.

The languages of India are all comprehended in these three classes. The first contains *Sanscrĭt*, a most polished tongue, which was gradually refined until it became fixed in the classic writings of many elegant poets, most of whom are supposed to have flourished in the century preceding the Christian æra. It is cultivated by learned *Hindus* throughout India, as the language of science and of literature, and as the repository of their law civil and religious. It evidently draws its origin (and some steps of its progress may even now be traced) from a primeval tongue which was gradually refined in various climates, and became *Sanscrĭt* in India; *Pahlaví*

* *Sanscrĭta* is the passive participle of a compound verb formed by prefixing the preposition *sam* to the crude verb *crĭ*, and by interposing the letter *s* when this compound is used in the sense of embellishment. Its literal meaning then is "adorned;" and when applied to a language, it signifies "polished." *Prácrĭta* is a similar derivative from the same crude verb, with *pra* prefixed: the most common acceptation of this word is "outcast, or man of the lowest class;" as applied to a language, it signifies "vulgar." *Apabhrans'a* is derived from *bhras'* to fall down: it signifies a word, or dialect, which falls off from correct etymology. Grammarians use the *Sanscrĭta* as signifying "duly formed or regularly inflected;" and *Apabhrans'a* for false grammar.

Pahlavi in Persia, and Greek on the shores of the Mediterranean. Like other very ancient languages, *Sanscrĭt* abounds in inflections, which are, however, more anomalous in this, than in the other languages here alluded to; and which are even more so in the obsolete dialect of the *Védas*, than in the polished speech of the classick poets. It has nearly shared the fate of all antient tongues, and is now become almost a dead language; but there seems no good reason for doubting that it was once universally spoken in India. Its name, and the reputed difficulty of its grammar, have led many persons to imagine that it has been refined by the concerted efforts of a few priests, who set themselves about inventing a new language; not like all other tongues, by the gradually improved practice of good writers and polite speakers. The exquisitely refined system by which the grammar of *Sanscrĭt* is taught, has been mistaken for the refinement of the language itself. The rules have been supposed to be anterior to the practice, but this supposition is gratuitous. In *Sanscrĭt*, as in every other known tongue, grammarians have not invented etymology, but have only contrived rules to teach what was already established by approved practice.

There is one peculiarity of *Sanscrĭt* compositions which may also have suggested the opinion that it could never be a spoken language. I allude to what might be termed the euphonical orthography of *Sanscrĭt*. It consists in extending to syntax the rules for the permutation of letters in etymology. Similar rules for avoiding incompatible sounds in compound terms exist in all languages; this is sometimes effected by a deviation from orthography in the pronunciation of words, sometimes by altering one or more letters to make the spelling correspond with the pronunciation. These rules have been more profoundly investigated by *Hindu* grammarians than by those of any other nation, and they have completed a system of orthography which may be justly termed euphonical. They require all compound terms to be reduced to this standard, and *Sanscrĭt* authors, it may be observed, delight in compounds of inordinate length; the whole sentence too, or even whole periods, may, at the pleasure of the author, be combined like the elements of a single word, and good writers generally do so. In common speech this could never have been practised. None but well known compounds would be used by any speaker who wished to be understood, and each word would be distinctly articulated independently of the terms which precede and follow it. Such indeed is the present practice of those who still speak the *Sanscrĭt* language; and they deliver themselves with such fluency as is sufficient to prove that *Sanscrĭt* may have been spoken in former times with as much facility as the contemporary dialects of the Greek language, or the more modern dialects of the Arabic tongue. I shall take occasion again to allude to this topick after explaining at large what are, and by whom were composed, those grammatical institutes in which the *Sanscrĭt* language is framed, according to the author above quoted; or by which (for the meaning is ill conveyed by a literal translaation) words are correctly formed and inflected.

PÁṄINI, the father of *Sanscrĭt* grammar, lived in so remote an age, that he ranks among those ancient sages whose fabulous history occupies a conspicuous place in the *Puráńas*, or Indian theogonies*. The name is a patronymick,

* Every *Puráná* treats of five subjects: the creation of the universe, its progress, and the renovation of worlds; the genealogy of gods and heroes; chronology, according to a fabulous system; and heroick history, containing the achievements of demi-gods and heroes. Since each *Puráná* contains a cosmogony, with mythological and heroick history, the works which bear that title may not unaptly be compared to the Grecian Theogonies.

patronymick, indicating his descent from *Pan'in*; but according to the *Paurán'ica* legends, he was grandson of DÉVALA, an inspired legislator. Whatever may be the true history of PÁN'INI, to him the *Sútras*, or succinct aphorisms of grammar, are attributed by universal consent. His system is grounded on a profound investigation of the analogies in both the regular and the anomalous inflections of the *Sanscrit* language. He has combined those analogies in a very artificial manner; and has thus compressed a most copious etymology into a very narrow compass. His precepts are indeed numerous*, but they have been framed with the utmost conciseness; and this great brevity is the result of very ingenious methods which have been contrived for this end, and for the purpose of assisting the student's memory. In PÁN'INI's system the mutual relation of all the parts marks that it must have been completed by its author; it certainly bears internal evidence of its having been accomplished by a single effort, and even the corrections, which are needed, cannot be interwoven with the text. It must not be hence inferred, that PÁN'INI was unaided by the labours of earlier grammarians; in many of his precepts he cites the authority of his predecessors †, sometimes for a deviation from a general rule, often for a grammatical canon which has universal cogency. He has even employed some technical terms without defining them, because, as his commentators remark, those terms were already introduced by earlier grammarians‡. None of the more ancient works, however, seem to be now extant; being superseded by his, they have probably been disused for ages, and are now perhaps totally lost §.

2 D 2 A PER-

* Not fewer than 3996.

† SA'CALYA, GA'RGYA, CA'SYAPA, GA'LAVA, SA'CAT'A'YANA, and others.

‡ In a few instances he quotes former grammars to refute them.

§ Definitions of some technical terms, together with grammatical axioms, are also cited from

A PERFORMANCE such as the *Pán'iníya* grammar must inevitably contain many errors. The task of correcting its inaccuracies has been executed by CÁTYÁYANA *, an inspired saint and law-giver, whose history, like that of all the Indian sages, is involved in the impenetrable darkness of mythology. His annotations, entitled *Vártícas*, restrict those among the *Pán'iníya* rules which are too vague, enlarge others which are too limited, and mark numerous exceptions which had escaped the notice of PÁN'INI himself.

THE amended rules of grammar have been formed into memorial verses by BHARTRI-HARI, whose metrical aphorisms, entitled *Cáricá*, have almost equal authority with the precepts of PÁN'INI, and emendations of CÁTYÁYANA. If the popular traditions concerning BHARTRI-HARI be well founded, he lived in the century preceding the Christian æra†; for he is supposed to be the same with the brother of VICRAMADITYA, and the period when this prince reigned at *Ujjayiní* is determined by the date of the *Samvat* Æra.

THE studied brevity of the *Pán'iníya Sútras* renders them in the highest degree obscure. Even with the knowledge of the key to their interpretation, the student finds them ambiguous. In the application of them when

those ancient works in the commentaries on PA'N'INI. They are inserted in a compilation entitled *Paribháshá*, which will be subsequently noticed. The various ancient grammars of the *Sanscrit* tongue, as enumerated in a memorial verse, are eight in number, and ascribed to the following authors; viz. INDRA, CHANDRA, C'AS'A, CRITSNA', PI'SA'LI', S'A'CATA'YANA, PA'N'INI, and AMERA JINE'NDRA.

* This name likewise is a patronymick.

† A beautiful poem has been composed in his name, containing moral reflections, which the poet supposes him to make on the discovery of his wife's infidelity. It consists of either three or four *S'atacas*, or centuries of couplets.

when understood, he discovers many seeming contradictions; and, with every exertion of practised memory, he must experience the utmost difficulty in combining rules dispersed in apparent confusion through different portions of PÁN'INI's eight lectures. A commentary was therefore indispensably requisite. Many were composed by ancient grammarians to elucidate the text of PÁN'INI. A most copious one on the emendations of his rules was compiled in very ancient times by an uncertain author. This voluminous work, known by the title of *Mahábháshya*, or the great commentary, is ascribed to PATANJALI, a fabulous personage, to whom mythology has assigned the shape of a serpent. In this commentary every rule is examined at great length. All possible interpretations are proposed: and the true sense and import of the rule are deduced through a tedious train of argument, in which all foreseen objections are considered and refuted; and the wrong interpretations of the text, with all the arguments which can be invented to support them, are obviated or exploded.

VOLUMINOUS as it is, the *Mahábháshya* has not exhausted the subject on which it treats. Its deficiencies have been supplied by the annotations of modern grammarians. The most celebrated among these scholiasts of the *Bháshya* is CAIYÁT'A, a learned Cashmirian. His annotations are almost equally copious with the commentary itself. Yet they too are loaded by numerous glosses; among which the old and new *Vivaranás* are most esteemed.

THE difficulty of combining the dispersed rules of grammar, to inflect any one verb or noun through all its variations, renders further aid necessary. This seems to have been anciently afforded in vocabularies, one of which exhibited the verbs classed in the order implied by the system of PÁN'INI, the other contained nouns arranged on a similar plan. Both probably cited the precepts which must be remembered in conjugating and declining each verb and noun. A catalogue of verbs, classed in regular order, but with few references to the rules of etymology, is extant, and is known by the title of *D'hátupát'a.* It may be considered as an appendix to the grammar of PÁN'INI; and so may his own treatise on the pronunciation of vocal sounds, and the treatise of YASCA on obsolete words and acceptations peculiar to the *Véda.* A numerous class of derivative nouns, to which he has only alluded, have been reduced to rule under the head of *Un'ádi,* or the termination *u,* &c.; and the precepts, respecting the gender of nouns, have been in like manner arranged in *Sútras,* which are formed on the same principles with PÁN'INI's rules, and which are considered as almost equally ancient. Another supplement to his grammar is entitled *Gan'apát'a,* and contains lists of words comprehended in various grammatical rules under the designation of some single word with the term "&c." annexed to it. These supplements are due to various authors. The subject of gender alone has been treated by more than one writer reputed to be inspired, namely by CÁTYÁYANA, GO'BHILA, and others.

THESE subsidiary parts of the *Pán'iníya* grammar do not require a laboured commentary; excepting only the catalogue of verbs, which does need annotation; and which is in truth a proper ground work for a complete review of all the rules of etymology, that are applicable to each verb*. The

* The number of verbal roots amounts to 1750 nearly; exclufive of many obfolete words omitted in the *D'hátupáta,* but noticed in the *Sútras* as the roots of certain derivatives. The crude verbs, however, are more numerous, because many roots, containing the same radical letters, are variously conjugated in different senses: the whole number of crude verbs separately noticed in the catalogue exceeds three thousand. From each of these are deduced many compound verbs by prefixing one or

The *Vrĭtti nyása*, a very celebrated work, is, I believe, a commentary of this sort*. It is mentioned by MAITRE'YA RACSHITA, the author of the *D'háta pradípa*, as the work chiefly consulted by him in compiling his brief annotations on the *D'hátupát'a*. A very voluminous commentary on the catalogue of verbs was compiled under the patronage of SAYAN'A, minister of a chieftain named SANGAMA, and is entitled *Mád'havíyá vrĭtti*. It thoroughly explains the signification and inflection of each verb; but at the same time enters largely into scholastick refinements on general grammar.

SUCH vast works as the *Mahábháshya* and its scholia, with the voluminous annotations on the catalogue of verbs, are not adapted for general instruction. A conciser commentary must have been always requisite. The best that is now extant is entitled the *Cás'icá vrĭtti*, or commentary composed at *Varán'as'í*. The author VA'MANA, in a short preface, explains his design: 'to gather the essence of a science dispersed in the early commentaries, in the *Bháshya*, in copious dictionaries of verbs and of nouns, and in other works.' He has well fulfilled the task which he undertook. His gloss explains in perspicuous language the meaning and application of each rule: he adds examples, and quotes, in their proper places, the necessary emendations from the *Várticas* and *Bháshya*. Though he never deviates into frivolous disquisitions, nor into tedious reasoning, but expounds the text as succinctly as could consist with perspicuity, his work is

more prepositions to the verbal root. Such compounds often deviate very widely in their signification, and some even in their inflections, from the radical verb. The derivative verbs again are numerous; such as causals, frequentatives, &c. Hence it may be readily perceived how copious this branch of grammar must be.

* I have not yet had an opportunity of inspecting either this or its gloss. It has been described to me as a commentary on the *Cásicá vrĭtti*.

is nevertheless voluminous; and yet, copious as it is, the commentaries on it, and the annotations on its commentaries, are still more voluminous. Amongst the most celebrated is the *Padamanjarí* of HARADATTA MIS'RA; a grammarian whose authority is respected almost equally with that of the author, on whose text he comments. The annotators on this again are numerous; but it would be useless to insert a long list of their names, or of the titles of their works.

EXCELLENT as the *Cás'icà vrĭtti* undoubtedly is, it partakes of the defects which have been imputed to PÁN'INI's text. Following the same order, in which the original rules are arranged, it is well adapted to assist the student in acquiring a critical knowledge of the *Sanscrĭt* tongue. But for one who studies the rudiments of the language, a different arrangement is requisite, for the sake of bringing into one view the rules which must be remembered in the inflections of one word, and those which must be combined even for a single variation of a single term. Such a grammar has been compiled within a few centuries past by RÁMACHANDRA, an eminent grammarian. It is entitled *Pracríya-caumudí.* The rules are PÁN'INI's, and the explanation of them is abridged from the ancient commentaries; but the arrangement is wholly different. It proceeds from the elements of writing to definitions; thence to orthography: it afterwards exhibits the inflections of nouns according to case, number, and gender; notices the indeclinables; and proceeds to the uses of the cases: it subjoins the rules of opposition, by which compound terms are formed; the etymology of patronymicks and other derivatives from nouns; and the reduplication of particles, &c. In the second part, it treats of the conjugation of verbs arranged in ten classes: to these primitives succeed derivative verbs, formed from verbal roots, or from nouns. The rules concerning

cerning different voices follow: they are succeeded by precepts regarding the use of the tenses; and the work concludes with the etymology of verbal nouns, gerunds, supines, and participles. A supplement to it contains the anomalies of the dialect in which the *Véda* is composed.

The outline of PÁN'INI's arrangement is simple; but numerous exceptions and frequent digressions have involved it in much seeming confusion. The two first lectures (the first section especially, which is in a manner the key of the whole grammar,) contain definitions; in the three next are collected the affixes, by which verbs and nouns are inflected. Those which appertain to verbs, occupy the third lecture: the fourth and fifth contain such as are affixed to nouns. The remaining three lectures treat of the changes which roots and affixes undergo in special cases, or by general rules of orthography, and which are all effected by the addition or by the substitution of one or more elements *. The apparent simplicity of the design vanishes in the perplexity of the structure. The endless pursuit of exceptions and of limitations so disjoins the general precepts, that the reader cannot keep in view their intended connexion and mutual relation. He wanders in an intricate maze; and the clew of the labyrinth is continually slipping from his hands.

The order in which RÁMACHANDRA has delivered the rules of grammar is certainly preferable; but the *sútras* of PÁN'INI thus detached from their context are wholly unintelligible. Without the commentator's exposition, they are indeed what Sir WILLIAM JONES has somewhere termed them, dark as the darkest oracle. Even with the aid of a comment, they cannot be fully understood until they are perused with the proper context. Notwithstanding

2 E

* Even the expunging of a letter is considered as the substitution of a blank.

withstanding this defect, BHÁT'T'O'JI' DI'CSHITA *, who revised the *Caumudí*, has for very substantial reasons adhered to the *Pa'n'iníya sútras*. That able grammarian has made some useful changes in the arrangement of the *Pracríya*: he has amended the explanation of the rules, which was in many places incorrect or imperfect: he has remedied many omissions; has enlarged the examples; and has noticed the most important instances where the elder grammarians disagree, or where classical poets have deviated from the strict rules of grammar. This excellent work is entitled *Sidd'hánta Caumudí*. The author has very properly followed the example of RÁMACHANDRA, in excluding all rules that are peculiar to the obsolete dialect of the *Véda*, or which relate to accentuation; for this also belongs to the *Véda* alone. He has collected them in an appendix to the *Sidd'hánta Caumudí*; and has subjoined, in a second appendix, rules concerning the gender of nouns. The other supplements of PÁN'INI's grammar are interwoven by this author with the body of his work.

THE *Hindus* delight in scholastick disputation. Their grammarians indulge this propensity as much as their lawyers and their sophists †. BHÁT'T'O'JI' DI'CSHITA has provided an ample store of controversy in an argumentative commentary on his own grammar. This work is entitled *Prant'a menóramá*. He also composed a very voluminous commentary on the eight lectures of PÁN'INI, and gave it the title of *S'abda Caustubha*. The only portion of it I have yet seen reaches no farther than to the end of the first section of PÁN'INI's first lecture. But this is so diffusive, that, if the whole have been executed on a similar plan, it must triple the ponderous

* Descendants of BH'A'T'T'O'JI' in the fifth or sixth degree are, I am told, now living at Benares. He must have flourished then between one and two centuries ago.

† Many separate treatises on different branches of general grammar are very properly considered as appertaining to the science of logick.

ponderous volume of the *Mahábhashya* itself. I have reason, however, for doubting that it was ever completed.

THE commentaries on the *Sidd'hánta Caumudí* and *Manóramá* are very numerous. The most celebrated shall be here briefly noticed. 1. The *Tatwa bód'hiní* expounds the *Sidd'hánta*: it is the work of INYÁNE'NDRA SARASWATI, an ascetick, and the pupil of VAMANE'NDRA SWA'MI'. 2. The *Sábdéndu s'éc'hara* is another commentary on BHÁT'T'O'JI''s grammar. It was composed by a successor, if not a descendant, of that grammarian. An abridgment of it, which is very generally studied, is the work of NÁGE'S'A, son of S'IVA BHAT'T'A, and pupil of HARIDI'CSHITA. He was patronised, as appears from his preface, by the proprietor of *Sríngavéra púra**. Though called an abridgment, this *Laghu S'abdéndu* is a voluminous performance. 3. The *Laghu S'ábdaratna* is a commentary on the *Manóramá* of BHAT'T'O'JI' DI'CSHITA, by the author's grandson, HARI' DICSHITA. This work is not improperly termed an abridgment, since it is short in comparison with most other commentaries on grammar. A larger performance on the same topicks, and with the same title of *S'ábda ratna*, was composed by a professor of this school. 4. BÁLA SARMAŃ PÁGOŃDIYA, who is either fourth or fifth in succession from BHAT'T'O'JI', as professor of grammar at Benares, has written commentaries on the *Caustubha*, *Sábda retna*, and *Sabdéndu s'éc'hara*. His father, BAIDYARAT'HA BHAT'T'A, largely annotated the *Paribháshéndu s'éc'hara* of NÁGO'J'I' BHAT'T'A, which is an argumentative commentary on a collection of grammatical axioms and definitions cited by the glossarists of PA'N'INI. This compilation, entitled *Paribháshá*, has also furnished the text for other controversial performances bearing similar titles.

2 E 2 WHILE

* A town on the Ganjes, marked *Singbore* in Rennel's maps. It is situated above *Illahabad*.

While so many commentaries have been written on the *Sidd'hánta Caumudí*, the *Pracríya Caumudí* has not been neglected. The scholiasts of this too are numerous. The most known is Crishńa Pand'ita; and his work has been abridged by his pupil Jayanta, who has given the title of *Tatwa chandra* to a very excellent compendium *. On the other hand, Cri'shńa Pand'ita has had the fate common to all noted grammarians; since his work has employed a host of commentators, who have largely commented on it.

The *Caumudís*, independently even of their numerous commentaries, have been found too vast and intricate for young students. Abridgments of the *Sidd'hánta Caumudí* have been therefore attempted by several authors with unequal degrees of success. Of three such abridgments, one only seems to deserve present notice. It is the *Mad'hya Caumudí*, and is accompanied by a similar compendium of annotations, entitled *Mad'hya Ménoramá*. The name indicates, that it holds a middle place between the diffuse original, and the jejune abstracts called *Laghu Caumudí*, &c. It contains such of Pa'ńini's rules as are most universal, and adds to each a short but perspicuous exposition. It omits only the least common exceptions and limitations.

When *Sanscrit* was the language of Indian courts, and was cultivated not only by persons who devoted themselves to religion and literature, but also by princes, lawyers, soldiers, physicians, and scribes; in short, by the first three tribes, and by many classes included in the fourth; an easy and

* Finished by him, as appears from a postscript to the book, in the year 1687 of the *Samvat era*. Though he studied at Benares, he appears to have been born on the banks of the *Tapati*, a river marked *Taptee* in Rennel's map.

and popular grammar must have been needed by persons who could not waste the best years of their lives in the study of words. Such grammars must always have been in use; those, however, which are now studied are not, I believe, of very ancient date. The most esteemed is the *Sáraswata*, together with its commentary named *Chandricá*. It seems to have been formed on one of the *Caumudís*, by translating PAŃINI's rules into language that is intelligible, independently of the gloss, and without the necessity of adverting to a different context.

ANOTHER popular grammar, which is in high repute in Bengal, is entitled *Mugd'habód'ha*, and is accompanied by a commentary. It is the work of VÓPADÉVA, and proceeds upon a plan grounded on that of the *Caumudís;* but the author has not been content to translate the rules of PÁN'INI, and to adopt his technical terms. He has on the contrary invented new terms, and contrived new abbreviations. The same author likewise composed a metrical catalogue of verbs alphabetically arranged. It is named *Cavicalpadruma*, and is intended as a substitute for the *D'hátupát'a.*

The chief inconvenience attending VÓPADÉVA's innovation is, that commentaries and scholia, written to elucidate poems and works of science, must be often unintelligible to those who have studied only his grammar, and that the writings of his scholars must be equally incomprehensible (wherever a grammatical subject is noticed) to the students of the *Páníniya.* Accordingly the *Pandits* of Bengal are cut off in a manner from communication on grammatical topics with the learned of other provinces in India. Even etymological dictionaries, such as the commentaries on the metrical vocabularies, which I shall next proceed to mention, must be unintelligible to them.

It appears from the prefaces of many different grammatical treatises, that works entitled *Dhátu* and *Náma páráyańa*, were formerly studied. They must have comprehended, as their title implies, "the whole of the verbs and nouns" appertaining to the language; and, since they are mentioned as very voluminous, they must probably have contained references to all the rules applicable to every single verb and noun. HARADATTA's explanation of the title confirms this notion. But it does not appear that any work is now extant under this title. The *D'hátupát'a*, with its commentaries, supplies the place of the *D'hátupárayańa*. A collection of dictionaries and vocabularies in like manner supplies the want of the *Náma párayańa*. These then may be noticed in this place as a branch of grammar.

The best and most esteemed vocabulary is the *Amera cósha*. Even the bigotry of SANCAR ACHÁRYA spared this, when he proscribed the other works of AMERA SINHA *. Like most other *Sanscrĭt* dictionaries, it is arranged

* AMER-SINH was an eminent poet, and one of the nine gems (for so these poets were called), who were the ornament of VICRAMA'DITYA's court. Unfortunately he held the tenets of a heterodox sect; and his poems are said to have perished in the persecutions fomented by intolerant philosophers against the persons and writings of both JAINAS and BAUDD'HAS. The persecution instigated by SANCARA and UDAYAN A'CHA'RYA, were enforced, perhaps from political motives, by princes of the *Vaishn'ava* and *S'aiva* sects, who compelled the BAUDD'HA monarchs to retire from *Hindustán*, and to content themselves with their dominions of *Lásat'a* and *Bhót'a*. It would be curious to investigate the date of this important revolution. The present conjecture, for it is little more than mere conjecture, is partly founded upon some acknowledgments made by *Pandits*, who confess that SANCARA and UDAYANA persecuted the heterodox sects, and proscribed their books; and partly on the evidence of the engraved plate found at *Mudgagiri*, and of the inscription on the pillar found at *Bedál* (See As. RES. v. I. p. 123 & 133), from which it appears, that DE'VAPA'LA DE'VA belonged to the sect of BUDD'HA; and that he reigned over *Bengal* and *Car'nát'a* as well as *Lásat'* and *Bhót*; and had successfully invaded *Cambója*, after traversing as a conqueror the *Vind'hya* range of mountains. His descendants, as far as the fourth generation, governed a no less extensive empire; as appears from the inscription on the pillar at *Bedál*. I must however acknowledge, that this last mentioned inscription

ranged in verse to aid the memory. Synonymous words are collected into one or more verses, and placed in fifteen different chapters, which treat of as many different subjects. The sixteenth contains a few homonymous terms, arranged alphabetically in the Indian manner by the final consonants. The seventeenth chapter is a pretty full catalogue of indeclinables, which European philologists would call adverbs, prepositions, conjunctions, and interjections; but which *Sanscrĭt* grammarians consider as indeclinable nouns. The last chapter of the *Ameracósh* is a treatise on the gender of nouns. Another vocabulary by the same author is often cited by his commentators under the title of *Ameramálá*.

Numerous commentaries have been written on the *Amera cósh.* The chief object of them is to explain the derivations of the nouns, and to supply the principal deficiencies of the text. *Sanscrĭt* etymologists scarcely acknowledge a single primitive amongst the nouns. When unable to trace an etymology which may be consistent with the acceptation of the word, they are content to derive it according to grammatical rules from some root to which the word has no affinity in sense. At other times they adopt fanciful etymologies from *Puránas* or from *Tantras.* But in general the derivations are accurate and instructive. The best known among these commentaries

inscription does not indicate any attachment to the sect of Budd'ha. This may be accounted for by supposing that the worshippers of Crĭshn'a and of Ra'ma were then as cordial to the followers of Budd'ha, as they now are towards each other. The king and his minister might belong to different sects.

Amera is mentioned in an inscription at *Budd'ha gayá* as the founder of a temple at that place. (As. Res. v. I. p. 284). This circumstance may serve to explain why his works have been proscribed with peculiar inveteracy, as it is acknowledged by many *Pandits* that they have been. He was probably a zealous sectarist.

This is, however, by no means certain: and Bha'nuji' D'ischita, in his commentary on the *Amera cósha,* denies that there is any evidence to prove that the author belonged to the sect of Jainas.

commentaries of the *Amera cósha* is the *Padra chandricá*, compiled from sixteen older commentaries by VRĬHASPATI surnamed MUCUT'A, or at full length RÁYA MUCU'TA MAN'I. It appears from the incidental mention of the years then expired of astronomical eras, that MUCU'TA made this compilation in the 4532d year of the *Cali yug*, which corresponds with A. D. 1430. ACHYUTA JALLACI' has abridged MUCUTA's commentary, but without acknowledgment, and has given the title of *Vyác'hyá pradípa* to his compendium. On the other hand, BHÁNUJI'-DI'CSHITA has revised the same compilation, and has corrected the numerous errors of MUCUT'A: who often derives words from roots that are unknown to the language; or according to rules which have no place in its grammar. BHÁNUJI' has greatly improved the plan of the work, by inserting from other authorities the various acceptations of words exhibited by AMERA in one or two senses only. This excellent compilation is entitled *Vyách'ya sud'há*.

THE *Amera cósha*, as has been already hinted, gives a very incomplete list of words that have various acceptations. This defect is well supplied by the *Médiní*, a dictionary so named from its author MÉDINICAR. It contains words that bear many senses, arranged in alphabetical order by the final consonants; and a list of homonymous indeclinables is subjoined to it. A similar dictionary, compiled by MAHÉS'WARA, and entitled *Vis'wa pracás'a*, is much consulted, though it be very defective, as has been justly remarked by M'EDINICAR. It contains, however, a very useful appendix on words spelt more than one way; and another on letters which are liable to be confounded, such as *v* and *b*; and another again on the gender of nouns. These subjects are not separately treated by M'EDINICAR; but he has on the other hand specified the genders with great care in the body of the work. The exact age of the *Médini* is not certainly known;

but it is older than MUCUT'A's compilation, since it is quoted by this author.

AMERA's dictionary does not contain more than ten thousand different words. Yet the *Sanscrĭt* language is very copious. The insertion of derivatives, that do not at all deviate from their regular and obvious import, has been very properly deemed superfluous. Compound epithets, and other compound terms, in which the *Sanscrĭt* language is peculiarly rich, are likewise omitted; excepting such as are especially appropriated, by a limited acceptation, either as titles of Deities, or as names of plants, animals, &c. In fact compound terms are formed at pleasure, according to the rules of grammar; and must generally be interpreted in strict conformity with those rules. Technical terms too are mostly excluded from general dictionaries, and consigned to separate nomenclatures. The *Ameracósh* then is less defective than might be inferred from the small number of words explained in it. Still, however, it needs a supplement. The *Háràvalí* may be used as such. It is a vocabulary of uncommon words, compiled by PURUSHÓTTAMA, the author of an etymological work, and also of a little collection of monograms, entitled *E'cácshara.* His *Háràvalí* was compiled by him under the patronage of D'HRĬTA SINHA. It is noticed by MÉDINICAR, and seems to be likewise anterior to the *Vis'wa.*

The remaining deficiencies of the *Ameracósh* are supplied by consulting other dictionaries and vocabularies; such as HELÁYUD'HA'S, VÁCHESPATI's, the *Dharańícósha,* or some other. *Sanscrĭt* dictionaries are indeed very numerous. PURUSHÓTTAMA and MÉDINICAR name the *Utpaliní, Sabdárńáva* and *Sansárávárta,* as works consulted by them. PURUSHÓTTAMA adds the names of VÁCHESPATI, VYÁD'I and VICRAMÁDITYA; but it is not quite clear whether he mentions them as the authors and patrons of these, or of other dictionaries. M'EDINICAR adds a fourth vocabulary called *Námamálá*, and with similar obscurity subjoins the celebrated names of BHÁGURI, VARARUCHI, SÁS'WATA, BÓPÀLITA and RANTIDÉVA. He then proceeds to enumerate the dictionaries of AMERA, S'UBHÁNGA, HELÁYND'HA, GÓVERD'HANA, RABHASA PÁLA, and the *Ratnacósha*; with the vocabularies of RUDRA, DHANANJAYA, and GANGÁD'HARA; as also the *Dharan'icósha, Háràvalì, Vrïhadamara, Tricán'd'asésha* and *Ratnamálà*. Many of these are cited by the commentators on AMERA, and by the scholiasts on different poems. The following are also frequently cited; some as etymologists, the rest as lexicographers: SWÁMÍ, DURGA, SARVADHARA, VÁMANA, CHANDRA, and the authors of the *Vaijayantí Námanid'hána, Haima, Vrïhat-nighanti, &c.* To this list might be added the *Anécárt'ha, dwani manjari Nánárt'ha*, and other vocabularies of homonymous terms; the *Dwiructi, Bhuriprayóga cósha*, and other lists of words spelt in more than one way; and the various *Nighantis* or nomenclatures, such as the *Dhanwantari-nighanta* and *Rájanighanta*, which contain lists of the materia medica; and the *Nighanti* of the *Véda*, which explains obsolete words and unusual acceptations *.

BEFORE I proceed to mention other languages of India, it may be proper to mention, that the school of *Benares* now uses the *Sidd'hánta caumudí*, and other works of BHATTÓJI, as the same school formerly did the *Cás'icá vrïtti*. The *Pracríyà caumudí*, with its commentaries, maintains its ground among the learned of *Mit'hilà* or *Tirhút*. In both places, however, and indeed

* The *Niructi*, as explained in Sir WILLIAM JONES's treatise on the literature of the *Hindus*, belongs to the same class with the *Nighanti* of the *Véda*: and a small vocabulary under both these titles is commonly annexed to the *Rïgvéda* to complete the set of *Upavédas*: There is however a much larger work entitled *Niructi*; and the commentators of it are often cited upon topics of general grammar.

indeed throughout India, the *Mahábháshya* continues to be the standard of *Sanscrit* grammar. It is therefore studied by all who are ambitious of acquiring a critical knowledge of the language. The *Haricáricá*, with its commentaries by HÉLÁRÁJA and PUNJARÁJA, was probably in use with a school that once flourished at *Ujjayiní*: but it does not seem to be now generally studied in any part of India.

The second class of Indian languages comprehends the written dialects which are now used in the intercourse of civil life, and which are cultivated by lettered men. The author of a passage already quoted includes all such dialects under the general denomination of *Prácrit*: but this term is commonly restricted to one language, namely to the *Saraswatí bála bání*, or the speech of children on the banks of the *Saraswatí**. There is reason to believe that ten polished dialects formerly prevailed in as many different civilized nations, who occupied all the fertile provinces of *Hindustán* and the *Dekhin*. Evident traces of them still exist. They shall be noticed in the order in which these *Hindu* nations are usually enumerated.

The *Sáreswata* was a nation which occupied the banks of the river *Sáraswatí*. *Bráhmanas* who are still distinguished by the name of their nation, inhabit chiefly the *Penjáb* or *Panchanada*, west of the river from which they take their appellation. Their original language may have once prevailed through the southern and western parts of *Hindustán* proper, and is probably the idiom to which the name of *Prácrit* is generally appropriated. This has been more cultivated than any other among the dialects which will be here enumerated, and it occupies a principal place

2 F 2 in

* The term will bear a different interpretation: but this seems to be the most probable explana- of it. The other (youthful speech of Saraswatí) is generally received.

in the dialogue of most dramas. Many beautiful poems, composed wholly in this language, or intermixed with stanzas of pure *Sanscrït*, have perpetuated the memory of it, though perhaps it have long ceased to be a vernacular tongue. Grammars have been compiled for the purpose of teaching this language and its prosody, and several treatises of rhetorick have been written to illustrate its beauties. The *Prácrïta manóramà* and *Prácrïta Pingala* are instances of the one, and the *Saraswatì Cant'ábharan'a* of Bhójadéva may be named as an example of the other, although both *Sanscrït* and *Prácrit* idioms furnish the examples with which that author elucidates his precepts. For the character of the *Prácrit* language I must refer the reader to Sir William Jones's remarks in his preface to the translation of the Fatal Ring.

The *Cányacubjas* possessed a great empire, the metropolis of which was the ancient city of *Cányacubja* or *Canój*. Theirs seems to be the language which forms the ground-work of modern *Hindustánì*, and which is known by the appellation of *Hindí* or *Hindevì*. Two dialects of it may be easily distinguished, one more refined, the other less so. To this last the name of *Hindí* is sometimes restricted, while the other is often confounded with *Prácrit*. Numerous poems have been composed in both dialects, not only before the *Hindustánì* was ingrafted on the *Hindí* by a large intermixture of Persian, but also in very modern times, by *Muhammedan* as well as *Hindu* poets. *Dóhrás* or detached couplets, and *Cabits* or stanzas, in the *Hindevì* dialect, may be found among the works of *Muslemán* authors; it will be sufficient to instance those of Melic Muhammed Jaisí, Muhammed Afzel, and Amírkhán Anjám. Most poems in this dialect are, however, the exclusive production of *Hindu* poets*. On examining them, the affinity of *Hindí*

* Among the most admired specimens of *Hindí* poetry, the seven hundred couplets of Bihárílál,

6

Hindí with the *Sanscrĭt* language is peculiarly striking; and no person acquainted with both can hesitate in affirming that *Hindí* is chiefly borrowed from *Sanscrĭt*. Many words of which the etymology shows them to be the purest *Sanscrĭt*, are received unaltered; many more undergo no change but that of making the final vowel silent; a still greater number exhibits no other difference than what arises from the uniform permutation of certain letters; the rest too, with comparatively few exceptions, may be easily traced to a *Sanscrĭt* origin. That this is the root from which *Hindí* has sprung, (not *Hindí* the dialect whence *Sanscrĭt* has been refined,) may be proved by etymology, the analogy of which is lost in *Hindí* and preserved in *Sanscrĭt*. A few examples will render this evident.

CRÍYÁ signifies action, and *Carma* act, both of which are regularly derived from the root *Crĭ* to do. They have been adopted into *Hindustání*, with many other regular derivatives of the same root; (such, for example, as *Caran'a* [contracted into *Carná*] the act of doing; *Cartá* the agent; *Cáran'* cause, or the means of doing; *Cárya* [*Cárj*, *Cáj*,] the thing to be done, and the intent or purpose of the action.) But I select these two instances, because both words are adopted into *Hindustání* in two several modes. Thus *Críá* signifies action, and *Ciriá* expresses one metaphorical sense of the same *Sanscrĭt* word, viz. oath or ordeal. Again, *Ciriá-caram* signifies funeral rites; but *Cám* is the most usual form in which the *Sanscrĭt Carma* is exhibited in the *Hindustání*; and it thus assumes the same form

LA'L, and the amatory verses of SU'NDER and of MATIRA'M, are conspicuous. But their dialect is not pure *Hindevi*; since they sometimes borrow from the Persian language. SU'NDER wrote his poems in the reign of SHA'HJEHA'N, and seems to have been patronized by that prince, whom he praises in his preface. BIHA'RI'LA'L flourished at the court of *Ambhér*, towards the beginning of the sixteenth century of the Christian era. His poems were arranged in their present order for the use of the unfortunate prince A'ZEM SHA'H; and the modern edition is therefore called *A'zemsháhí*. The old edition has been elegantly translated into *Sanscrĭt* verse, by HERIPRESA'DA' PAN-[illegible]nder the patronage of CHE'T SIN'H, when *Raja* of *Benares*.

form with *Cám*, desire, a very different word taken from the *Sanscrït* derivative of the root *Cam*, to seek: here then, *Hindustání* confounds two very different words in one instance, and makes two words out of one in the other instance.

SAT literally signifies existent, it is employed in the acceptation of truth; *Satya*, a regular derivative from it, signifies true; or, employed substantively, truth. The correspondent *Hindí* word, *sach*, is corrupted from the *Sanscrït satya*, by neglecting the final vowel, by substituting *j* for *y*, according to the genius of the *Hindevì* dialect, and by transforming the harsh combination *tj* into the softer sound of *ch*. Here then is obviously traced the identity of the *Hindustánì sach*, and *Bengáli shótyo*, which are only the same *Sanscrït* word *satya* variously pronounced.

YUVAN signifies young, and *yauvana* youth; the first makes *Yuvá* in the nominative case: this is adopted into *Hindustánì* with the usual permutation of consonants, and becomes *Jubá*, as *Yauvana* is transformed into *Jóban*. The same word has been less corrupted in Persian and Latin, where it stands *Juwán* and *Juvenis*. In many inflections the root of *Yuvan* is contracted into *Yún*, the possessive case, for example, forms in the three numbers, *Yúnas, Yunós, Yúnám*: here, then, we trace the origin of the Latin comparative *Junior;* and I cannot hesitate in referring to these *Sanscrït* roots, the Welsh *Jevangk*, and Armorican *Jovank*, as well as the Saxon *Yeong*, and finally the English *Young*. This analogy, which seems evident through the medium of the *Sanscrït* language, is wholly obscured in *Hindustánì*.

THESE examples might be easily multiplied, but unprofitably, I fear; for after proving that nine tenths of the *Hindí* dialect may be traced back

to

to the *Sanscrĭt* idiom, there yet remains the difficulty of accounting for the remaining tenth, which is perhaps the basis of the *Hindí* language. Sir WILLIAM JONES thought it so, and he thence inferred, that the pure *Hindí* was primeval in Upper India, into which the *Sanscrĭt* was introduced by conquerors from other kingdoms in some very remote age *. This opinion I do not mean to controvert. I only contend, that where similar words are found in both languages, the *Hindí* has borrowed from *Sanscrĭt*, rather than the *Sanscrĭt* from *Hindí*. It may be remarked too, that in most countries the progress has been from languages rich in inflections, to dialects simple in their structure. In modern idioms, auxiliary verbs and appendant particles supply the place of numerous inflections of the root: it may, for this reason, be doubted, whether the present structure of the *Hindí* tongue be not a modern refinement. But the question, which has been here hinted rather than discussed, can be decided only by a careful examination of the oldest compositions that are now extant in the *Hindí* dialect. Until some person execute this task, a doubt must remain, whether the ground-work of *Hindí*, and consequently of *Hindustánì*, be wholly distinct from that of *Sanscrĭt*.

ON the subject of the modern dialect of Upper India, I with pleasure refer to the works of *(a very ingenious member of this society)* Mr. GILCHRIST, whose labours have now made it easy to acquire the knowledge of an elegant language, which is used in every part of *Hindustán* and the *Dekhin;* which is the common vehicle of colloquial intercourse among all well educated natives, and among the illiterate also in many provinces of India, and which is almost every where intelligible to some among the inhabitants of every village. The dialects, which will be next noticed, are of more limited use.

GAURA,

* Third anniversary discourse.

GAURA *, or, as it is commonly called, *Bengalah*, or *Bengáli*, is the language spoken in the provinces, of which the ancient city of *Gaur* was once the capital; it still prevails in all the provinces of Bengal, excepting perhaps some frontier districts, but is said to be spoken in its greatest purity in the eastern parts only; and, as there spoken, contains few words which are not evidently derived from *Sanscrit*. This dialect has not been neglected by learned men. Many *Sanscrit* poems have been translated, and some original poems have been composed in it; learned *Hindus* in Bengal speak it almost exclusively; verbal instruction in sciences is communicated through this medium, and even publick disputations are conducted in this dialect. Instead of writing it in the *Dévanágarì*, as the *Prácrit* and *Hindeví* are written †, the inhabitants of Bengal have adopted a peculiar character, which is nothing else but *Déva-nágarí*, difformed for the sake of expeditious writing. Even the learned amongst them employ this character for the *Sanscrit* language, the pronunciation of which too they in like manner degrade to the *Bengálí* standard. The labours of Mr. HALHED and Mr. FORSTER have already rendered a knowledge of the *Bengálí* dialect accessible, and Mr. FORSTER's further exertions will still more facilitate the

* It is necessary to remark, that although *Gaura* be the name of *Bengal*, yet the *Bráhmanas*, who bear that appellation, are not inhabitants of *Bengal* but of *Hindustán* proper. They reside chiefly in the *Suba* of *Delhi*; while the *Bráhmanas* of Bengal are avowed colonists from *Canój*. It is difficult to account for this contradiction. The *Gaura Bráhmanas* alledge a tradition, that their ancestors migrated in the days of the *Pándavas*, at the commencement of the present *Cali Yuga*. Though no plausible conjecture can be founded on this tradition, yet I am induced to retract a conjecture formerly hazarded by me; that the *Gar* of our maps was the original country of the *Gaura* priests.

† *Prácrit* and *Hindì* books are commonly written in the *Dévanágarì*; but a corrupt writing, called *Nágarí*, is used by *Hindus* in all common transactions where *Hindí* is employed by them; and a still more corrupted one, wherein vowels are for the most part omitted, is employed by bankers and others in mercantile transactions. I must here confess that I can give no satisfactory explanation of the term. The common etymology of *Nágarí* is unsatisfactory; unless *Nagara* be taken as the name of some particular place emphatically called the city.

the acquisition of a language, which cannot but be deemed greatly useful, since it prevails throughout the richest and most valuable portion of the British possessions in India.

Mait'hila, or *Tirhutíya*, is the language used in *Mit'hilà*, that is, in the *Sircár* of *Tirhút*, and in some adjoining districts, limited however by the rivers *Cusí (Causicí,)* and *Gandhac (Gandhací,)* and by the mountains of *Népál*: it has great affinity with *Bengálí*; and the character in which it is written differs little from that which is employed throughout Bengal. In *Tirhút*, too, the learned write *Sanscrĭt* in the *Tirhutíya* character, and pronounce it after their own inelegant manner. As the dialect of *Mit'hilà* has no extensive use, and does not appear to have been at any time cultivated by elegant poets, it is unnecessary to notice it further in this place.

Utcala, or *Od'radés'a*, is co-extensive with the *Subá* of *O'résá*, extending from *Médinípúr* to *Mánacapattana*, and from the sea to *Sammall-púr*. The language of this province, and the character in which it is written, are both called *Uríya*. So far as a judgment can be formed from imperfect specimens of this language, it contains many *Sanscrĭt* words variously corrupted, with some Persian and Arabick terms borrowed through the medium of *Hindustání*, and with others of doubtful origin. The letters are evidently taken from the *Dévanágarí*; and the *Bráhmens* of this province use the *Uríya* character in writing the *Sanscrĭt* language: its deviations from the *Dévanágarí* may be explained, from the practice of writing on palm leaves with an iron style, or on paper with a pen cut from a porcupine's quill. It differs in this respect from the hand-writing of northern tribes, and is analogous to that of the southern inhabitants of the peninsula.

THE five *Hindu* nations, whose peculiar dialects have been thus briefly noticed, occupy the northern and eastern portions of India; they are denominated the five *Gaurs.* The rest, called the five *Drávirs*, inhabit the southern and western parts of the peninsula. Some *Pandits* indeed exclude *Car'náta*, and substitute *Càsmíra;* but others, with more propriety, omit the *Cáshmirian* tribe; and, by adding the *Cánaras* to the list of *Drávirs*, avoid the inconsistency of placing a northern tribe among southern nations. There is reason too for doubting whether *Cáshmíra* be occupied by a distinct nation, and whether the inhabitants of it be not rather a tribe of *Cányacubjas.*

DRÁVIRA is the country which terminates the peninsula of India. Its northern limits appear to lie between the twelfth and thirteenth degrees of north latitude. The language of the province is the *Támel*, to which Europeans have given the name of *Malabar* *, from *Malay-wár*, a province of *Drávira.* They have similarly corrupted the true name of the dialect into Tamul, Tamulic, and Tamulian †: but the word, as pronounced by the natives, is *Támla*, or *Támalah;* and this seems to indicate a derivation from *Támra*, or *Támraparn'í* a river of note, which waters the southern *Máthura*, situated within the limits of *Drávir.* The provincial dialect is written in a character which is greatly corrupted from the parent *Dévanágarí*, but which nevertheless is used by the *Bráhmens* of *Drávir* in writing the *Sanscrít* language. After carefully inspecting a grammar published by Mr.

* A learned *Bráhmen* of *Drávira* positively assures me, that the dialect of Malabar, though confounded by Europeans with the *Támel*, is different from it; and is not the language to which Europeans have allotted that appellation.

† The Romish and Protestant missionaries who have published dictionaries and grammars of this dialect, refer to another language, which they denominate *Grandam* and *Grandonicum.* It appears that *Sanscrít* is meant, and the term thus corrupted by them is *Grant'ha*, a volume or book.

Mr. DRUMMOND at Bombay, and a dictionary by missionaries at Madras, I can venture to pronounce that the *Túmla* contains many *Sanscrĭt* words, either unaltered or little changed, with others more corrupted, and a still greater number of doubtful origin.

THE *Mahárúshtra* or *Mahrátta* is the language of a nation which has in the present century greatly enlarged its antient limits. If any inference may be drawn from the name of the character in which the language is written, the country occupied by this people was formerly called *Múru* *; for the peculiar corruption of the *Dévanágarì*, which is employed by the *Mahárásh'tras* in common transactions, is denominated by them *Múr*. Their books, it must be remarked, are commonly written in *Dévanàgarì*. The *Mahrátta* nation was formerly confined to a mountainous tract situated south of the river *Nermada*, and extending to the province of *Cócán*. Their language is now more widely spread, but is not yet become the vernacular dialect of provinces situated far beyond the antient bounds of their country. Like other Indian tongues, it contains much pure *Sanscrĭt*, and more corruptions of that language intermixed with words borrowed from Persian and Arabick, and with others derived from an unknown source. If the bards of *Múru* were once famous, their supposed successors, though less celebrated, are not less diligent. The *Mahrátta*s possess many poems in their own dialect, either translated from the *Sanscrĭt*, or original compositions in honour of CRĬSHNÁ, RAMÁ, and other deified heroes. Treatises in prose too, on subjects of logick and of philosophy, have been composed in the *Mahrátta* dialect.

* Mentioned in the royal grant preserved at a famous temple in *Carnát'a*. See As. RES. *v.* III. *p.* 48. However, the *Mahráttas* themselves affirm, that the *Múru* character was introduced amongst them from the island of *Silán*.

Carnát'a, or *Cárnara,* is the antient language of *Carnát'aca,* a province which has given name to districts on both coasts of the peninsula. This dialect still prevails in the intermediate mountainous tract, but seems to be superseded by other provincial tongues on the eastern coast. A peculiar character formed from the *Dévanágarì,* but like the *Támla,* much corrupted from it through the practice of writing on palm-leaves with an iron style, is called by the same name with the language of *Carn'á'tic. Bráhmens* of this tribe have assured me that the language bears the same affinity to *Sanscrìt* as other dialects of the *Dacshin.* I can affirm too, from their conversation, that the *Cánaras,* like most other southern tribes, have not followed the ill example of Bengal and the provinces adjacent to it, in pronouncing the *Sanscrìt* language in the same inelegant manner with their own provincial dialects.

Tailanga, *Télingah,* or *Tilanga,* is at once the name of a nation, of its language, and of the character in which that language is written. Though the province of *Telingána* alone retain the name in published maps of India, yet the adjacent provinces on either bank of the *Crìshná* and *Gódáverí,* and those situated on the north-eastern coast of the peninsula, are undoubtedly comprehended within the ancient limits of *Tilanga,* and are inhabited chiefly by people of this tribe. The language too is widely spread: and many circumstances indicate that the *Tailangas* formerly occupied a very extensive tract, in which they still constitute the principal part of the population. The character in which they write their own language is taken from *Dévanágarì,* and the *Tailanga Bráhmens* employ it in writing the *Sanscrìt* tongue, from which the *Tailanga* idiom is said to have borrowed more largely than other dialects used in the south of India. This language appears to have been cultivated by poets, if not by prose writers, for the *Tailangas* possess many compositions in their own provincial dialect, some of which are said to record the ancient history of the country.

THE province of *Gúrjara** does not appear to have been at any time much more extensive than the modern *Guzrát*, although *Bráhmanas* distinguished by the name of that country, be now spread over the adjoining provinces on both sides of the *Nermadá*. This tribe uses a language denominated from their own appellation, but very nearly allied to the *Hindí* tongue, while the character in which it is written conforms almost exactly with vulgar *Nágarí*. Considering the situation of their country, and the analogy of language and writing, I cannot hesitate in thinking that the *Gurjaras* should be considered as the fifth northern nation of India, and the *U'ríyas* should be ranked among the tribes of the *Dacshin*.

BRIEF and imperfect as is this account of the *Prácrits* of India, I must be still more concise in speaking of the languages denominated *Mágad'hi* and *Apabhransa* in the passages quoted at the beginning of this essay. Under these names are comprehended all those dialects which, together with the *Prácrits* above noticed, are generally known by the common appellation of *Bháshá*, or speech. This term, as employed by all philologists from PA'N'INI down to the present professors of grammar, does indeed signify the popular dialect of *Sanscrït*, in contradistinction to the obsolete dialect of the *Véda*; but in common acceptation, *Bhákhá* (for so the word is pronounced on the banks of the Ganges) denotes any of the modern vernacular dialects of India, especially such as are corrupted from the *Sanscrït*: these are very numerous. After excluding mountaineers, who are probably aborigines of India, and whose languages have certainly no affinity with *Sanscrït*, there yet remain in the mountains and islands contiguous to India, many tribes that seem to be degenerate *Hindus*; they have certainly retained some

* The limits of *Gúrjara*, as here indicated, are too narrow. It seems to have been co-extensive with the antient, rather than the modern *Guzrát*, and to have included the whole, or the greatest part of Candesh and Malwa.

some traces of the language and writing which their ancestors had been taught to employ.

WITHOUT passing the limits of *Hindustán*, it would be easy to collect a copious list of different dialects in the various provinces, which are inhabited by the ten principal *Hindu* nations. The extensive region, which is nearly defined by the banks of the *Saraswatí* and *Gangá* on the north, and which is strictly limited by the shores of the eastern and western seas towards the south, contains fifty-seven provinces according to some lists, and eighty-four according to others. Each of these provinces has its peculiar dialect, which appears, however, in most instances, to be a variety only of some one among the ten principal idioms. Thus *Hindustánì*, which seems to be the lineal descendant of the *Cányacubja*, comprises numerous dialects from the *Orduzebán*, or language of the royal camp and court, to the barbarous jargon which reciprocal mistakes have introduced among European gentlemen and their native servants. The same tongue, under its more appropriate denomination of *Hindí*, comprehends many dialects strictly local and provincial. They differ in the proportion of Arabick, Persian and *Sanscrit*, either pure or slightly corrupted, which they contain; and some shades of difference may be also found in the pronunciation, and even in the basis of each dialect.

NOT being sufficiently conversant with all these idioms, I shall only mention two, which are well known, because lyrick poets have employed them in songs, that are still the delight of natives of all ranks. I allude to the *Penjábí* and to the *Brij-bhákhá*. The first is the language of *Panchananda*, or *Penjáb*, a province watered by the five celebrated rivers which fall into the *Sind'hu*. The songs entitled *Khéáls* and *Teppas*, which are no doubt familiar to all who have a taste for the vocal music of India, are composed almost exclusively in this dialect; as the *Dhurpeds* and regular *Rags* are in *Hindí*, and *Rékhtah* *, in the language of the court of *Hindustán.*

THE *Brij-bhákhá*, or *Vraja-bháshá*, is the dialect supposed to have been anciently spoken among the peasants in the neighbourhood of *Mat'hura.* It derives its name from the cowpens *(Vraja)* and dairies in the forest of *Vrĭndá*, where CRĬSHN'A was educated among the wives and daughters of the cowherds. His amorous adventures with RA'D'HA' and the *Gópís* furnish the subject of many favourite songs in this dialect. It is still spoken with much purity throughout a great part of the *Antarbéd*, or *Dóáb*, and in some districts on the opposite banks of the *Yamunà* and *Gangá.*

To these cursory observations might be fitly added a specimen of each language, and of the character in which it is written, together with a list of the most common terms in the various dialects of India, compared with words of similar sound and import in the ancient languages of Europe. I have indeed made collections for this purpose, but the insertion of a copious list would exceed the limits of a desultory essay. For this reason, and because the collection is yet incomplete, I suppress it; and shall here close the present essay abruptly, with the intention of resuming the subject, should the further prosecution of these inquiries at any future time enable me to furnish the information called for by this society, concerning the number of *Hinduwí* dialects, and the countries where they are spoken.

VIII.

* The author of the *Tezcareh Shúárá Hind* explains *Rékhtah* as signifying any poetry composed in the language of the royal court of *Hindustán*, but in the ſtyle and metre of Persian poetry.

John Borthwick Gilchrist

'Preface'. *The Strangers' East Indian Guide to the Hindoostanee; or Grand Popular Language of India*. London: W. Bulmer, 1808.

PREFACE.

NOTHING can be so discouraging to the student of a living language in this country, as the chance of being, by future proficiency therein, under the disagreeable necessity of unlearning whatever pronunciation or lessons he may have acquired at the outset of his oriental career. Few of my readers, who are in the smallest degree acquainted with Indian affairs, need now be apprized that they will be exposed to the irksome situation I have just stated, provided they still prefer to this little volume the inaccurate and inadequate performances of my predecessors, as their guides to the Hindoostanee tongue. To them we may apply the following lines with great propriety:

Aut inertes, aut insani, aut quibus egestas imperat,
Qui sibi semitam non sapiunt, alteri monstrant viam.

That it is as easy to learn at first the polished and grammatical style of any speech, as it can be to acquire its corrupt and barbarous idiom, is a fact which will stand the test of every person's experience through all quarters of the globe, and in none more satisfactorily than among the various nations of Hindoostan. It is true, that such a jargon, as the intelligent writer, quoted in page 8th mentions, may be acquired very imperceptibly, though in reality the trouble is not less in doing this, than the small portion of manly exertion which is requisite, when properly directed, to attain so useful an object as the Hindoostanee language.

The late philological performance of a Mr. Lebedeff, who sojourned as a musician for some years in India, hath, by its appearance in this hemisphere, stamped a real value on Hadley's labours, for he may now comparatively be termed a classic in *Moorish* lore, by the acquisition of a second in that department, much more pernicious to learners than the principal ever could have proved at any period of his reign. It is a melancholy reflexion, that a space of thirty or forty years has rather heaped error upon error in the Hindoostanee publications from the London press, than evinced the smallest tendency to eradicate them entirely. The presence of a Hindoostanee *Moonshee*, even in the metropolis, has apparently produced as yet no other than the preposterous effect of prefixing to the corrupt dialect of that most useful language, a Bungalee alphabet, although we are informed in the same breath by Hadley's editors, that there is little or no affinity between these two dialects. This, however, is nothing to the discordant medley of Oriental tongues, prepared by Mr. Lebedeff for the instruction of his readers, who will find, by a few months residence in this part of the world, that all their previous labour and pains to acquire its languages by his aid, have proved wholly in vain. To obviate as soon as possible, to the utmost of my ability, so serious and galling a loss of time to my countrymen on their way to India, I have been once more induced to devote my leisure hours to their service. Having the fullest conviction, that no future stage of their progress will afford them cause to upbraid me with the charge here preferred against other authors, for that ignorance and incapacity which are still so evident in all the successive attempts at a grammar of the grand popular speech of Hindoostan, I can surely feel no hesitation to express my sentiments accordingly,

Feliciter is sapit qui periculo alieno sapit.

The experience of my friends, as well as my own observations, hath fully convinced me, that in a climate like India, we cannot at starting sufficiently shorten and smooth the road to the acquisition of its most useful tongue, I have therefore submitted this abstract to the suffrages of an indulgent public, but with no intention of entering the lists as an author against Mr. Lebedeff, or any such writers, whatever I may do with more creditable opponents. That there are many very respectable individuals, whose stay is too transitory, or whose duties are too laborious and important in India, to admit of other than desultory study, is a truth which every one must allow, as well as the necessity for such persons still possessing a certain knowledge of the Hindoostanee or current tongue. For people in either of those predicaments I may safely recommend these sheets, as they deviate very little from the grammatical rules observed in my larger works, which many persons cannot always refer to or employ. This advice is offered in the conviction, that the present introduction is on the whole much easier and plainer than any thing yet published on the colloquial speech of India. To superficial students, whose ears cannot accurately discriminate sounds, a reversed vocabulary would rather prove embarrassing at first than useful, it has therefore been omitted, because when leisure, duty, interest, or inclination stimulate any learner's exertions farther than this preliminary step, he will not hesitate to furnish his library with the large Grammar and Linguist, and apply to them with the best effect accordingly. To insert the oriental letters in a scheme like this, would at once defeat the very object of so small a performance, and render it nearly as discouraging, from the intricacy of its character, as a complete Hindoostanee grammar has hitherto been deemed tremendous by its bulk alone. In the multitude of counsellors there may be safety, when these are duly qualified to offer the advice required ; every stranger, therefore, will do well before he follows any, relative to his own application to the languages, to ask his advisers to translate the following easy sentence in the Hindoostanee or popular language. "Hindee zuban murboot toom seek,ho to seek,ho, pur myn ne aj tuluk yoon hee seek,hee hy."

If this be readily complied with, by furnishing a translation and analysis in writing, the new comer ought implicitly to follow the plan his friends may lay down for the future prosecution of his studies, otherwise he should hesitate, and advert to the fate of the blind leading the blind in any pursuit whatever. At all events, good reader! my solicitude at the very commencement of your literary labours in this country is so far pardonable, as I honestly wish you should trust *neque cæcum ducem, neque amentem consultorem*, in all important matters of this kind.

Were the learner to task his self every day with one page of the Vocabulary, he would soon be master of the whole by heart, and by acquiring only those words first which occur next to the English, he would very quickly lay in a stock of the utmost consequence to a beginner. When these objects have been attained, the marginal spaces may be appropriated solely to encrease the original store, or to a reversed scheme of the whole, including such remarks and observations, as the learner's progress may enable him occasionally to make on the subject of his studies. As he proceeds, his labour will be smoothed by the pleasing conviction, that almost every word acquired from these sheets may be brought to the profit side of his account at once, without the smallest apprehension of being constrained by experience to insert many items to the score of loss, as he must inevitably do with the most of his acquisitions from Hadley, and others of that stamp.

On the theme of this small work, I feel particular satisfaction in subjoining the following extract from the learned and ingenious philological lucubrations of Mr. H. T. Colebrooke, in the 7th volume of the Asiatic Researches, page 223. " On the subject of the modern dialect of Upper India, I with pleasure refer to the works of Mr. Gilchrist, whose labours have now made it easy to acquire the knowledge of an elegant language, which is used in every part of *Hindoostan* and the *Dukhin*;

which is the common vehicle of colloquial intercourse among all well-educated natives; and among the illiterate also in many provinces of India; and which is almost every where intelligible to some among the inhabitants of every village.

"Without passing the limits of *Hindoostan*, it would be easy to collect a copious list of different dialects, in the various provinces, which are inhabited by the ten principal *Hindoo* nations. The extensive region, which is nearly defined by the banks of the *Suruswutee* and *Gunga* on the north, and which is strictly limited by the shores of the eastern and western seas towards the south, contains fifty-seven provinces according to some lists, and eighty-four according to others. Each of these provinces has its peculiar dialect, which appears, however, in most instances to be a variety only of some one among the ten principal idioms. Thus *Hindoostanee*, which seems to be the lineal descendant of the *Kanyukoobju*, comprises numerous dialects, from the *Oordoo zuban*, or language of the royal camp and court, to the *barbarous jargon which reciprocal mistakes* have introduced among *European gentlemen* and their *native servants.* The same tongue, under its more appropriate denomination of *Hindee,* comprehends many dialects strictly local and provincial. They differ in the proportion of Arabick, Persian, and *Sunskrit,* either pure or slightly corrupted, which they contain: and some shades of difference may be also found in the pronunciation, and even in the basis of each dialect." (1)

To enable the Hindoostanee student to judge and decide for his self as soon as possible, after his arrival in this country, I have here also deemed it my duty to insert the very judicious and irrefragable arguments in Mr. W. B. Bayley's Collegial Thesis, just published, on the importance and utility of that language.

" The language which in my proposition I have specified by the name of Hindoostanee, is also frequently denominated Hindee, Oordoo, and Rekhtu. It is com-

---

(1) The slight orthographical deviations, in a few words, from Sir William Jones's plan to my own, will surely be pardoned here, as every author has the same right, on such occasions, to make free with mine.

pounded of the Arabic, Persian, and Sunskrit, or B,hak,ha, which last appears to have been in former ages the current language of Hindoostan.

" Owing in some measure to the intercourse of the merchants of Arabia with this country, but more particularly to the frequent invasions of it by the M*oo*sulmans, and their ultimate settlement in it, a considerable number of Arabic and Persian words became engrafted on the original language of the natives, and out of this mixture arose a new language, the Hindoostanee, like a modern superstructure on an ancient foundation.

" By degrees it assumed its present appearance and estimation; and the court of Dihlee made choice of it, as the medium in all affairs depending on colloquial intercourse. Hence its influence gradually spread abroad so widely, that it became universally used in the courts of the M*oo*sulman princes. Many of the native inhabitants also grew familiarized to it, and used it in all concerns, the validity of which did not depend upon written documents.

"As the intercourse and communication of the *Moo*sulmans with the natives of India was greater or less, according to certain circumstances and situations, the Hindoostanee naturally varied considerably, with respect to the prevalence of one or other of the languages composing it. This circumstance will sanction a division of it into three distinct dialects; namely, the pristine, or country; the middle, or familiar; and the learned, or court dialect; each of which are respectively useful in different districts, situations, and families.

"In the first, or pristine dialect, there is a smaller admixture of foreign words; hence this is more nearly related to the original dialects of the country.

"In the second, or familiar dialect, the number of foreign words bears nearly an equal proportion to the original ones.

"In the third, or court dialect, Arabic and Persian words are by far the most numerous.

"It is unnecessary for me to explain the various moral and physical causes, which have rendered the Hindoostanee less prevalent in some parts of India than in others, since they must be evident to every reflecting mind. This circumstance, however, by no means invalidates my proposition; for although I can grant that particular dialects are spoken by the inhabitants of several districts and provinces of India, yet I assert, that none of them, taken individually, is so generally useful and necessary as the Hindoostanee. Nor will my assertion appear too bold, when it be considered, that however extensive a country may be, and how numerous soever the dialects spoken in it, still the language of its court and metropolis will always be most generally known and understood, and must of consequence be that most worthy of attention and cultivation by foreigners.

"I shall now advert to a few arguments, which I trust will be convincing and satisfactory proofs of the truth of my proposition.

"In the whole of the vast country of Hindoostan, scarce any M*oo*sulman will be found, who does not understand and speak the Hindoostanee.

"Every Hindoo also, of any distinction,

or who has the least connection either with the M*oo*sulman or the British government, is, according to his situation, acquainted, more or less, with this language.

" It is moreover the general medium by which many persons of various foreign nations settled in Hindoostan, communicate their wants and ideas to each other. Of the truth of this, indeed, we ourselves are an evidence, as are the Portugueze, Dutch, French, Danes, Arabs, Turks, Greeks, Armenians, Georgians, Persians, M*o*ghuls, and Chinese.

" In almost all the armies of India this appears to be the universally used language; even though many of the individuals composing them, be better acquainted with the dialects peculiar to their respective districts.

" Nearly from Cape Comorin to Kab*oo*l, a country about 2000 miles in length, and 1400 in breadth within the Ganges, few persons will be found in any large villages or towns, which have ever been conquered or much frequented by M*oo*sulmans, who are not sufficiently conversant in the Hindoostanee; and in many places beyond the Ganges, this language is current and familiar.

"An accurate knowledge of the customs and manners of a nation, depends principally on an acquaintance with its colloquial languages; and in no country, perhaps, is this knowledge more essential, or a more desirable object of attainment, than in Hindoostan, the inhabitants of which differ so widely in religion, laws, customs and prejudices.

"When the conquerors and rulers of a country are unacquainted with the current speech of their subjects, the natural consequences must evidently be injustice on the one part and disaffection on the other.

"Although in the popular language of any country, there may be a deficiency of books of science, still that language is the most proper and necessary for conducting the affairs of civil government and commerce, of military as well as judicial concerns. I may here observe, that many centuries have not elapsed since the learning, laws, and religion of our own country were preserved and studied in a foreign language; that language, however, has been superseded by the English, a sufficient proof that the current language of the country was deemed most worthy of cultivation and study.

"Although the Hindoostanee language does not boast of very many prose compositions, or works of science, yet how many elegant tales and beautiful poems have been composed in it! How universally are commercial and military concerns, and even political correspondence of the highest consequence, connected with it, and carried on in it! And in this place, I may observe, that the instructions of the learned natives, and all their disputations and arguments on subjects of literature, are conducted in it; and that in every case, where a native of this country wishes either to compose or to dictate any thing to be written, he constantly arranges his ideas, and explains his meaning, in the Hindoostanee.

"Lastly, a correct and general knowledge of this language greatly facilitates the acquisition of many others, and is the only mean by which we can effectually prevent injustice and imposition.

"If the assertions which I have here made be founded on truth, what argument can be brought to invalidate my proposition? The conclusion from the premises is this; that to the merchant, the traveller, the civil and military officer, the philosopher and physician; in short, to every one who carries on concerns of any moment in India, the Hindoostanee language is more generally necessary and advantageous than any other; and on this account, it ought to be the most cultivated and esteemed."

During the first six months residence in India, I have seldom known the attendance of a native teacher, or Moonshee, upon a scholar, produce much benefit; on the contrary, except in the mere pronunciation of a few letters, such interference generally does a great deal of harm. To those readers who will so far confide in my judgment, as to follow my advice, I shall candidly impart it by desiring them, in the above period to acquire, if possible, the difficult sounds from some of their well-informed European friends; and at the same time to make their selves complete masters of every word and rule in this minute volume at least, before they sit regularly down to study the language with any Moonshee. Indeed, if they can prevail on their selves to include the Oriental Linguist, or Anti-jargonist, in this counsel, they never will have cause to repent such precaution, as it may save them much vexation, trouble, disgust, a great deal of time, and even some cash, on the score of native instructors, of whom not one in a thousand has sufficient ability and sagacity combined to conduct the studies of a new comer, with propriety and effect, in the Hindoostance, or any other Oriental tongue. If the assistance, however, of such men be in the beginning unavailing and tormenting, the aid of those among them who have a smattering of English, is still more pernicious and delusive; every scholar, therefore, who intends ultimately to make his self a proficient in Hindoostanee, will find it his interest in many respects to believe, that I expect no adequate advantages, which can instigate me to mislead and deceive him in any pursuit of this kind, by communicating my undisguised sentiments of these people, on the present occasion, and by deprecating all such premature equivocal aid accordingly.

CALCUTTA,
15th July, 1802.

TO WRITERS AND GADETS.

THAT gentlemen going to India, under the auspices of the Honourable East India Company, may not plead ignorance of existing regulations concerning their servants' acquirement of the oriental languages, the following extracts from the public orders of the Governor-General in Council at Bengal, are now laid before them.

Fort William, Public Department,
Dec. 11, 1798.

" The Right Honourable the Governor-General in Council, considering that the due administration of the internal government and affairs of the Company in Bengal, requires that no civil servant should be nominated to certain offices of trust and responsibility, until it shall have been ascertained that he is sufficiently acquainted with the laws and regulations enacted by the Governor-General in Council, and the several languages, the knowledge of which is requisite for the due discharge of the respective functions of such offices: His Lordship in Council hereby apprizes the civil servants of the Company in Bengal, that from and after the 1st of January 1801, no servant will be deemed eligible to any of the aforementioned offices, until he shall have passed an examination (the nature of which will be hereafter determined) in the laws and regulations, and in the languages, a knowledge of which is hereby declared to be an indispensable qualification for such respective offices.

" The languages, a knowledge of which will be considered requisite in the several offices in the judicial, revenue, and commercial departments, are—

" For the office of judge, or register, of any court of justice, in the provinces of Bengal, Behar, Orissa, or Benares, the Hindoostanee and the Persian languages.

" For the office of collector of revenue, or of customs, or commercial resident, or salt agent, in the provinces of Bengal or Orissa, the Bengal language.*

" For the office of collector of revenue, or of customs, or commercial resident, or agent, for the provision of opium, in the provinces

---

* It has been generally allowed, that a judge in Bengal should also know the local dialect of that province; nor can it be denied, that the collectors, &c. there, would be greatly benefited by adding the Hindoostanee and Persian to the Bengal tongue.

of Behar, or Benares, the Hindoostanee language.

G. H. BARLOW,
Secretary to Government."

To British Officers, and Gentlemen of every description, proceeding to India.

Since the above orders were published, a more regular System of Oriental Education has been adopted by the Bengal government for the civil and military establishments of Bengal, Madras, and Bombay, in all of which, the Hindoostanee (or Moors) has been justly considered an object of primary acquisition and importance, and taught accordingly to all writers and cadets on their arrival in India.

A knowledge of the Hindoostanee is not only essential for every stranger in British India, who must have a personal communication with the natives at large, but, moreover, paves the way for the speedy acquirement of the Persian and other oriental tongues, in that country, where alone they can be generally learned, as local classic languages, through the medium of the Hindoostanee, which is the vernacular speech of the people, and necessarily of all the Moonshees, or native teachers, in Hindoostan.

In the armies, maritime, and domestic affairs of India, no other language than the Hindoostanee is universally spoken or understood; nor is any other required from the cadets now studying it and tactics at the military academies, lately established in the three presidencies of Bengal, Madras, and Bombay.

As several modern and ancient tongues may be deemed both useful and ornamental to men of liberal education in Europe, the Sunskrit, Persian, Arabic, &c. will prove equally so in India; but it should always be recollected, that to every person there, the Hindoostanee is no less indispensable, than a knowledge of English evidently is to the inhabitants of the United Kingdom; and consequently should be treated as the most requisite qualification for gentlemen bound to the East Indies; because they will sooner or later find, that, comparatively, the learned languages are secondary considerations, which may be afterwards acquired in India, with greater facility, less expence, and much more effectually, than they can yet be attained in this country.

If the above reasoning be founded in facts, well known and established for some years past both at home and abroad, the public may reasonably hope, that the oriental departments of the civil and military colleges at Hertford and Marlow, will speedily embrace the Hindoostanee as an object of the first consideration to the students destined for India; since we must admit, that however learned our British judges, civil and military officers, might otherwise be, they would all prove now-a-days wholly unfit for their respective offices in our country, without an adequate knowledge of their mother tongue; and the Hindoostanee being exactly to India, what the English language is colloquially to the United Kingdom, or what the Turkish is to that empire, the inference is so very plain, that he who runs may read.

To students who wisely commence their oriental career with the grand popular speech of India, which has hitherto been very undeservedly superseded by the Persian, while degraded and misrepresented under the absurd term of Moorish Jargon, or Moors, all the Works enumerated in the Catalogue will necessarily prove of the highest utility and importance, either at their outset or progress through the most useful, to beginners, of all the Eastern tongues.

These Publications most essential are inserted first, that should circumstances render economy unavoidable, even in such purchases, three, four, or five only may suffice, till the student can in India more conveniently supply his self with the rest, also procurable there, as they become requisite in the course of his more advanced studies, at his own expence, when not less willing, and probably more able, to defray every progressive charge of this sort.

Fanny Parkes

[Account of a suttee] *Wanderings of a Pilgrim in Search of the Picturesque during Four-and-Twenty Years in the East*. London: Pelham Richardson, 1850. 2 vols.

and an English officer; her mother afterwards married a native buniyā (shop-keeper). She had a sister; both the girls lived with the mother, and employed themselves in embroidering saddle-cloths for the horses of the rich natives. They were both very plain; nevertheless, one of them sent her picture to his majesty, who, charmed with the portrait, married the lady. She had money in profusion at her command: she made her father-in-law her treasurer, and pensioned her mother and sister.

The Suttee.

A rich buniyā, a corn chandler, whose house was near the gate of our grounds, departed this life; he was an Hindoo. On the 7th of November, the natives in the bazār were making a great noise with their tom-toms, drums, and other discordant musical instruments, rejoicing that his widow had determined to perform suttee, *i. e.* to burn on his funeral-pile.

The magistrate sent for the woman, used every argument to dissuade her, and offered her money. Her only answer was, dashing her head on the floor, and saying, "If you will not let me burn with my husband, I will hang myself in your court of justice." The shāstrs say, "The prayers and imprecations of a suttee are never uttered in vain; the great gods themselves cannot listen to them unmoved."

If a widow touch either food or water from the time her husband expires until she ascend the pile, she cannot, by Hindoo law, be burned with the body; therefore the magistrate kept the corpse *forty-eight* hours, in the hope that hunger would compel the woman to eat. Guards were set over her, but she never touched any thing. My husband accompanied the magistrate to see the suttee: about 5000 people were collected together on the banks of the Ganges: the pile was then built, and the putrid body placed upon it; the magistrate stationed guards to prevent the people from approaching it. After having bathed in the river, the widow lighted a brand, walked round the pile, set it on fire, and then mounted cheerfully: the flame caught and blazed up instantly; she sat down, placing the head of the corpse on her lap, and repeated several times the usual form,

" Ram, Ram, suttee ; Ram, Ram, suttee ;" *i. e.* " God, God, I am chaste."

As the wind drove the fierce fire upon her, she shook her arms and limbs as if in agony ; at length she started up and approached the side to escape. An Hindoo, one of the police who had been placed near the pile to see she had fair play, and should not be burned by force, raised his sword to strike her, and the poor wretch shrank back into the flames. The magistrate seized and committed him to prison. The woman again approached the side of the blazing pile, sprang fairly out, and ran into the Ganges, which was within a few yards. When the crowd and the brothers of the dead man saw this, they called out, " Cut her down, knock her on the head with a bamboo ; tie her hands and feet, and throw her in again ;" and rushed down to execute their murderous intentions, when the gentlemen and the police drove them back.

The woman drank some water, and having extinguished the fire on her red garment, said she would mount the pile again and be burned.

The magistrate placed his hand on her shoulder (which rendered her impure), and said, " By your own law, having once quitted the pile you cannot ascend again ; I forbid it. You are now an outcast from the Hindoos, but I will take charge of you, the Company will protect you, and you shall never want food or clothing."

He then sent her, in a palanquin, under a guard, to the hospital. The crowd made way, shrinking from her with signs of horror, but returned peaceably to their homes ; the Hindoos annoyed at her escape, and the Mussulmans saying, " It was better that she should escape, but it was a pity we should have lost the *tamāshā* (amusement) of seeing her burnt to death."

Had not the magistrate and the English gentlemen been present, the Hindoos would have cut her down when she attempted to quit the fire ; or had she leapt out, would have thrown her in again, and have said, " She performed suttee of *her own accord*, how could *we* make her? it was the will of God." As a specimen of their religion the woman said, " I have transmigrated six times, and have been burned six times with six different husbands; if I do not burn the seventh time, it will prove unlucky for me!" "What good will burning do you?" asked a bystander. She replied, "The women of my husband's family have all been suttees, why should I bring disgrace upon them? I shall go to heaven, and afterwards re-appear on earth, and be married to a very rich man." She was about twenty or twenty-five years of age, and possessed of some property, for the sake of which her relatives wished to put her out of the world.

If every suttee were conducted in this way, very few would take place in India. The woman was not much burned, with the exception of some parts on her arms and legs. Had she performed suttee, they would have raised a little cenotaph, or a mound of earth by the side of the river, and every Hindoo who passed the place returning from bathing would have made sālām to it; a high honour to the family. While we were in Calcutta, many suttees took place; but as they were generally on the other side of the river, we only heard of them after they had occurred. Here the people passed in procession, flags flying, and drums beating, close by our door. I saw them from the verandah; the widow, dressed in a red garment, was walking in the midst. My servants all ran to me, begging to be allowed to go and see the tamāshā (fun, sport), and having obtained permission, they all started off, except one man, who was pulling the pankhā, and he looked greatly vexed at being obliged to remain. The sāhib said, the woman appeared so perfectly determined, he did not think she would have quitted the fire. Having performed suttee according to her own account six times before, one would have thought from her miraculous incombustibility, she had become asbestos, only purified and not consumed by fire. I was glad the poor creature was not murdered; but she will be an outcast; no Hindoo will eat with her, enter her house, or give her assistance; and when she appears they will point at her and give her abuse. Her own and her husband's family would lose caste if they were to speak to her: but, as an example, it will prevent a number of women from becoming suttees, and do infinite good: fortunately, she has no children. And these are the people called in Europe the "mild inoffensive Hindoos!"

The woman was mistress of a good house and about 800 rupees; the brothers of her deceased husband would, after her destruction, have inherited the property.

The burning of the widow is not commanded by the shāstrs: to perform suttee is a proof of devotion to the husband. The mountain Himalaya, being personified, is represented as a powerful monarch: his wife, Mena; their daughter is called Parvuti, or mountain-born, and Doorga, or difficult of access. She is said to have been married to Shivŭ in a *pre-existing* state when she was called Sŭtēē. After the marriage, Shivŭ on a certain occasion offended his father-in-law, King Dŭkshŭ, by refusing to make sālām to him as he entered the circle in which the king was sitting.

To be revenged, the monarch refused to invite Shivŭ to a sacrifice which he was about to perform. Sŭtēē, the king's daughter, however, was resolved to go, though uninvited and forbidden by her husband. On her arrival, Dŭkshŭ poured a torrent of abuse on Shivŭ, which affected Sŭtēē so much that she died.

In memory of this proof of great affection, a Hindoo widow burning with her husband on the funeral-pile, is called a Sŭtēē.

The following passages are from the Hindoo Shāstrs:—

"There are 35,000,000 hairs on the human body. The woman who ascends the pile with her husband, will remain so many years in heaven."

"As the snake draws the serpent from its hole, so she, rescuing her husband (from hell), rejoices with him."

"The woman who expires on the funeral-pile of her husband, purifies the family of her mother, her father, and her husband."

"So long as a woman, in her successive transmigrations, shall decline burning herself, like a faithful wife, on the same fire with her deceased lord, so long shall she not be exempted from springing again to life in the body of some female animal."

"There is no virtue greater than a chaste woman burning

herself with her husband:" the term Sŭtēē, here rendered "chaste" is thus explained; "commiserating with her husband in trouble, rejoicing in his joys, neglecting herself when he is gone from home, and dying at his death."

"By the favour of a chaste woman the universe is preserved, on which account she is to be regarded by kings and people as a goddess."

"If the husband be out of the country when he dies, let the virtuous wife take his slippers (or any thing else which belongs to his dress) and binding them, or it, on her breast, after purification, enter a separate fire."

Mothers collect the cowries strewn by a sŭtēē as she walks round the pile, ere she fires it, and hang them round the necks of their sick children as a cure for disease.

In the plate entitled "Superstitions of the Natives," fig. 3 represents the cowrie shells. (Cypræa moneta.)

The suttee took place on the banks of the Ganges, under the Bund between the Fort and Raj Ghat, a spot reckoned very holy and fortunate for the performance of the rite.

Several of our friends requested me, in case another suttee occurred, to send them timely notice. Five days afterwards, I was informed that a rānee[1] was to be burned. Accordingly I sent word to all my friends. Eight thousand people were assembled on the suttee-ground, who waited from mid-day to sun-set: then a cry arose—"The mem sāhiba sent us here! the mem sāhiba said it was to take place to-day! see, the sun has set, there can now be no suttee!" The people dispersed. My informant told me what he himself believed, and I mystified some 8000 people most unintentionally.

TEMPLE OF BHAWĀNĪ AND SUTTEES, ALOPEE BAGH.

In Alopee Bagh, in the centre of a large plantation of mango-trees, is a small temple dedicated to Bhawānī; there is no image in it, merely a raised altar, on which victims were, I suppose, formerly sacrificed. Each of the small buildings on the

[1] A Hindoo queen or princess.

John William Kaye

[Female Infanticide]

Administration of the East India Company.

London: R. Bentley, 1853.

CHAPTER V.

Infanticide—Varieties of the Crime—Love of Offspring among the Hindoos——Rajpoot Honor—Its Excesses—Causes of the prevalence of the Evil—Our First Remedial Efforts—Jonathan Duncan—Colonel Walker—Failure of our First Endeavours — Disparity of the Sexes—Renewed Attempts—Mr. Willoughby—Major Ludlow—Increased Success—Present State of Infanticide in India.

In this Christian country it is to be feared that the dark crime of infanticide is painfully on the increase. This much at least has been said of late by wise judges on the bench, and by earnest writers in the public journals; and the records of our criminal courts unhappily show that this is no imaginary complaint.* It is a grave fact, wretchedly significant of the state of morals amongst us. Still it is only a crime—incidental, exceptional. In some parts of India it has been, for many generations, a *custom.*

It is curious to contrast the causes of the crime in the two countries. A sagacious Rajpoot arguing the question with us, might, perhaps, point triumphantly to the circumstances which engender the crime in England, in justification of the custom which obtains among his own people. It is, he might say, in anticipation and prevention of those very circumstances that the dreadful practice has been instituted. But to demonstrate the fact is not to prove the justification.

* Mr. Raikes, in his very interesting volume of "Notes on the North-Western Provinces of India," says: "Infanticide is a world-wide crime. Except the land of our own Saxon forefathers, we can scarce name a country unstained by the blood of its infant children." Would to God that we were free from the stain!

In England infant life is secretly destroyed by unmarried females. In an agony of shame and terror a poor girl who has become a mother, but is not a wife, strangles or suffocates her illegitimate babe. In all probability she has been betrayed and deserted, and there is a male offender, of whom the law takes no cognizance, more guilty than the actual murderess. Still, it is the unchastity of the female that is the proximate cause of the crime. The Rajpoot assumes that unchastity is the necessary condition of unmarried life. And to preserve the purity of his daughters, and the honor of his family, he murders his female children a few hours after their birth.

Marriage, in both cases, is the remedy; but the difficulties in the way of its application are diametrically the reverse. In England, marriage is honorable; but celibacy is not disgraceful. In India, celibacy *is* disgraceful. An unmarried daughter is a reproach to her parents, and a reproach to herself.* Indeed, more or less, the birth of a daughter is always a calamity. It is a disappointment in the first instance, because to beget sons is glorious in the estimation of a Hindoo, and there cannot be too many born into his house. And it is a care to him afterwards, because marriage is a necessity, and the circle of suitability is narrowed by the exclusiveness of caste. The higher the social degree of the family, the greater the difficulty. In England infanticide is peculiar to the lower orders; in India it is peculiar to the higher. In England it is the activity of degradation; in India the activity of pride. In England male and female infants are murdered with equal recklessness. In India the destroying hand is laid only on the latter. But in both cases, it is the non-attainment

* "So great a disgrace," says Ward, in his account of the Hindoos, "is incurred by remaining unmarried, that on one occasion a number of old maids were married to an aged Koolin Brahmin, as his friends were carrying him to the river to die."

of honorable marriage in *esse*, or in *posse*, which impels to the commission of the crime.

In a country where polygamy is common, and concubinage not dishonorable—where an unconnected man, indeed, is rarely to be found—it might seem that women would be too much in demand to warrant, at any stage of existence, the destruction of female life. And, in truth, the customs of the country are such that any widely-diffused system of female infanticide must be wholly incompatible with them. Their co-existence would be a physical impossibility. The number of child-murders, committed in the worst of times, has never been sufficiently great to have any general effect upon the population. But confined as it has been to certain localities, and to certain tribes, the sacrifice of life, viewed in connexion with those limits, has been something terrible to contemplate. It has amounted, indeed, to an almost total annihilation of female life in a large number of high-caste families.

The infanticide of which I am now writing is, the systematic female infanticide of Central and Western India. Child-murder among the Hindoos has assumed other forms, but the evil has been less extensive, and more easily repressible when it has been the growth of religious superstition, and has taken a more overt and violent shape. In the latter case, it has been an open sacrifice, with the intent of propitiating one of the bloody deities of the Hindoo mythology. In Southern and Eastern Bengal, children of both sexes have been offered up by their parents sacrifices to Gunga. Here, however, the object that is sought to be attained by the commission of the atrocity, is the very opposite of that which the Rajpoot of Malwah, Jusselmere, or Goojrat sets before him when he commits, or decrees the commission of the crime. In Bengal and Orissa these sacrifices have been consummated in fulfilment of a vow, and are thank-offerings in return for a favorable response to the prayers for offspring with which childless women have wearied their gods, when the curse of barrenness has seemed to press heavily upon them. Slaves to a dreadful superstition, they vow to offer up their firstborn to Gunga if the deity will answer their prayers. In the fulness of time the vow is consummated. The child, doomed from the hour of its birth, is suffered to live long enough to root itself deeply in the affections of its parents, and then, on a given day, is deliberately thrust into the cruel stream.* These, however, are exceptional cases—accidental crimes. The law can reach them, and has reached them; and it may be said that they are now almost blotted out from the catalogue of Pagan atrocities. The love of offspring—the desire to surround themselves with children—has driven these wretched people to offer up these dreadful sacrifices to their false gods. But among the Rajpoots of Central and Western India, it is the desire to lessen the number of their children that impels them to destroy the infant life of their female offspring. There is nothing of a religious sacrifice about it. It is simply a matter of convenience. In very many parts of the world infanticide is a common thing—a rite, a custom. But I believe that in no part of the world is there anything nearly resembling the female infanticide of which I am now writing.

In all parts of India the desire for offspring is very strong. A childless woman is a miserable woman—a

* "The people in some parts of India, particularly the inhabitants of Orissa, and of the eastern parts of Bengal, frequently offer their children to the Goddess Gunga. The following reason is assigned for the practice: When a woman has been long married, and has no children, it is common for the man, or his wife, or both of them, to make a vow to the Goddess Gunga, that if she will bestow the blessing of children upon them, they will devote their firstborn to her. If after this vow they have children, the eldest is nourished till a proper age, which may be three, four, or nine years, according to circumstances, when, on a particular day, appointed for bathing in a holy part of the river, they take the child with them and offer it to this goddess; the child is encouraged to go further and further into the water till it is carried away by the stream, or is pushed off by its inhuman parents."—[*Ward on the Hindoos.*]

hissing, a reproach. She believes that a curse is upon her. She is despised by herself, and scorned by her husband. She thinks—and if she gives birth to children who are taken away from her by death, the same thought comes upon her—that she is thus afflicted for some grievous sin committed in a pre-existent state. The parental instinct is as strong among them as among any people in the world. And even where the parental instinct is not, the tenderness with which strong bearded men devote themselves to the care of young children, is as touching as it is remarkable. It is not indifference, therefore, to infant life, out of which this horrid practice emanates. It is simply the existence among these "chivalrous" Rajpoots of a strong delusion, which some call honor, some pride of birth, and others grossness of ignorance, deadness of conscience — barbarism — devilry—what you will.

It is hard to designate the feeling aright. I shall not attempt to provide the fitting nomenclature. It would be better to illustrate than to define. A score of examples of the strange working of Rajpoot honor readily suggest themselves; but I know not one more striking than the following, which Mr. Forbes, an old Bombay civilian, has set down in his "Oriental Memoirs:"—"About four years before my appointment to Baroche," he writes, of the last quarter of the eighteenth century, "some Mahomedans, walking through a village where a family of Rajpoots resided, approached their house, and accidentally looked into a room where an elderly woman was eating. They intended no insult; they saw her at her meal, and immediately retired. But this accident occasioned a disgrace on the Rajpoot lady for which, on her part, there could be no expiation. She at that time lived with her grandson, a fine young man, who was absent when the Mahomedans committed their trespass;

on his return home she related the circumstance, and her determination not to survive it. She therefore entreated him earnestly to put her to death—a step which she had only deferred that she might fall by his hand. The youth's affection and good sense induced him to remonstrate with his venerable parent, whom he endeavoured to dissuade from her purpose, by alleging that none but her own family knew of the disgrace, the very men who were the innocent cause of it being unconscious of the offence. Persevering, however, in her resolution, but unable to persuade either her grandson or any other person to perform the sacrifice, she calmly waited until he next went from home, and then beat her head against the wall with dreadful violence. On his return he found his venerable parent in this agonising and shocking state. She again entreated he would finish the sacrifice, and release her from misery; he then stabbed her to the heart."*

This is Rajpoot honor—Rajpoot chivalry. It may be called by ennobling names, but, in reality, it is nothing but the densest barbarism. It is easy to understand, and even to admire, the feeling which impels the Tartar warrior, at the approach of a victorious enemy, to slaughter his wives and children. All nations, more or less, comprehend the great aphorism, "Death is better than dishonor." We know what is that dishonor which follows the assault and capture of a hostile town. But the dishonor incurred by an old woman seen, by a

* *Forbes' Oriental Memoirs*, vol. i., p. 490.—The sequel of this story is worth telling, if only as a proof that in those days such atrocities were not sheltered, under any plea of religion or custom, from the just vengeance of the law. "By the English laws," says Mr. Forbes, "he was secured as a murderer, sent to Bombay for trial, and confined in the common prison until the ensuing sessions. The grand jury found a bill for murder; the petty jury, composed half of Europeans and half of natives, found him guilty; and the judges condemned him to death. The Rajpoots in general have a noble mien and dignified character; their high caste is stamped on their countenance; this young man possessed them all. I saw him receive his sentence, not only with composure, but with a mingled look of disdain and delight not easy to de-

passing stranger, in the act of eating her dinner, is not very readily appreciable. The only thing that is very clear about the matter, is that, if a woman is so easily dishonored, it were better that she should eat her dinner in a place where curious travellers cannot see her.

But such being the turgid sense of honor which inflates these chivalrous Rajpoots, it is not strange that the disgrace of unmarried daughters—a disgrace of which all Hindoos are more or less sensible—should be keenly appreciated by them. An overweening idea of the necessities of caste and the suitability of matrimonial alliances renders marriage a matter of difficult achievement. A husband is to be found for the Rajpootnee damsel among the members of her own caste. On no account must she ally herself with one of inferior rank. Within this narrow circle she must find a husband, or the family is disgraced. Nor does the difficulty end with the attainment of the husband. Among the Hindoos there is always a wretched waste of money, varying, of course, according to the rank of the parties, on occasion of marriage ceremonies. Among the people of whom I am speaking, it is a point of honor that these festivals should be celebrated at a cost which must press heavily upon the financial resources of men with whom poverty and pride are too often yoke-fellows. It is not

scribe. Unconscious of the crime laid to his charge, he said that he had nothing to accuse himself of except disobedience to his parent, by permitting humanity and filial affection to supersede his duty and the honor of his caste; that life was no longer desirable; nor, if acquitted by the English laws, would he survive the ignominy of having been confined with European culprits and prisoners of the lowest castes, with whom he had been compelled to eat and associate in a common prison—acts so contrary to everything which he esteemed right and honorable, that the sooner he was transferred to another state of existence the better. However inclined the Government might be to clemency, it would evidently have been fruitless; the noble Rajpoot would not survive the disgrace, and the sentence of the law was executed, in the hope that it might prevent others from following his example."

convenient, therefore, that daughters should grow up in the house. They must be *sarf-kard*, or cleared away.

Such are the causes of female infanticide as it exists in certain parts of Hindostan. There is no religious warrant for it. The Hindoo Shastres are sufficiently clear on the subject of the enormity of child-murder. Indeed, it is almost the one exceptional case of a barbarous custom, that has not the sanction expressed or implied, by precept or example, of the monstrous faith which these people profess. There are, doubtless, some obscure fables, some dim traditions, among them, in which it is pretended that the origin of the enormity is to be found; but even these do not impute to it a divine origin. No god commanded the horrid rite, or set the example of its perpetration. The patron saint of female infanticide is at best no better than "a powerful Rajah."*

It was not likely that on such an iniquity as this the English in India would look with passive unconcern. It was an evil very palpable to the understandings of men, but the proper remedy was not equally apparent. It was, indeed, something very difficult to deal with—an abomination propped up and sustained by feelings deeply implanted in men's hearts, and not to be eradicated without such rendings and revulsions of the whole social and domestic system as might be fraught with the most dangerous results. Still the effort was to be

* Colonel Walker says: "The Jharigahs relate that a powerful Rajah of their caste, who had a daughter of singular beauty and accomplishments, desired his Raj-goor, or family priest, to affiance her to a prince of rank and descent equal to her own. The Raj-goor travelled over many countries without discovering a chief possessed of the requisite qualities. In this dilemma the Rajah consulted the Raj-goor, and he advised him to avoid the disgrace which would attend the princess's remaining unmarried, by having recourse to the desperate expedient of putting his daughter to death. The Rajah was long averse to this expedient. The Raj-goor at length removed his scruples by consenting to load himself with the guilt, and to become in his own person responsible for all the consequence of the sin. Accordingly the princess was put to death, and female infanticide was from that time practised by the Jharigahs."

made—made, wheresoever British influence extended, not merely in districts under our immediate administration, but in parts of the country where the native princes held dominion; and we could only exercise indirect control over the acts of the people through the agency of the British Residents at these foreign Durbars. And it is to the honor of the Company and their officers, that, in spite of all discouragements and denials, all difficulties and all obstacles, they have now for half a century been engaged in this good work, and have achieved an amount of success which, if not full and entire, is at least meet reward and glorious compensation for all the painful labor it has cost.

In the van of those active and benevolent British officers, who have endeavoured to suppress this inhuman practice, stands Jonathan Duncan, many years Resident of Benares, and afterwards Governor of Bombay. He was a simple-minded man, of enlarged benevolence, who, wheresoever his lot was cast in the East, made for himself a place in the affections of the people by whom he was surrounded. Mackintosh said of him that he had been *Brahmanised* by long residence in India; but the word, coined for the purpose by the accomplished Recorder of Bombay, conveys but a half-truth. Inasmuch as that Duncan knew the people of India well, conversed with them as freely as though they had been his own countrymen, and from long intercourse with them, had contracted some Oriental rust, which, in the eyes of one fresh from the literary coteries of the English capital, was something new and strange, he had been *Brahmanised.* But the word unfitly describes the character of one who regarded the people around him, from the highest to the lowest, with deep paternal interest, and whose enlarged toleration and extended sympathies partook not at all of the cruel exclusiveness of the priestly aristocracy of Hindostan. He had been Indianised indeed, but not Brahmanised. He had no toleration of things, which Brahmanism not only tolerates, but encourages; and he set himself against the iniquities which were done in the name of the religion, and sanctioned by the priesthood of the country. And foremost among these iniquities was the female infanticide of Central and Western India. He had first been made acquainted with the existence of the evil in the neighbourhood of Juanpore,* about the year 1789; and had subsequently, on his removal to Western India, clearly traced the extension of the cruel system to the provinces of Cutch and Kattywar. "I am well assured," he wrote, with respect to the former, "and it is, indeed, here generally believed (and being so, it is my duty not to keep such enormities, however sanctioned by usage, from the knowledge of Government), that it is no unfrequent practice among the tribe of Rajkoomar to destroy their daughters, by causing the mothers to refuse them nurture; whence this race of men do often, from necessity, marry into other Rajpoot families. The greatest exception to this melancholy truth that I can find is, that men—and these the more wealthy Rajkoomars—will sometimes spare and bring up their female issue, especially when they happen to have none of the male line. This horrid custom is said to exist also among some other tribes, more especially in the Vizier's dominions, and it is thought to be founded in the extravagant desire of independency enter-

* Sir John Shore, in 1794, speaks of this in a communication to the Asiatic Society:—"That the practice of infanticide," he says, "should ever be so general as to become a custom with any sect or race of people, requires the most unexceptionable evidence to gain belief; and I am sorry to say that the general practice, as far as regards female infants, is fully substantiated with respect to a particular tribe on the frontiers of Juanpur, a district of the province of Benares, adjoining to the country of Oude. A race of Hindoos called Rajkoomars reside here; and it was discovered in 1789 only that the custom of putting to death their female offspring had long subsisted, and did actually then very generally prevail among them. The Resident at Benares (Mr. Duncan, afterwards Governor of Bombay), in a circuit which he made through the country where the Rajkoomars dwell, had an opportunity of authenticating the existence of the custom from their own confessions; he conversed with several; all unequivocally admitted it, though all did not fully admit its atrocity."

tained by this race of men, joined, perhaps, to the supposed necessity of procuring a suitable settlement in marriage for those devoted females were they allowed to grow up, and the disgrace which would ensue from any omission in that respect. Nor is this species of atrocity of recent institution ; for a similar prejudice, as existing among the Indians, was known by the ancient Greeks and Romans, as is found in the relations they have left of this quarter of the world."*

This was written in October, 1789, and is remarkable as containing the first official notice of the subject of female infanticide in India. In less than three months from the day on which Jonathan Duncan announced his discovery of the horrid custom, he wrote to Lord Cornwallis that he had taken measures for its suppression. "I have prevailed on those situated within our frontier," he wrote, "to agree to renounce in future this horrid practice, to which effect they have entered into the engagement which will be found translated in the accompanying extract of my proceedings." The words of the covenant are worth quoting:—"Whereas," proceeds this curious document, "it hath become known to the Government of the Honorable East India Company, that we of the tribe of *Rajkumar* do not suffer our female children to live; and whereas, this is a great crime, as mentioned in the *Brehma Bywant Purana*, where it is said that killing even a fœtus is as criminal as killing a Brahman; and that for killing a female or woman, the punishment is to suffer in the Naraka, or Hell called *Kat Shutala*, for as many years as there are hairs on the female's body, and that afterwards such person shall be born again, and successively become a leper and afflicted with the *jakhima ;* and whereas, the British Government in India, whose subjects we are, hold in detestation such mur-

* *Jonathan Duncan to Lord Cornwallis, October 2, 1789. Moore's Hindoo Infanticide.*

derous practices, and we do ourselves acknowledge that although customary among us, they are highly sinful; we do therefore hereby agree not to commit any longer such detestable acts, and any among us who shall (which God forbid!) be hereafter guilty thereof, or who shall not bring up and get our daughters married to the best of our abilities among those of our own caste, shall be expelled from our tribe, and shall neither eat nor keep society with us, besides suffering hereafter the punishments denounced in the above Purana and Shastra. We have therefore entered into this engagement.—(*Dated 17th December*, 1789.)"

For many years it was believed that this engagement had been observed, and that the Rajkoomars had ceased to murder their female infants. But excellent as was the intention of the covenant, and undeniable as were the truths set forth in its preamble, this great measure had everything in the world to recommend it but practical success.

Meanwhile, happy in the belief of the beneficent issue of his ameliorative efforts in Central India, Jonathan Duncan, now appointed Governor of Bombay, was endeavouring, in like manner, to suppress the barbarous custom as he found it to exist among the Jareejah Rajpoots of Cutch and Kattywar. He was fortunate in the agency he employed. In Major Walker he found an officer combined in whom were the purest philanthropic zeal, sound intelligence, and unfailing perseverance. The difficulties to be encountered were many and formidable. The natives around him declared that the custom would never be suppressed until the Company should take possession of the country in their own name. But, in spite of these discouragements, Walker entered on the great undertaking with sanguine expectations of success. "I conceived," he said, "that reason and feeling would effect the relinquishment of a barbarous custom unconnected with the principles of society, and which all the passions of the human mind, and all the forms and maxims of religion were combined to destroy. As it was evident, also, that the most disinterested humanity had led the Honorable Company to interfere for the abolition of female infanticide, I conceived that this reflection, and the respect due to their mediation, would have disposed the Jareejahs to comply with a request which it was scarcely to be supposed could be at variance with their own sentiments." All this, however, was a mere amiable delusion, and Major Walker was compelled presently to acknowledge that "sentiments of nature and humanity have no influence with the Jareejahs," and reluctantly to abandon his favorable expectations of success.

Undaunted, however, by the discovery that nothing was to be hoped for from the good feelings of the Jareejahs, Walker began now to turn his thoughts towards a new course of action. It was a distasteful—a sickening game that he was called upon to play. The amount of selfishness and bigotry—of falsehood and avarice—of cowardice and chicanery—that he had to encounter, can hardly be over-estimated. But the English officer looked it all steadily in the face. He made this great matter of Female Infanticide the subject of continual discussion, oral and written, with the Jareejah chiefs. He believed that it would be no small thing to familiarise their minds with the idea that the practice of female infanticide, so long unquestioned, was something at least of questionable propriety—something which other nations, and especially that great nation from which springs the paramount power in India, regarded with horror and detestation. And, at all events, from this constant obtrusion of the subject there came this amount of good—that the chiefs seeing how extreme was the eagerness of the British Government to carry this point of the abolition of Female Infanticide, bethought themselves of turning our solicitude to profitable account, and trading upon our humanity. These chivalrous Rajpoots seemed not unwilling to yield, for a consideration, at least an outward assent to the proposals of the British officer. And it seems to have been mainly in expectation of some advantage to themselves that at last they consented, in a cowardly reluctant manner, each endeavouring to push the other forward, to become parties to an engagement similar to that which Mr. Duncan had extracted from the Rajkoomars in the neighbourhood of Juanpore. They *did* sign the covenant at last; and Major Walker saw many good reasons for believing that they would fulfil the promises they had made. And so it came to be considered that, both in Central and in Western India, Infanticide had been suppressed by Duncan and Walker; and learned writers in Encyclopædias, and in brave independent quartos of their own, set forth the gratifying announcement without a doubt of its truth.

But though Duncan and Walker deserved success, it was not in their power to command it. They were the pioneers of humanity and civilisation in that direction, and bravely they labored with axe and hatchet to clear away the dense jungle of barbarism that lay before them; but they did not apply the fire to the root, and the noxious wilderness soon sprung up again above the delusive clearings they had made. For a while it was believed that the horrid custom had been suppressed, alike in the East and the West; little or nothing was heard of the abomination, and no new efforts were made to suppress it. But about the year 1816 it was officially announced that the Rajkoomars were murdering their children after the old fashion. Mr. Shakespear, then acting as Superintendent of Police, reported that though the Regulations of 1795 and 1804 "contain provisions for the prevention and punishment of the inhuman practice prevalent among the tribe of Rajkoomars of causing the female infants to be strangled to death, there is reason to believe that this practice still obtains among them to nearly the same extent as formerly, though a greater degree of caution is preserved to prevent detection;" and the Governor-General in Council expressed his regret that " the measures adopted by Mr. Duncan whilst Resident at Benares, and the provisions of the Regulations, had failed to prevent the inhuman practice." The same lamentable tidings came also from Western India. Major Carnac, Resident at Baroda, officially reported to the Bombay Government, that " the abolition of the inhuman practice in Cutch had not been accomplished." And in the following year Captain Ballantine reported, with reference to the Rajpoots of Goozrat, that " the object of our interference for the suppression of this singular custom has too generally failed to select any individual party for the just vengeance of Government and offended nature." To make the extent of the evil, as then existing, more apparent, this energetic officer drew up a statistical report, containing a register of all the Jareejah families known in Kattywar, with " the age and number of their female offspring saved, or now living, since the introduction of the Infanticide arrangement by Colonel Walker in 1808;" and from this census it appeared that during the space of ten years only sixty-three female Jareejah children had been preserved in the whole of Kattywar; that in none of the large *talooks*, or estates, of the Jareejah chiefs, was there more than one female child to be found, and in some not even one, though containing four hundred families.* Such, in spite of the laudable efforts of Duncan and Walker, was the result of our first humane efforts to suppress this dreadful abomination.

But this mortifying discovery moved the Company's

* Parliamentary Papers, quoted in the *Calcutta Review*, whose admirable summary I have mainly followed.

Government and the Company's servants to order, and to prosecute new efforts for the suppression of the great crime. The Court of Directors wrote out to the Bombay Government, "enjoining them in the most serious and earnest manner to be unremitting in their endeavours to accomplish this humane object in the countries where British influence can be felt and exerted." But it was not very clear, even to the most humane and energetic servants of the Company, how these unremitting endeavours were to be prosecuted, so as to accomplish the great object. The difficulty, indeed, was very great, and, seemingly, insurmountable. Some of the most large-minded men, believing that we could make an impression on the evil only by the adoption of measures so objectionable that it might be questioned whether the remedy were not worse than the disease, seemed, in spite of the strong instincts of humanity which urged them forward, almost inclined to counsel an adherence for the future to the old measures of moral discouragement, which had proved so abortive in the past. The great standing difficulty was this. The general prevalence of the crime was acknowledged. Its results were sufficiently apparent in the fact, that the number of female children to be found among the Jareejahs was only *one-sixth* of the number of males. But it was difficult—indeed, impossible—to bring to light specific acts of infanticide without such an intrusion into the domestic privacy of high-caste Rajpoot families as would be regarded with horror, and resented with indignation. This systematic child-murder, indeed, was altogether an affair of the Zenana. The mother was herself the executioner. She rubbed the nipples of her breasts with opium, and the babe sucked in poison with its first milk.* Every-

* A significant hint from the fathers, not conveyed in words, generally sealed the fate of the child. "Simtook Ram, minister of Amjherra," writes Sir John Malcolm in his *Central India*, "told me he was sitting with Premun Singh, the present Thakoor, when he heard the birth of a female child whispered in his ear. He saw him preparing between his fingers the

thing was done so secretly behind the ***purdah;*** even the very birth of the child was so little noised abroad, that the disappearance of whole families of female children, one after another, in individual succession, could not be clearly traced. Public notoriety pointed vaguely to the general fact. But the lips of all who were competent to speak to individual offences were closed. No man willingly bore witness against his neighbour. How, then, were we to penetrate the obscurity, and break down the exclusiveness of domestic life—an exclusiveness so jealously guarded, so religiously maintained, that it almost seemed as though dishonor would enter the female apartments with the sunbeams or the west wind? It was proposed that hired informers should be employed; but the proposal did not find favor in the eyes of authority. Mount-Stuart Elphinstone—a statesman of equal wisdom and humanity—set his face steadfastly against it. "No effectual check," he wrote, "can be imposed on this atrocious practice, so long as it is so completely congenial to the general feelings of the people, unless by employing hired agents, as proposed by Major Ballantine, whose duty it should be to detect offenders of this description; and such a measure would lead to so much intrusion into the most private and domestic proceedings of the superior castes (among whom alone infanticide prevails), and would be open to so many abuses on the part of the informers, that I do not think the chance of success would compensate for the disaffection which it would create. It may also be doubted how far we have a right to interfere to such an extraordinary pitch with the private life of a people, with whose civil government and internal policy we do not pretend to have any concern. We must therefore be content to follow the foot-

fatal pill of opium (the usual signal), but he implored that the child might live: his request was granted, and this little girl (added Simtook Ram), now eight years of age, is always called my daughter."

steps of our predecessors (without attempting to go beyond them) in their most meritorious endeavours to discountenance this enormity; and we may safely flatter ourselves, that as the manners of the people become softened by a continuance of tranquillity and good order, they will gradually discontinue a practice which is not more inconsistent with reason than repugnant to natural instinct."

This was written in 1821. There was, seemingly, nothing very hopeful in it. The *laisser-faire* system was to be tried again. Moral discouragements were to be left to work out their slow results. "In speaking to those natives," writes Sir John Malcolm, with reference to the Rajpoots of Central India, "who enjoyed superior rank and station under the authority or control of the British Government, I have always expressed my horror at self-immolation (Suttee), and my hope that through their influence in society, and their desire not to outrage the feelings of their European superiors, it would in time be abolished. But with regard to infanticide I have ever, when it was mentioned, stated my abhorrence of the murders that were committed under the plea of this usage, and refused to see those who practiced it. Such sentiments," he added, "were never known to give offence." In Western India the same discouragements were at work; and they were not wholly without success. Many good and able European officers, among whom may be especially named Colonel Miles, Major Barnewell, and Mr. Blaine; and, subsequently, in the regions of Cutch, Henry Pottinger and Alexander Burnes exerted themselves to put down the abomination by such gentle, moral force as they conceived themselves justified in applying, and the result was not wholly a blank. It is officially reported, that whilst the number of female children belonging to the murderous tribes in Kattywar, preserved from destruction in 1808, only amounted to 32, it had risen, in 1817, to 63; and in 1824, to 266. In Cutch, the numbers had increased from 93, in 1823, to 143 in 1826; and, a few years later, Captain Burnes reported that the number had risen to 211. This last calculation was made from a census of more than a hundred villages, in which it was ascertained that there were, at the same time, 1167 male children; the girls being thus shown, in proportion to the boys, to be little more than as one to six. These returns, however, must be received with some caution. It is difficult to obtain a correct census of the people in these Rajpoot villages; and the returns, therefore, must be regarded rather as approximations, than as accurately ascertained results.

In the interval, however, of which I am now writing, between the years 1820 and 1830, there is one successful episode in the history of this great war against infanticide, which is worthy of especial recital. Among the rude people of Mairwarra, Colonel Hall had exerted himself to some purpose; for in a report dated July 31st, 1827, he reported "the complete and voluntary abolition of the two revolting customs—female infanticide and the sale of women." "Both crimes," he wrote, "were closely connected, having had their origin in the heavy expense attending marriage contracts. The sums were payable by the male side, were unalterable, equal for the rich and the poor, without any abatement whatever in favor of the latter. What first established the payment is unknown; but it was so sacred and inviolable, and even a partial deviation so disgraceful, that the more necessitous of the tribe would not incur the imputation. . . . Hence arose Infanticide. The sums payable were beyond the means of so many, that daughters necessarily remained on hand after maturity, entailed immortal disgrace, and thus imposed a necessity for all female progeny becoming victims to their family honor. On the establishment of

British rule, both evils gradually diminished. . . . . . Female Infanticide was at once prohibited, and though many, no doubt, still fell secret sacrifices from the great facility of undetected destruction, yet the danger, aided by improved feeling, increased the survivors so considerably, as to force upon the Mairs a due sense of the root of the evil, and a general wish for its removal by a reduction of the regulated sum of contract; but they were averse—indeed, declared their inability—to alter their long-established sacred custom themselves, and earnestly entreated that it might be done by an order of authority, binding all to obedience by heavy penalties. This was promised in a general way in case of necessity; but as there were many points to be settled, and it was advisable to ascertain the general feeling with accuracy, as well as to avoid interference, if possible, a general *punchayut* was strongly urged either to decide the matter, or, at all events, aid in the framing of appropriate regulations. After the lapse of a few months allowed for consideration, the whole was settled in public punchayut, and its resolutions were confirmed without the slightest alteration; so that the proceeding originated with, and has been carried through by, the inhabitants themselves; nor has there been a single petition against it, either pending or subsequent to adjustment. They have lowered the sum payable on marriage contracts, abolished all right of subsequent sale, and fixed a year's imprisonment, or 200 rupees fine, with exclusion from caste, as the punishment for deviation."* The result seems to have justified the sanguine expectations of Colonel Hall. Writing more than twenty years afterwards, his successor, Colonel Dixon, says: "Thus Infanticide received its death-blow through the diminution of the expenses attending on marriage, which was now brought within the reach of all sections of society. For many years

* *Report of Colonel Hall, July,* 1827, *quoted in Dixon's Mairwarra.*

past no female children have been put to death. The practice has fallen altogether into desuetude. Indeed, so greatly have the ideas of the people changed on this and other usages since the introduction of our rule, that the commission of such an act would now be viewed as a most heinous crime."*

Thus the first unequivocal success resulted from the establishment of sumptuary regulations. But it was easier to deal with these rugged Mairs, just rescued from a state of extreme barbarism, than with the "chivalrous" Rajpoots of Central and Western India. It is not improbable that if the British, or any other Government, had undertaken to portion the Jharijah girls, the dreadful custom would have been annihilated. The plan was, indeed, proposed, and negatived by the higher authorities. And the extreme alternative of putting down the abomination by force was rejected upon the ground that the Rajpoots of Western India were not our subjects, but our allies, and that such a mode of procedure would be inconsistent with the terms of our treaties. In 1831 Sir John Malcolm, then Governor of Bombay, went down to Booj and addressed the assembled Jharijah chiefs on the enormity of the crime so prevalent among them. He told them that so strong in England was the feeling against such abominations, that the nation would call upon the East India Company to sever their connexion with a people so polluted. The chiefs, seemingly abashed, falsely denied their participation in the prevailing guilt—and promises and pledges were not wanting. Indeed, the "chivalrous" Rajpoots were at no time chary of their promises and pledges—and now, as our English officers became more and more energetic in their efforts to put down the abomination, these promises and pledges became more and more plentiful.

In Central India, promises were as readily made and

* *Dixon's Mairwarra.*

as readily broken as in the West. Many earnest-minded men were exerting themselves, about this time, in Rajpootana, to push forward the good work. Distinguished among these was Mr. Wilkinson, whose name is ever to be held in remembrance by those who would record the good deeds of the Company's servants. He was a man of the kindliest and the most catholic sympathies, of large intelligence, and unwearying perseverance. He lived and toiled for the people, and he died, at his post, amongst them, warmly loved and deeply deplored. All that earnest desire and energetic action could do to wean the Rajpoots of Central India from the accursed practice of Infanticide, was now done by this full-hearted civilian. He assembled the chiefs; he addressed them; he reasoned with them; he expostulated with them; and at last he persuaded them to adopt certain resolutions, by an adherence to which it seemed probable that the iniquity might be suppressed. And many of the petty sovereigns of Rajpootana not only undertook to prohibit the practice, but issued proclamations declaring it illegal. Other officers in Central India, as Colonel Sutherland, Captain Richards, Captain Ludlow, and others, had been exerting themselves in the same good cause, and there were many encouraging promises and seemingly genuine renunciations to reward their labors.

The Rana of Oudipore, the chief of the independent sovereigns of Rajpootana, was forward to set the example —a potential one—of prohibition; and in January, 1834, Lord William Bentinck wrote to express the "pure and unmixed satisfaction" which he felt, and to utter words of further encouragement; but all these promises and renunciations were mere unmeaning words. The princes and chiefs had not been convinced, or they feared to reduce their convictions to practice. At all events, Wilkinson, who had labored so long and so diligently, and whose heart was so thoroughly in his work, was forced back upon the mortifying conclusion that no real impression had been made upon the minds of the magnates of the land. Only two months after he had explained to the chief people the enormity of the crime of infanticide and received their assurances of renunciation, he ascertained that two of their number had since put their daughters to death. The promised proclamations might have been issued; but no pains were taken to circulate them. He found, in the course of his circuits, that some of the states had not even heard of the prohibitory edict ; and, under the government of that very Rana of Oudipore whom Lord William Bentinck had so commended, some of the people told Mr. Wilkinson that it was true they had heard it whispered "that female infanticide had been prohibited some time before along with the killing of peacocks."

All this was very discouraging—but still Mr. Wilkinson did not despair of the effect of moral influence. He secured the services of some learned Brahmins to write pamphlets condemnatory of the crime, which he circulated among the people. He bethought himself, too, of the effect upon their minds of pictorial representations ; but all this was of no avail. "It has been my object," he wrote, "to excite such a genuine and general feeling of execration as should lead to a voluntary abandonment of the practice. Still, when we reflect on the inveteracy of habit, and the extreme tardiness with which new ideas are spread in the world, it would be idle to hope that the abandonment of the practice will be effected by the measures already taken."

In the mean while a great experiment was being initiated in Western India. In 1831, Mr. J. P. Willoughby, of the Bombay Civil Service, was appointed Political Agent in Kattywar. He soon began to give his thoughts to the painful subject of Female Infanticide, and collected all the information he could acquire regarding the dreadful practice and all that had been done towards its suppression. Reviewing the labors of his predecessors, and deriving wisdom from the past, he sent in an elaborate report to Government, in which he took a retrospective view of the results of our bygone efforts, and then sketched out a plan of future proceedings.

The measures suggested by Mr. Willoughby were these. *First,* that steps should be taken to obtain a complete census of the Jharijah population, as without it no data could exist for computing the number of female infants who were born, and thence deducing an approximation to the number actually destroyed. *Second,* that every Jharijah chief should be called upon to furnish a half-yearly register of all the marriages, betrothals, births, and deaths occurring among his tribe residing in his district; and that, if he failed in this obligation, or furnished a false return, he should be severely punished.* *Third,* that the Political Agent should furnish an annual report on the subject of Infanticide, together with a register of all marriages, betrothals, births, and deaths that have occurred among the tribe within the year reported on. *Fourth,* that a proclamation should be issued by the British Government throughout Kattywar, requiring the Jharijah chiefs to enforce the observance of their Infanticide engagements, and noticing in terms of approbation or condemnation their adherence to or departure from these engagements, and guaranteeing to all able or willing to supply information relating to the commission of the crime, a reward in proportion to the rank of the

* Mr. Willoughby, in the admirable Report which contains these suggestions, shows that this important matter had not escaped the attention of the Court of Directors. "This is no new suggestion," he says, "on my part, for in the correspondence on my records I find allusion made to instructions issued many years ago to the Honorable Court of Directors, that in addition to such intermediate reports as might become necessary, one general statement should be submitted at the end of each year, showing how far the amended system had been acted on and observed, what deviations are known or suspected to have been made from its rules, and what measures pursued for their enforcement, with an estimate of the number of lives saved."

party convicted, and the protection of the British Government. ***Fifth***, that every Rajpoot in Kattywar should be enjoined to make it an express stipulation in every marriage contract on giving his daughter to a Jharijah chief that the issue of the union should be preserved. ***Sixth***, that presents of cloth, money, &c., should be made, out of the ***Infanticide Fund***, to the chiefs and inferior members of the Jharijah tribes who preserved their female children.*

These measures, approved and sanctioned by the higher authorities, were pushed forward with promptitude and energy. The vigilance of the British officers was not without its results. In the course of eighteen months, it was reported that seventy-three female infants were preserved by the Jharijah tribes; of these, forty, it was said, would have perished but for our humane intervention. Still, in spite of all our efforts, there remained the lamentable fact, that at least one-half of the female infants born were murdered by their remorseless parents. It was, however, no small thing to convict certain offenders of specific acts of infanticide ; and charges were now brought and fully established against the chief of Rajkote. "The barbarous insensibility evinced by him on the occasion, proved him to have little claim to forgiveness." He was fined 12,000 rupees, to be paid to the Infanticide Fund; and his estate was attached as security for its payment. This conviction produced the most salutary effect throughout Kattywar, and was soon followed by other cases. Another petty chief, convicted on the clearest evidence of

* "The Infanticide Fund was established in 1825. It is composed of all fines, under 20,000 rupees, imposed upon the tributaries for breaches of the peace or other misconduct, and of realisation under the head of Mohsullee. The British Government set the example. His Highness the Guicowar, being subsequently induced to consent that all fines imposed upon his tributaries should be similarly appropriated. From this source occasional remissions of tribute, presents to the chiefs, and pecuniary assistance on the marriage of their daughters, have been granted to those who have practically renounced the custom; and another mode of testifying approbation to those who have preserved their daughters, is by postponing the payment of the tribute to suit their convenience." — [***Mr. Willoughby's Report.***]

the same offence, was sentenced to suffer twelve months' imprisonment, and to pay a fine of 3000 rupees. These were followed by other cases of detection and punishment. But though the evil sensibly diminished under these influences, it was not entirely suppressed. Here and there a case was brought struggling into light, but scores of cases of cruel child-murder, behind the sanctity of the purdah, escaped detection and exposure.

Perhaps, it would have been unreasonable to expect in such a case anything more than progressive improvement. It was, indeed, the hardest task that we had ever set ourselves—the hardest we have ever set ourselves since. I believe that in this country, where we all of us live comparatively out of doors—*coram populo*—an extensive system of Female Infanticide might be carried on without detection. I believe that married women in England might murder their sucklings by hundreds without suspicion. A little seemingly accidental neglect—a little want of active care at particular periods, will snap the thread of infant life, and give no sign of premeditated crime. But the nursery of the Hindoo woman, even of the poorest, is surrounded by social screens and fences which, however flimsy may be their material structure, are morally so impassable, so impenetrable, that the vigilance and activity of authority is utterly baffled and repelled by them. It was this that rendered the task so difficult—that rendered success, even under the best and most encouraging circumstances, so vague and uncertain. With such formidable obstructions before us it was a great thing to make any progress. It was a great thing that the Bombay Government should be enabled to write: "The complete suspension of the crime, originating in ignorance, prejudice, and false pride, must doubtless be the work of time; yet, looking back to the past, and seeing how much had been accomplished within the last few years, they were encouraged strongly to hope that a steady and constant perseverance in the measures in operation would, in the end, be rewarded by full and complete success."

Mr. Willoughby, promoted to higher office, quitted Kattywar in 1835, and was succeeded in the Political Agency by Mr. Erskine, who continued the good work which had been pushed forward so energetically by his predecessor. But it was plain still that there was much to be done. In 1837, upon a census of twenty-seven districts, it appeared that there were 1422 boys, and only 409 girls. In 1841, Captain Jacob, who was associated with Mr. Erskine on this great field of humanising labor, reported that the number of males under the age of twenty was 2923, whilst the females reached the encouraging amount of 1209, little less than one-half of the entire juvenile population. The result, indeed, led Captain Jacob to observe: "It must be highly gratifying to those benevolent men who had labored for the suppression of Infanticide, to see the progressive return to the order of nature, in the relative proportion of sexes, that must be attributed to their labor alone;" and called forth the commendatory remark of the Bombay Government, which I have quoted above.

Nor were these anticipations of the gradual suppression of the horrid practice unjustified by the result. I cannot afford to trace, year by year, the progressive improvement in the appearance of the census of the male and female population of Kattywar. But, perhaps, the good effects of our humanising measures may be best illustrated by passing on at once to the cheering details contained in the two last Infanticide Reports which have made their way into official record. In the Infanticide Report for the year 1849, from Kattywar, of which Major Lang, who has long been zealously employed in that province, is now Political Agent, there is this cheering announcement: "The proportion of female children to males in all the tribes is now so nearly equal, and the progressive increase of the female population so regular, that if the returns can be depended upon in other respects, there would appear to be every ground for believing that the practice of Infanticide must have become almost entirely extinct in this province." And then he goes on to report these encouraging statistical facts. "When the census for 1845 was forwarded with my Report of the 25th of August, 1846, there were two Jharijahs with five daughters each, 19 with four, 105 with three, and 387 with two. . . . . By the returns now submitted there are one Jharijah with six daughters, 11 with five, 49 with four, 159 with three, and 522 with two."* The Report of the following year, though less detailed, is equally satisfactory. It shows that the female Jharijah population has increased to a greater extent than the male. The former had increased, during the year 1850, by 186; the latter only by 149. "The only accusation of Infanticide," writes Major Lang, "which was brought forward during the year under review, was that reported in my letter of the 25th of September, 1850, which was found on investigation by my assistant, Captain Barr, to be entirely groundless."† But to make the progressive results of these great measures fully apparent, it would be well to give a brief tabular statement of the male and female Jharijah population of Kattywar, extending over the six years from 1845 to 1850, inclusive :‡

* *Major Lang to Bombay Government. MS. Records, December* 31, 1850. I have omitted the details of the smaller tribes, which are no less gratifying.

† *Major Lang to Bombay Government, December* 26, 1851. *MS. Records.*

‡ Well might Mr. Willoughby, when a seat in the Bombay Council gave him an opportunity of commenting on such results as these, congratulate himself on the success of his measures.

"I trust I shall be pardoned the expression," he wrote, "of the high gratification I have derived from the perusal of this and other similar Reports, establishing that the success which has attended our measures for the extirpation of the crime of Female Infanticide from Kattywar and Cutch has been far greater and much more rapid than the most sanguine could have anticipated. It was my good fortune to have been the originator of these measures, the success of which is mainly to be attributed to the vigorous manner in which I dealt with several proved cases of Infanticide before I left the province. I recollect that, by some whose opinion I valued, I was thought to have invaded too strictly the sanctity of Rajpoot domestic privacy, and that the measures I had

	1845.	1846.	1847.	1848.	1849.	1850.
Males	6617	6600	6844	7356	7353	7502
Females	2334	2429	2779	3090	3273	3423

It must necessarily take many years to restore the balance of the sexes, fearfully disturbed as it has been from generation to generation; but with such results as these before me, remembering that the time was when the number of female children to be found among the Jharijahs was only *one-sixth* of the number of males, and that on some large estates containing as many as 400 families not one female child was to be found,* I think I am justified in saying that what has been done is most honorable to the British nation, and that the rest is but "a work of time."

Whilst these measures were being thus energetically pursued in Western India, another group of British officers were carrying out the same good work in the Central Rajpoot states, with the approval and co-operation of the princes and chiefs themselves. The process, however, by which they hoped to attain the same great result, differed from that which Mr. Willoughby had introduced into Kattywar. It was based upon the admitted fact, that in those states the one great sustaining cause of the unholy practice was the extreme costliness of marriage ceremonials. To marry his daughter was often to ruin a man. There was a wretched brood of men known as "Charans" and "Bhats," who turned to vile uses two of the noblest functions of humanity, and degraded the priestly and the bardic office into a sort of

recourse to were too harsh, and likely to outrage the feelings of the whole Rajpoot community. But I argued that those philanthropic men, Governor Duncan and Colonel Walker, never intended that the engagements which they induced the Jharijahs to enter into should be waste paper; and although I was aware that I was touching on delicate ground, I felt assured that I should find a powerful ally in those feelings of parental affection which exist in the human breast in every stage and degree of civilisation. The result has certainly proved I was not mistaken."—[*Minute, March* 28, 1851. *Bombay Consultations. MS. Records.*]

* See *ante*, pages 559, 560.

tyrannous mendicancy, which the Rajpoots feared to resist. The exorbitant fees claimed by these men,* who would have cursed the grudging giver, or, worse still in the estimation of the proud and sensitive Rajpoot, pilloried him with ridicule, constituted the heaviest tax levied upon the luckless father. It was admitted that these large sums of money were reluctantly paid—that the thraldom of this aristocratic custom sat heavily upon the tribes.† They would have escaped from it if they could, but they feared to take the responsibility of such an innovation upon themselves. The Durbars, timid and hesitating, though not unwilling to co-operate for the suppression of what they knew and acknowledged to be an abomination, shrunk from an authoritative demonstration without the open support and encouragement of the paramount power. They were fearful, indeed, of taking the initiative in such a procedure ; but if they could push forward the British Government as the instigators of the needed reform, they might venture to co-operate with us and set their seal upon the sumptuary enactments which our officers were eager to suggest.

The right men were in Rajpootana. Colonel Sutherland, Major Thoresby, and Major Ludlow, all gave their hearts to the work. The two great objects were these: firstly to limit the influx of these bards on the occasion of nuptial ceremonies—to keep out the incursion of foreigners,‡ who swelled the chorus of hungry appli-

* It is said that the Rana of Odeypore, though in an impoverished state at the time, gave a lakh of rupees to the chief bard. The profession, being a lucrative and not a laborious one, is considerably over-stocked. The Joudpore Vakeel stated that there were 20,000 Charans in Marwar, and sometimes 4000 or 5000 graced the nuptials of an important chief.

† This is very clearly stated by one of our political officers in Rajpootana, who has been forward in the good work of Infanticide-suppression. "Far from having prejudices to combat (as we should unquestionably have as regards the rite of Suttee, and to a certain extent in the question of Surna), we shall in the course proposed carry with us the sense of the whole of the Rajpoot tribes, who have hitherto been forced reluctantly by the tyranny of custom to destroy their female offspring."—[*Major Ludlow to Major Thoresby. MS. Records.*]

‡ That is, of Charans and Bhats not

cants; and secondly, to fix a ratable amount to be paid to the domestic bards who were suffered to have a legitimate right to enrich themselves on these occasions. It was not difficult to persuade the princes of Rajpootana to enter into engagements for the enforcement of these measures, and to issue edicts enunciating them. Thus, instigated by Major Ludlow, the Jyepore Durbar, which was then the organ of an infant prince, sent forth "a proclamation of the Raj of Jyepore made by Major Ludlow and the Council of Regency," containing a forcible denunciation of the crime of Infanticide* and a clear specification of the suggested remedies. The lawful tax thenceforth to be paid was not to exceed a tithe of the annual income of the father of the bride. This was to be the maximum sum payable by the Jagheedars, but people with a less settled income were allowed only to disburse a smaller amount. The Jyepore authorities enforced these regulations with good effect; and Ludlow was soon able to report that an incursion of foreign bards had been successfully resisted, and had withdrawn, ungorged, unsatisfied, without a breach of the peace.

Nor was this all that was done. The other states, through Ludlow's instrumentality, were induced to follow the example of Jyepore. They responded, indeed, with acclamation to the appeal, and followed the letter of the Jyepore proclamation. Not one of the states, after these edicts were issued, admitted the foreign bards to their nuptial ceremonies. Indeed, so glad were the

belonging to the particular part of the country in which the marriage was celebrated, but who scented a far-off wedding as a jackal scents carrion, and hurried in flocks to their prey.

* "It is notorious that many Rajpoots kill their female daughters at the birth, and the cause would appear to exist in the distress and annoyance arising from the demand of Tyag (nuptial presents) on marriage occasions made by Charans, Bhats, &c., and from the abuse and revilings showered by these persons upon those who are not in circumstances to satisfy them to the extent of their demands. The act of Infanticide is a grievous tyranny and a great sin, which attaches alike to those who perpetrate it, and the sovereign in whose territory it occurs, and therefore the amounts receivable in future by Bhats, Charans, &c., are represented in this proclamation, &c., &c." —[*MS. Records.*] Cause and effect are here very plainly indicated. *Sublatâ causâ tollitur effectus.*

Thakoors to rid themselves entirely of the intolerable tyranny under which they had groaned so long, that they made the proclamations an excuse for not listening to the claims of their own "Bhats," and "Charans," whom they now learnt to send away empty-handed, under the pretext that the order of the Durbar for their payment must be first obtained. These people were the terror of Rajpootana. Their influence is now thoroughly broken down ; and they dare not even enforce the payment of the tithe permitted by the Sumptuary Regulations.

The effect of these measures on the great crime itself in Central India does not so distinctly appear as in the case of the Jharijah and other tribes of Kattywar, inasmuch as the results are not represented by a detailed census of the population. But it is not to be doubted that at least one great thing had been done. A change had been wrought in public opinion. It was clearly the interest of all classes of Rajpoots to resist a tax which often involved them in frightful pecuniary embarrassments. Nor was this all that was done. There was something more than an appeal to their purses. In Jyepore, Ludlow, seeing clearly where lay the only real remedy, exerted himself to appeal to their intelligence. He did everything that he could to encourage the diffusion of education in the states. And neither Suttee, nor Infanticide, nor Thuggee, nor human sacrifice, nor any other kindred abomination, can long stand up against so mighty a conqueror as that.

These measures for the suppression of Female Infanticide in Kattywar and in the Rajpoot states of Central India, it must be understood by the European reader, were carried on not within the dominions of the East India Company, but in the territories of the native princes over which we exercise only a moral control through the agency of our British Residents. But it may be asked whether, all this time, in our own provinces, there was no such thing as Female Infanticide. And I am afraid it must be answered that there *was*. The extent to which the crime was perpetrated, under our own immediate rule, was very limited; and it was confined to one or two collectorates. But still under the very eyes of British authority child-murder was going on, for some time, unchecked. The Purdah screened it from our sight. It was long before we ascertained the fact. And when we did ascertain its existence, both in Western and Central India, the evil appeared to be one not easily to be held in subjection. It may be thought that nothing could be easier than to drag the offenders into our criminal courts, and to convict them of the capital offence. And so it would have been if a woman had beaten out the brains of her child against the walls of the cutcherry or the magistrate's house. But perpetrated as the crime was in secret, nothing was more easy than accusation—nothing more difficult than conviction. The Regulations, powerful as they were, could not deal with this abstruse abomination.

The districts in Western and Central India, under which it was discovered that the crime of Infanticide was practised by certain tribes, were Ahmedabad, in the Bombay Presidency, and Mynpooree, under the government of the North-Western Provinces. In Ahmedabad the existence of the crime was first brought to the notice of Government by Mr. Fawcett, at the end of 1847. The disparity of the sexes had been pointed out to him by a native functionary, and he knew the meaning of that terrible sign. The native officer was instructed to exert himself to bring the chief people into an arrangement tending to annihilate the dreadful practice. They were .not unwilling to discuss the subject. They assembled and set forth the facts of the case. Admitting the truth of the charge, they said it was simply the extreme costliness of marriage ceremonials which compelled the people of the child-murdering tribes to suppress the growth of female life. They knew that it was a great evil; and they entered into an agreement to reduce the sums paid, on these nuptial occasions, to less than an eighth of the old amount.* But, I fear that those compacts were not observed; and that the great evil was unsubdued. "Past experience," wrote Mr. Willoughby, in a Council-minute, "has unhappily elsewhere proved, that written agreements are insufficient to extirpate the offence, unless unceasing vigilance is exercised to secure adherence to them." And he then, in 1848, recommended that an annual census of the castes, in which the offence was supposed to be committed, should be forwarded to Government; and that the Sudder Judges should be requested to issue a circular to all magistrates, directing them to institute inquiries as to whether the crime was perpetrated in any part of the country within their jurisdiction. The result of that investigation was, that only among the marked tribes in the Ahmedabad and the Kaira collectorates were there any indubitable traces of the existence of the atrocity. Broach was suspected, but upon closer examination the suspicion was shown to be unfounded.†

* The compact was entered into by fifty-eight villages, inhabited by the Lewa Koombee tribe. The chief people promised to reduce the expenses paid them from 3800 to 480 rupees. The Lewa Koombees of the city of Ahmedabad afterwards came into the arrangement, and undertook to reduce their expenses to one-third of the whole amount.—[*Minute of Mr. Willoughby, Sept.* 9, 1848—1851. *MS. Records.*]

† In one of the answers returned, a circumstance is mentioned which illustrates the benefits derived from the publication of those summaries of facts which make up the staple-contents of "review articles:"

"Opposed to the conclusions thus derived," wrote one of the magistrates, "I confess to having approached the subject with no knowledge of my own, nor did the records of this magistracy in any way assist me; they were absolutely silent on the subject. Neither should I up to the present time have improved my stock of information, but for accidentally meeting with an able article in the *Calcutta Review* for August, 1844, from which, it appears, that Parliamentary Papers have been published giving the results of all the inquiries set on foot into the practice of female infanticide in Central and Western India; and I must here be permitted to suggest respectfully that a copy of this record would be of material importance in every Zillah, not only as conveying the most authentic information hitherto collected upon a most interesting topic, but as leading the uninformed into approved channels of further inquiry."—[*MS. Records.*]

Turning now to another part of the country, I would show what has recently been done in the neighbourhood of Mynpoorie. A statement on this subject was recently drawn up by Mr. Charles Raikes, magistrate and collector of that district. Originally published in a local periodical,* it was subsequently printed in a detached shape, and, in accordance with that system of diffusiveness of which I have spoken in another part of this work, widely circulated by order of the Government of the North-Western Provinces.† I cannot do better than quote from this paper the following statement of encouraging facts:

"Many of our readers will recollect the famine of 1838 (none, indeed, who were then in the N. W. Provinces will ever forget it), when mothers sold their children for a morsel of bread, when the rage of hunger obliterated even the distinctions of caste, and the Brahmin might be seen devouring the leavings of the Dhom. Nowhere did hunger and disease press heavier than in the plains of the mid Doab. Whole villages were depopulated, and every effort of public or private benevolence failed to meet the wants of a starving population. The Government did much to relieve the sufferers at the time, but a merely temporary assistance was not sufficient, and it became necessary to lower the revenue demand in many villages. Mr. Unwin, then collector of Mynpoorie, was in 1842 engaged in fixing the amount of this revision, and his camp was pitched in the midst of the villages of the Chohan Rajpoots. In the course of his proceedings it was found desirable to ascertain how far the population had been affected by the famine, and with this object Mr. Unwin determined to take ten villages in each pergunnah, and selecting one house in each of these villages, to count in person every head in it. 'In so doing,' we use his own words, 'I observed what previous information led me to expect, that no single Chohanee (female Chohan), young or old, was forthcoming. I remarked this to the Zemindars and people themselves, who, of course, were in numbers all about me on these occasions, and told them I knew the cause, and should look after them in future.'

* The *Benares Magazine.*

† It was subsequently embodied in Mr. Raikes' pleasant and instructive volume of "Notes on the North-Western Provinces of India," from which I now quote.

" Mr. Unwin acted with zeal and discretion, and above all things (in India) with *promptitude.* At once and on his own responsibility he established a system of watchful inspection, which was thus described by the officiating magistrate of Mynpoorie (in 1848), in reply to a call for information from the Court of Directors:

" ' In Chohan villages the watchmen are ordered to give information of the birth of a female child forthwith at the police-station. A burkundauze goes to the house and sees the child, the thanadar informs the magistrate, upon which an order is passed, that after one month the health of the new-born child should be reported. The watchmen are further bound to give information if any illness attack the child, when a superior police-officer (either thanadar, jemadar, or mohurrir) at once goes to the village, sees the child, and sends a report to the magistrate. In suspicious cases the body of the child is sent for and submitted to the civil surgeon.'

" The effect of Mr. Unwin's measures was soon felt in the district. Amongst other incidents we may quote the following, as partaking of that almost grotesque character which in these matter-of-fact days seems peculiar to India. The Government had watched Mr. Unwin's proceedings with approbation, and took an early opportunity to notify in a public manner the interest which was felt in the success of his measures.

" There is at Mynpoorie an old fortress, which looks far over the valley of the Esun river. This has been for centuries the stronghold of the Rajahs of Mynpoorie, Chohans whose ancient blood, descending from the great Pirthee Raj and the regal stem of Neem-rana, represents *la crême de la crême* of Rajpoot aristocracy. Here, when a son, a nephew, a grandson, was born to the reigning chief, the event was announced to the neighbouring city by the loud discharge of wall-pieces and matchlocks; but centuries had passed away, and no infant daughter had been known to smile within those walls.

" In 1845, however, thanks to the vigilance of Mr. Unwin, a little grand-daughter was preserved by the Rajah of that day. The fact was duly notified to the Government, and a letter of congratulation and a dress of honor were at once despatched from head-quarters to the Rajah.

" We have called this incident, the giving a robe of honor to a man because he did not destroy his grand-daughter, a *grotesque* one ; but it is very far from being a ridiculous incident. When the people see that the highest authorities in the land take an interest in their social or domestic reforms, those reforms receive an impetus which no lesser influences can give them. The very next year after the investiture of the Rajah, the number of female infants preserved in the district was *trebled!* Fifty-seven had been saved in 1845 ; in 1846, one hundred and eighty were preserved ; and the number has gone on steadily increasing ever since. This is the best answer to those who would sneer at the *paternal* style of government, and who would advocate mere red-tape, law, and bayonets for the people of India.

" Influence is everything in Hindostan. Indeed in all countries good government, like true religion, depends upon influences and motives quite as much as upon mere rules and restrictions. In England, influence does *much ;* in India, we repeat, it does *all.* To go against the *law* is nothing to the native of India, but he rarely consents to go against the *magistrate.* When a government of mere law comes in, when *codes* instead of *men* are to rule India, the sooner the English are off to their ships the better. Let us see what local influence, supported by the influence of the Government, but scarcely assisted by legal sanction, has done for the suppression of female infanticide in Mynpoorie. In 1843, not a single female Chohan infant was to be found in the district; at the present moment there are fourteen hundred girls living, between the ages of one and six. We subjoin an extract from the official Registers, from 1844 to 1850, inclusive. The girls born during the year, and still alive at the end of the year, are only entered.

Name of Thannah.	1844.	1845.	1846.	1847.	1848.	1849.	1850.	Total.	Girls of 6 years and under, living in May, 1851.
Koorowlie ...	7	2	19	1	15	15	24	83	119
Shekoabad ...	9	8	2	6	13	15	22	75	80
Bhowgong ...	5	4	3	8	8	7	10	45	60
Koosmurra	11	3	3	2	5	3	17	44	55
Kurhul	1	7	5	4	9	7	10	43	33
Sumao	58	8	35	44	53	46	43	287	145
Mynpoorie ...	28	10	57	57	77	97	108	434	353
Ghurour	15	9	21	41	36	61	57	240	234
Sirsa-gunge	0	2	2	2	1	0	1	8	8
Kyleyee	0	4.	25	43	29	38	43	182	140
Phurrah	0	0	8	1	15	13	13	50	38
Total	134	57	180	209	261	302	348	1491	1265

"To check these results, a census of the entire Chohan population of the district, of six years old and under, has been made in the present year. The plan adopted was, first to call upon the village accountants to report the number of boys and girls, up to the age of six, living in their respective villages. These returns were then tested as closely as possible by other independent officials, and, as the result of that examination, the number of females was reduced eleven per cent. The return thus corrected is as follows, and is given for pergunnahs, not for the thannahs, noted in the former table.

Names of Pergunnahs.	Boys 6 years and under.	Girls 6 years and under.
Ghurour	297	194
Souj	376	219
Kurhul	52	33
Koorowlie...	33	17
Mustúfabad and Shekoabad ...	474	299
Kishnee Nubbee Gunge... ...	261	102
Munchuna	364	246
Bhowgong...	283	150
Aleepoor Puttee	21	3
Total ...	2161	1263"

I will only add to this that Mr. Raikes himself has been active in this good work, and that he is now, I believe, pushing forward, with unabated energy and undiminished success, the good work of which he is here the exponent.

One more illustration of the good results of British interference must be adduced before I bring this chapter to a close. The practice of female infanticide was very prevalent on those Orissan hill-tracts, where Macpherson and Campbell achieved such great things for the suppression of the rite of human sacrifice. In some of the tribes it prevailed to such an extent, that no female infant was spared except when a woman's first child was a female. Villages containing a hundred houses were to be seen without a single female child. The practice had its origin in the social customs of the people, very different from those which obtain among the Rajpoots, of whom I have heretofore spoken. "So far," says Captain Macpherson, "is constancy to her husband from being required in a wife, that her pretensions do not, at least, suffer diminution in the eyes of either sex when fines are levied on her convicted lovers; while, on the other hand, infidelity on the part of a married man is held to be highly dishonorable, and is often punished by the deprivation of many social privileges. A wife, moreover, may quit her husband at any time, except within a year of her marriage, or when she expects offspring, or within a year after the birth of a child; and she may then return to her father's house, or contract a new marriage; while no man who is without a wife may, without entailing disgrace on himself and his tribe, refuse to receive any woman who may choose to enter his house and establish herself as its mistress. Now, a bridegroom gives for a wife of these tribes in which so few women are brought up, a large consideration in cattle and money. The sum is chiefly subscribed by his near relatives and his branch of his tribe, and is paid to his wife's father, who, again, distributes it amongst the heads of families of his own branch. But, when a wife quits her husband, he has a right to reclaim immediately from her father the whole sum paid for her; while the father, at the same time, becomes entitled to levy a like sum from any new husband to whom she may attach herself. And, it being observed that every man's tribe is at once answerable for all his debts, and bound in honor to enforce his claims, it will be understood that these restitutions and exactions, whether to be made betwixt persons belonging to different tribes or to different branches of the same tribe, must be, even in the simplest cases, productive of infinite difficulty and vexation; while they have given rise to three-fourths of the sanguinary quarrels and hereditary feuds which distract the Khond country. Thence, say the Khonds —'To any man but a rich and powerful chief, who desires to form connexions, and is able to make large and sudden restitutions, and to his tribe—a married daughter is a curse. By the death of our female infants before they see the light, the lives of men without number are saved, and we live in comparative peace.'"

I cannot afford to trace in detail the efforts which were made by Macpherson to root out this dreadful custom from among the Khonds. His exertions were characterised by the same energy and the same success as had attended his great crusade against human sacrifice. To use his own words: "The practice of female infanticide was suppressed in the greatest portion of the Khond country of Souradah, including Coradah, before the middle of 1844, and early in the present year throughout those Zemindaries—that the measures by which that change was accomplished materially affected the system of life and the chief interests of the Khond tribes, their aim being to establish an ascendancy over the Khond population founded upon a sense of benefits derived from their connexion with the Government—such as the benefit of justice, and that of protection in their intercourse with the low countries, and to remove the principal causes of infanticide, by preventing or settling disputes connected with property involved in marriage contracts, &c."* To this must be added, at least, an allusion to the interesting fact that the female victims, whom Macpherson had rescued, were given from time to time, when of ripe age, in marriage to men of the Khond tribes, and that these women put forth their influence most suc-

* *Capt. Macpherson to Mr. Halliday, Nov.* 11, 1846. *MS. Records.*

cessfully to wean the people from the hoary custom which had dwelt so cruelly among them.

I have every reason to believe that in this part of the country the efforts of our British officers have been attended with complete success, and that the good results of their humane efforts are likely to be abiding. The last report from the Khond agency contains these encouraging words:—"The lateness of the season," says Captain Campbell, "and the difficulty of procuring a sufficiency of water for my camp, prevented my visiting the infanticidal tribes, but many of the chiefs and a great number of the Meriah females, who had been married to Khonds of these tracts, visited me at Sooradah with their children, and from them I learnt with satisfaction that female children were now generally preserved; and in cases where they were destroyed it was done with great secrecy, and not openly as in former times. An officer of the Sebundies, well acquainted with the infanticidal tribes, and employed in superintending them, confirms this report."*

These good deeds require no gloss—I leave such statements to make their own way. It would be difficult to supply a fitting commentary, and impertinent to comment upon them in language not rising to the height of so great an argument. There are works which the English will leave behind them, mightier than any material fabrics which human skill can fashion and human labor construct. Let us rear what great substantial structures we may—and even in such works we are far surpassing the Moguls—History will be able to record nothing better of British rule in the East than that under the Government of the East India Company the widow ceased to burn herself on the funeral pile of her husband—the mother ceased habitually to destroy the

* *Colonel Campbell to the Government of India, April* 10, 1852. *MS. Records.*

infant life of her daughters—men ceased to purchase and to rear children for sacrifice to a cruel goddess—murder ceased to be a science and its practice an honorable profession—and that many wild tribes, by the conciliatory efforts of the servants of the Company, were weaned from a life of rapine, and raised from a state of barbarism, to become peaceful agriculturists and civilised rational men.*

* I have said nothing in this chapter about the suppression of Female Infanticide in Cutch, not because I was unmindful of the subject, but because I could not afford any further to extend the dimensions of this chapter. I believe that very gratifying progress has been made in that part of the world. My friend, Dr. Duff, when in Western India, was assured by the Rao (how interesting must have been a conversation on such a subject between two such men) that there had been, for some years, a gradual diminution of the great crime; and the assertion was satisfactorily proved by detailed statistics.

Talboys Wheeler

***The history of the imperial assemblage at Delhi, held on the 1st January, 1877, to celebrate the assumption of the title of Empress of India by Her Majesty the Queen. Including historical sketches of India and her princes past and present.* London: Longmans, Green, Reader, and Dyer, 1877.**

THE HISTORY

OF THE

IMPERIAL ASSEMBLAGE AT DELHI.

INTRODUCTION.

Political Significance of the Imperial Assemblage.—Antiquity of Imperial Assemblages in India.—Fitness of Delhi.—Reasons for Reviewing the History of India.—Three Empires in India: the Rajpút, the Muhammadan and the Mahratta.

THE Imperial Assemblage at Delhi has been held to celebrate the assumption of the title of "Empress of India" by her Majesty the Queen. The significance of the event may be overlooked amidst the general rejoicings; the event itself will stand out for all time as an epoch in the history of India. It is the natural outcome of the political changes which have moulded India into a British empire. The Muhammadan rule faded away. The great East India Company built up a new dominion, and then resigned its trust. Eighteen years have passed by since the Queen of the British Isles assumed the direct sovereignty of her eastern possessions. The Imperial Assemblage at Delhi has ratified the act. Henceforth

Her Majesty the Queen is Empress of India—not only in deed, but in name.

An Imperial Assemblage is one of the oldest institutions in India. From the remotest antiquity the Rajas and princes of India have assembled to celebrate the establishment of a new empire, or the accession of a new suzerain. The story of such gatherings is told in the earliest traditions of the two famous Hindu epics,—the Rámáyana and Mahá Bhárata.[1] To this day the memories are household words throughout India. In the age of Rajpút sovereignty such meetings were known as Raja-súyas and Aswamedhas. In the age of Muhammadan rule they were known by the name of Durbars.

There is no city in the British empire so fitted as Delhi for the assumption of the sovereignty of India. It is seated near one of the most ancient sites in all India. It is associated with nearly every era in the history of the past, —Rajpút, Muhammadan and Mahratta. Its streets and bazaars have grown up in historic times; their story is told in written annals. They stand in the midst of relics which belong to the remotest antiquity; the remains of a metropolis which may claim to be coeval with the oldest cities in the ancient world. The ruins of Indra-prastha, the "precinct of Indra," lie buried beneath the neighbouring mounds. The kings, the nobles, the once teeming population have shrivelled into dust and ashes. The traditions are preserved to this day in the Hindu epic of the Mahá Bhárata. Delhi and its surroundings are a monument of Indra-prastha. The legends of

[1] It is a moot point whether the Rámáyana or the Mahá Bhárata is the oldest poem. The Hindus consider that the Rámáyana is the more ancient.

Indraprastha and Delhi are for ever bound up with the history of India.[1]

A review of the past history of India may form a fitting introduction to the narrative of the proceedings of the Imperial Assemblage at Delhi. It may be well in the present place to recall some of the leading events in which the families of the princes who attended the Assemblage are interested or associated. Indeed, the ancestral houses of

[1] There are three cities known to tradition, which are associated with the site of Delhi :

(1) *Indra-prastha*, which was built between Delhi gate and the tomb of Humáyun, somewhere about fifteen centuries before Christ.

(2) *Mediæval Delhi*, which was founded round about the Iron Pillar and the Kutub tower about A.D. 750.

(3) *Modern Delhi*, which was built by the Moghul emperor Shah Jehan in the early half of the seventeenth century; it was called Jehanabad after the name of the founder.

Each of these cities will be noticed in turn in the following pages; but the following description of them by M. de Thevenot, who visited India in the seven teenth century, will be found interesting :—

"There are three towns of Delhi near to one another. The first, which is entirely destroyed, and whereof some ruins only remain, was very ancient; and the learned Indians will have it to have been the capital town of the states of King Porus, so famous for the war which he maintained against Alexander the Great. It was nearer the source of the Jumna than the two others which have been built since. The Indians say it had fifty-two gates; and there is still at some distance from its ruins a stone-bridge, from whence a way hath been made with lovely trees on each side, which leads to the second Delhi, by the place where the sepulchre of Humáyun is.

"The second town of Delhi is that which was taken by the Moghuls. It was then beautified with a great many stately sepulchres of the Afghan kings and other monuments, which rendered it a very lovely town; but Shah Jehan, the father of Aurungzeb, demolished it for the building of Jehanabad. Towards the sepulchre of Humáyun there is a pyramid or obelisk of stone [*i.e.*, the Iron Pillar], which by its unknown characters shows a great antiquity.

"The third town of Delhi is joined to the remains of the second. Shah Jehan resolved to give his name to a new town; he caused it to be built of the ruins of the second Delhi, and called it Jehanabad. It lies in an open champaign country upon the brink of the Jumna. The fortress of it is half a league in circuit, and hath good walls with round towers every ten battlements, and ditches full of water, wharfed with stone, as likewise lovely gardens round it. This fort is the palace of the king."

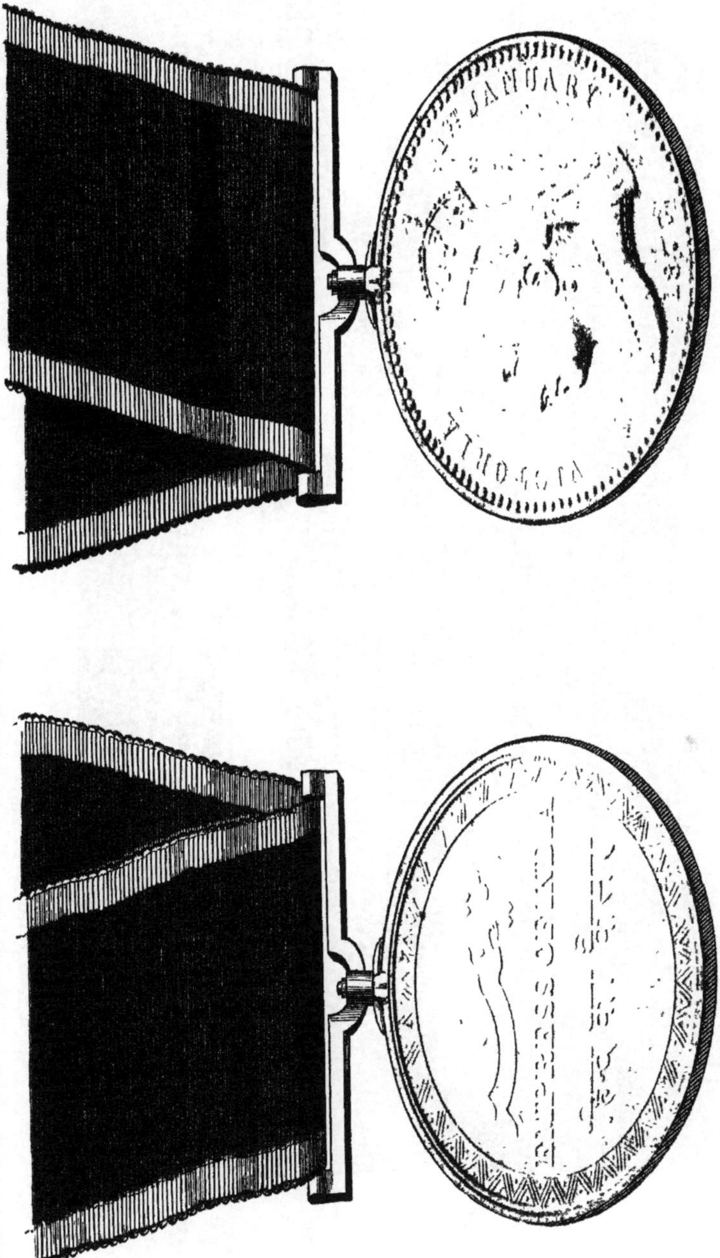

MEDAL STRUCK IN COMMEMORATION OF HER MAJESTY'S ASSUMPTION OF THE TITLE OF EMPRESS OF INDIA

H.H. THE LATE MAHARAJA JUNG BAHADUR, G.C.B., G.C S I.

all present have appeared upon the stage at one or other of the great epochs in Indian annals. Some claim descent from princes who fought in the wars of the Rámáyana and Mahá Bhárata; who joined in the royal and imperial assemblages which were celebrated in olden time. The forefathers of some may have flourished in the age when the galleys of Tyre and Sidon were plying in the eastern seas; when Alexander and his Greeks were advancing into the Punjab; when the ships of Roman merchants sailed to Indian ports. Other ancestors of existing families became famous under the imperial rule of Rajpúts, Muhammadans or Mahrattas. One and all have played a part in history during the rise and growth of the British empire in India. Their traditions have thus become interwoven with those of the English people. Henceforth all the great events in the history of India, from the foundation of Indra-prastha to the Imperial Assemblage of 1877, ought to be known and appreciated wherever the English language is spoken throughout the world.

The history of India before the advent of the British power tells of the rise and fall of three great empires,—the Rajpút, the Muhammadan and the Mahratta. Each in turn was a paramount power. Each in turn was broken up into small kingdoms, which became feudatory states of a new empire. The native princes of India are for the most part representatives of these bygone empires.

CHAPTER VII.

PROCLAMATION DAY.

1ST JANUARY, 1877.

The Imperial Assemblage.—The crowning event of the nineteenth century.—Good omens.—Scene of the Proclamation.—Throne Pavilion.—The Canopy.—Armorial bearings.—Amphitheatre.—Spectators' blocks.—Native Chiefs in the Amphitheatre.—European Governors and Administrators. The multitude.—British and Native Troops.—Guards of Honour.—Arrival of the Viceroy.—Chief Herald.—Imperial Proclamation.—Speech of His Excellency the Viceroy.—Concluding Ceremonies.

THE first of January eighteen hundred and seventy-seven was the great day of the Imperial Assemblage. Her Majesty the Queen of England was proclaimed Empress of India. The Governors and other High Officials of British India were assembled together with all the Ruling Native Chiefs to inaugurate the installation of the Empress as the Sovereign of Her Eastern Empire.

The nineteenth century has witnessed the regeneration of India; the proclamation of the Queen as Empress of India is the crowning event of the century. The India of the eighteenth century is as remote as the wars of the Heptarchy, or the invasions of Goths and Huns. The India of the nineteenth century is becoming like England of to-day. The railways and telegraphs are helping to draw princes and people nearer and nearer to the paramount power.

Throughout all the days of the Imperial Assemblage the weather was most propitious. There was no storm to disturb the ceremonial; not even a shower of rain to throw a damp on the proceedings. The morning of the proclamation was without a cloud. There was the same cool atmosphere and pleasant sunshine as on the day of the Viceroy's entry; and these conditions were specially desirable at a ceremonial which was to be carried out in tented pavilions and to some degree in the open air.[1]

The scene of the Proclamation was a turf-covered plain about four miles from Delhi. Three structures had been set up, namely, a Throne Pavilion for the Viceroy, an Amphitheatre for the High Officials and Ruling Chiefs, and blocks for Representatives of Foreign Governments and spectators.

The Throne Pavilion was a graceful building of blue, red, and gold, near the centre of the area. It was a hexagon; each of its sides was forty feet long; the whole was thus about two hundred and twenty-four feet round. The details are worth describing. The lower part was a solid structure of masonry ten feet from the ground. It was surrounded by a gilded railing. There was a flight of steps in front and another behind, also with gilded railings. The upper part was a canopy raised over the structure, supported on twelve slender clustered shafts. The Imperial Crown at the top rested upon a cushion. Beneath it depended a graceful drapery of red cloth embroidered with gold. On the upper cornice was worked a pattern of festooned laurel wreaths and Imperial Crowns. At each angle was a trophy of three satin

[1] It is a curious fact, which some may regard as a good omen, that within a day or two after the departure of the last visitor, Delhi was deluged with rain, which converted the camps into a swamp. Had it fallen earlier it might have spoiled much of the ceremonial.

bannerets, festooned outwards, displaying the Cross of St. George and the Union Jack. Below the cornice the canopy was continued in alternate stripes of red and white satin, embroidered with golden *fleurs de lis.* There was a lower frieze with an armorial vallance hanging from it. The frieze displayed the Rose, Shamrock, and Thistle, embroidered with the Lotos of India in gold, silver, and colours. It was adorned at each angle by a gilded crown and silken drapery. The vallance was composed of shield-shaped forms, on which were shown alternately the Irish Harp, the Lion Rampant of Scotland, and the Three Lions of England. The shafts of the canopy were hung with silver shields, about ten feet from the ground, bearing the imperial monogram in gold, surmounted by bannerets of various-coloured satins.

The base of the Throne Pavilion was broken up into panels, surmounted by a moulded cornice. The larger panels were filled in with gold embroidery on green velvet, representing the Imperial Crown boldly embossed in gold on a groundwork of symbolical foliage. The smaller panels were decorated with the Royal Arms of England richly worked in satin *appliqué.* All the panels were surrounded by gilded cable mouldings.

The Amphitheatre[1] for the reception of High Officials and Ruling Chiefs was a pavilion of blue, white, and gold, stretching out for nearly eight hundred feet in front of the Throne Pavilion. It was divided into thirty-six compartments, each of which was about twenty feet in length and thirty feet in depth, and had a separate entrance. The centre

[1] The term Amphitheatre is scarcely correct. It was properly speaking a semi-circle, whereas an Amphitheatre is elliptical in form. But the term Amphitheatre is intelligible, and conveys a general idea of the character of the structure. It is therefore employed in the present work.

of the arc was two hundred and twenty-six feet from the Throne Pavilion. Along the top front of the Amphitheatre were displayed *fleurs de lis* and gilded lance-heads supported on three sets of pillars of white and gold. An Imperial Crown was displayed on each pillar, also at the four corners of the Amphitheatre. The floor was covered with red cloth; the chairs were blue; a gilded railing ran along the front of the Amphitheatre.

The blocks for the spectators need no description. They were blue in colour, and raised behind the Throne Pavilion. Between the two blocks was the grand entrance to the area.

There was nothing oriental in these structures. They were not borrowed from any native designs. They were tented pavilions covered in to keep off the sun, otherwise they were exposed to the open air. They were rich in colour, as was suitable beneath an Indian sun.

The gathering together of Native costumes and European uniforms somewhat changed the appearance of these pavilions. The scene on the morning of the Proclamation assumed a varied and dazzling character. Every Ruling Chief and every European Governor and Lieutenant-Governor sat under his own banner, surrounded by Native nobles and European officials. Every effort was made to mingle the Ruling Chiefs with European officials, so as to avoid questions of precedence which have excited bitterness and heartburnings in India from the remotest antiquity. The result was such a display of oriental costumes and insignia with British uniforms and banners as was never witnessed before. Sixty-three Ruling Chiefs of India were present in the Amphitheatre. They and their retinues, all in gorgeous costumes of satin, velvet, or cloth of gold, were everywhere mixed up with

European officials in their uniforms of red and dark blue. Still it was generally possible to identify the Chiefs in their several compartments by their insignia and jewellery. In the centre of the Amphitheatre were the three boy princes of India,—the Nizam of Hyderabad, the Gaekwar of Baroda, and the Maharaja of Mysore. On the right were the Ruling Chiefs of Rajputana, including the young Maharana of Udaipur and the Maharajas of Jaipur and Jodhpur. On the left were the Ruling Chiefs of Central India, including Maharaja Scindia, Maharaja Holkar, and other representatives of the extinct Mahratta empire. At the extreme left were the Ruling Chiefs of the Punjab and the Maharaja of Kashmir. The remaining compartments were occupied by Chiefs of minor note, more or less dependent on the Governments of Madras, Bombay, Bengal, the North-West Provinces and the Central Provinces: feudatories in fact of the local Governments, rather than of the Government of India, which exercises the supreme jurisdiction over all.

Amongst the European authorities present in the Amphitheatre, it may suffice to name His Excellency the Duke of Buckingham, Governor of Madras; His Excellency Sir Philip Wodehouse, Governor of Bombay; Sir Richard Temple, Lieutenant-Governor of Bengal; Sir George Couper, Lieutenant-Governor of the North-West Provinces; General Sir Frederic Haines, the Commander-in-Chief in India; the Chief Commissioners of Oudh, the Central Provinces, Mysore, Burma, and Assam; Members of Council, Judges, Secretaries to Government, and other High Officials.

From an early hour there had been a general gathering towards the Imperial Assemblage. Ruling Chiefs drove by in state carriages accompanied by retainers and soldiers.

Groups of elephants crowded to the same spot clad in the trappings they had worn on the day of the entry. Vast multitudes also assembled to see the various Chiefs and High Officials pass by on their way to the place of Proclamation. The spectators' seats on either side of the Throne Pavilion were occupied by Ambassadors, Envoys, and Deputations, including those from Nipal and Siam ; also by Foreign Consuls, and a large number of European ladies and gentlemen. Here also were seated the Khan of Khelat, the Governor-General of the Portuguese Settlements in India, and numerous Native nobles and officials. The general public were also admitted in great numbers to the inclosure, behind the Amphitheatre.

All the British troops assembled at Delhi were drawn up on a plain to the north of the pavilions ; the Native chiefs and nobles had in like manner drawn up their retainers and followers on the opposite plain to the south of the pavilions.

Guards of honour were drawn up on either side of the Throne Pavilion, as well as at each of the several entrances to the Amphitheatre.

At noon a flourish of trumpets from the Heralds announced the arrival of His Excellency the Viceroy. All who were present in that vast assembly rose from their seats ; the military bands played a grand march. His Excellency, who was accompanied by Lady Lytton and the members of his family, alighted from his carriage and advanced towards the Throne Pavilion preceded by the Personal Staff. The bands struck up the National Anthem, and the guards of honour presented arms as the Viceroy took his seat upon the throne.

The proceedings were simple and impressive. His Excellency was arrayed in his robes as Grand Master of the

Star of India. He commanded the Chief Herald to read the Proclamation of the assumption of the Imperial Title by Her Majesty the Queen. The twelve Heralds sounded a flourish of trumpets. The Chief Herald then read the Proclamation in a loud voice, which was heard by the whole Assemblage.

"VICTORIA, R.

" WHEREAS an Act has been passed in the present Sessions of Parliament, intituled 'An Act to enable Her Most Gracious Majesty to make an addition to the Royal Style and Titles appertaining to the Imperial Crown of the United Kingdom and its Dependencies,' which Act recites that, by the Act for the Union of Great Britain and Ireland, it was provided that after such Union the Royal Style and Titles appertaining to the Imperial Crown of the United Kingdom and its Dependencies should be such as His Majesty by His Royal Proclamation under the Great Seal of the United Kingdom should be pleased to appoint: and which Act also recites that, by virtue of the said Act, and of a Royal Proclamation under the Great Seal, dated the 1st day of January 1801, Our present Style and Titles are 'VICTORIA, by the Grace of God of the United Kingdom of Great Britain and Ireland QUEEN, Defender of the Faith:' and which Act also recites that, by the Act for the better government of India, it was enacted that the Government of India, theretofore vested in the East India Company in trust for Us, should become vested in Us, and that India should thenceforth be governed by Us and in Our name, and that it is expedient that there should be a recognition of the transfer of government so made by means of an addition to be made to Our Style and Titles: and which Act, after the said recitals, enacts that it

H H. THE MAHARAJA OF JAIPUR, G.C.S.I.

shall be lawful for Us, with a view to such recognition as aforesaid, of the transfer of the Government of India, by Our Proclamation under the Great Seal of the United Kingdom to make such addition to the Style and Titles at present appertaining to the Imperial Crown of the United Kingdom and its Dependencies as to Us may seem meet; we have thought fit, by and with the advice of Our Privy Council, to appoint and declare, and We do hereby, by and with the said advice, appoint and declare that henceforth, so far as conveniently may be, on all occasions and in all instruments wherein Our Style and Titles are used, save and except all Charters, Commissions, Letters Patent, Grants, Writs, Appointments, and other like instruments, not extending in their operation beyond the United Kingdom, the following addition shall be made to the Style and Titles at present appertaining to the Imperial Crown of the United Kingdom and its Dependencies; that is to say, in the Latin tongue in these words: 'INDIÆ IMPERATRIX.' And in the English tongue in these words: 'EMPRESS OF INDIA.'

"And Our will and pleasure further is, that the said addition shall not be made in the Commissions, Charters, Letters Patent, Grants, Writs, Appointments, and other like instruments, hereinbefore specially excepted.

"And Our will and pleasure further is, that all gold, silver, and copper moneys, now current and lawful moneys of the United Kingdom, and all gold, silver, and copper moneys which shall on or after this day be coined by Our authority with the like impressions, shall, notwithstanding such addition to Our Style and Titles, be deemed and taken to be current and lawful moneys of the said United Kingdom; and further, that all moneys coined for and issued in any of the

Dependencies of the said United Kingdom, and declared by Our Proclamation to be current and lawful money of such Dependencies respectively bearing Our Style, or Titles, or any part or parts thereof, and all moneys which shall hereafter be coined and issued according to such Proclamation, shall, notwithstanding such addition, continue to be lawful and current money of such Dependencies respectively, until Our pleasure shall be further declared thereupon.

"Given at Our Court at *Windsor* the twenty-eighth day of *April* One thousand eight hundred and seventy-six in the thirty-ninth year of Our Reign.

"GOD SAVE THE QUEEN."

The Proclamation was then read aloud in the Urdu language by Mr. Thornton, the Officiating Foreign Secretary to the Government of India.

When the Proclamation was concluded, the Royal Standard was hoisted in honour of Her Majesty the Empress; and a grand salute of one hundred and one salvoes of artillery was fired, interspersed at intervals with more striking *feux de joie* from the long line of troops almost surrounding the Assemblage. Meanwhile mixed military bands played the National Anthem, followed by the stirring music of the march in "Tannhäuser." The scene, at this moment, was very impressive. The splendid semi-circle of Princes, the vast expanse of troops, brilliant retinues, state elephants, and crowds on crowds of human beings shading off into the distance; the strains of music sounding through the roar of artillery, and the reverberations of the *feux de joie*, combined to produce an effect never to be forgotten by those present. Some additional excitement was caused by the conduct of the elephants. They had stood the sounds of the artillery salvoes with wonderful equanimity, but as the roll of musketry approached them, many rushed wildly to and fro with trunks erect and trumpeting, and a murmur of excitement rose through the multitude. Fortunately, the *feux de joie* were not prolonged, and the elephants quickly recovered their composure without having caused serious accident.

The salutes and *feux de joie* occupied upwards of twenty minutes; then, as the sound of the last salvo died away, His Excellency the Viceroy arose and delivered the following speech to the Assemblage :—

"On the first day of November, in the year 1858, a Proclamation was issued by the Queen of England, conveying to the Princes and People of India those assurances of Her Majesty's good will which, from that day to this, they have cherished as their most precious political possession.

"The promises then made by a Sovereign, whose word has never been broken, need no confirmation from my lips. Eighteen years of progressive prosperity confirm them; and this great Assemblage is the conspicuous evidence of their fulfilment. Undisturbed in the enjoyment of their hereditary honours, protected in the prosecution of their lawful interests, both the Princes and the people of this Empire have found a full security for the future in the generosity and justice of the past.

"We are now assembled to proclaim the assumption by The Queen of the Title of Empress of India; and it is my duty, as Her Representative in this country, to explain the gracious intentions of Her Majesty in adding that title to the style and dignity of Her ancestral Crown.

" Of all Her Majesty's Possessions throughout the world, —possessions comprising a seventh part of the earth's surface, and three hundred millions of its inhabitants—there is not one that She regards with deeper interest than this great and ancient Empire.

" At all times, and in all places, the British Crown has had able and zealous servants, but none more illustrious than those whose wisdom and heroism have won and kept for it the dominion of India. This achievement, in which all Her Majesty's subjects, European and Native, have worthily co-operated, has also been aided by the loyalty of Her Majesty's great allies and feudatories; whose soldiers have shared with Her Armies the toils and victories of war; whose sagacious fidelity has assisted Her Government in preserving and diffusing the blessings of peace; and whose presence here to-day at the solemn inauguration of Her Imperial Title attests their confidence in the beneficence of Her power, and their interest in the unity of Her Empire.

" This Empire, acquired by Her Ancestors, and consolidated by Herself, The Queen regards as a glorious inheritance to be maintained and transmitted intact to Her descendants; and She recognises in the possession of it the most solemn obligations to use Her great power for the welfare of all its people, with scrupulous regard for the rights of Her feudatory Princes. For this reason, it is Her Majesty's Royal pleasure to add to the Titles of Her Crown one which shall be henceforth to all the Princes and Peoples of India the permanent symbol of its union with their interests, and its claim upon their loyal allegiance.

" The successive dynasties whose rule in India the power of the British Crown has been called by Providence to replace

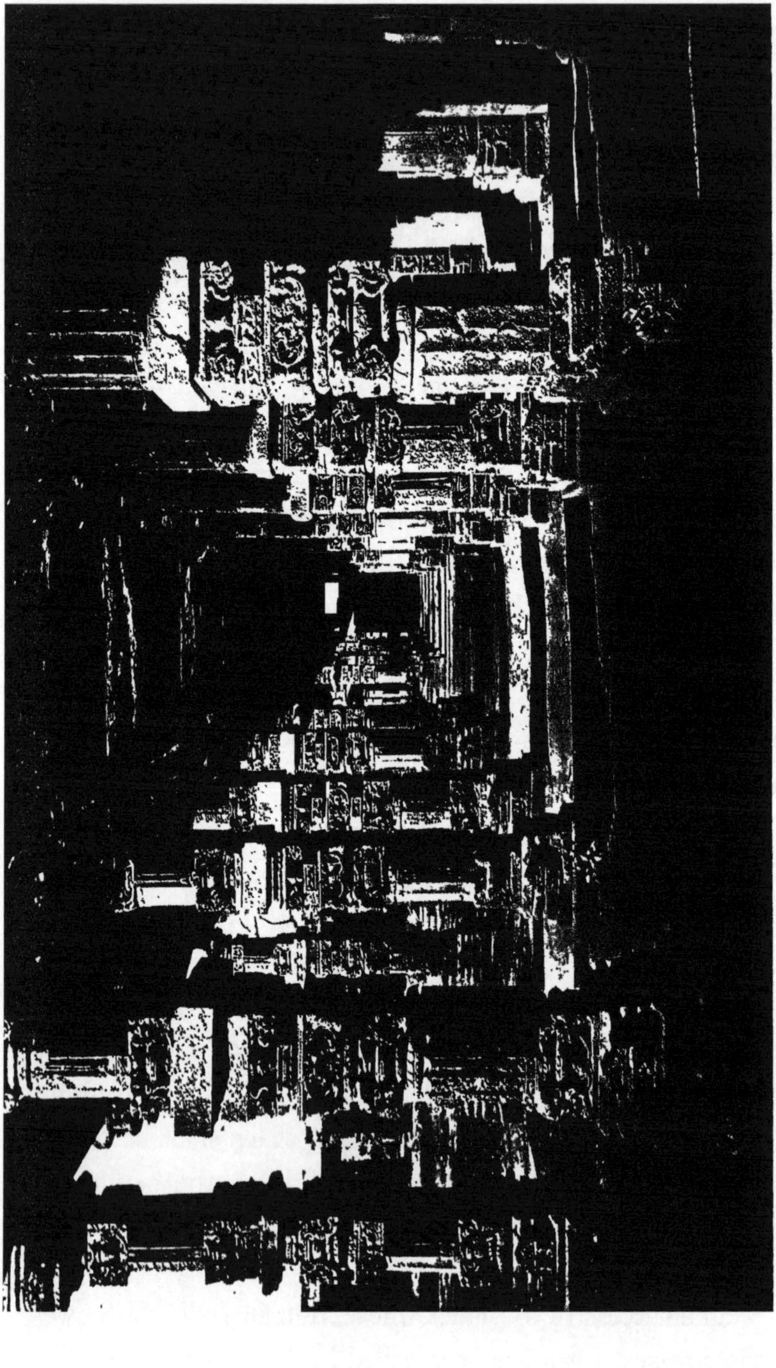

INTERIOR OF THE COLONNADE OF HINDOO PILLARS AT THE KOOTUB.

and improve, were not unproductive of good and great Sovereigns; but the polity of their successors failed to secure the internal peace of their dominions. Strife became chronic, and anarchy constantly recurrent. The weak were the prey of the strong, and the strong the victims of their own passions. Thus, sapped by incessant bloodshed and shaken by intestine broils, the great House of Tamerlane crumbled to decay; and it fell at last because it had ceased to be conducive to the progress of the East.

"Now, under laws which impartially protect all races and all creeds, every subject of Her Majesty may peacefully enjoy his own. The toleration of the Government permits each member of the community to follow without molestation the rules and rites of his religion. The strong hand of Imperial Power is put forth, not to crush but to protect and guide; and the results of British rule are everywhere around us in the rapid advance of the whole country, and the increasing prosperity of all its Provinces.

"British Administrators and faithful Officers of the Crown,—It is to your continued labours that these beneficent results are chiefly due: and it is to you, in the first instance, that I have now, in the name of Her Majesty, to express the gratitude and confidence of your Sovereign. Not less steadfastly than all your honoured predecessors, you have toiled for the good of this great Empire with a persevering energy, public virtue, and self-devotion, unsurpassed in history.

"The doors of fame are not open to all; but the opportunity of doing good is denied to none who seek it. Rapid promotion it is not often in the power of any Government to provide for its servants. But I feel assured that, in the service of the

British Crown, public duty and personal devotion will ever have higher incentives than the expectation of public honours or personal emoluments. Much of the most important and valuable work of Indian administration has always been, and always must be, done, not by persons in prominent positions, but by those district officers on whose patient intelligence and courage the efficient operation of its whole system is essentially dependent.

"I cannot give expression too emphatic to Her Majesty's grateful recognition of the admirable manner in which Her servants, both Civil and Military, have performed, and are performing, throughout India tasks as delicate and difficult as any which the Crown can confide to its must trusted subjects.

MEMBERS OF THE CIVIL AND MILITARY SERVICES,—placed at an early age in positions of immense responsibility, submitting with cheerful devotion to a severely exacting discipline, personally exercising the most important administrative functions among populations whose language, creed, and customs differ from your own,—may you ever be sustained in the firm, yet gentle, discharge of your arduous duties by the consciousness that, whilst you thus uphold the high character of your race, and carry out the benign precepts of your religion, you are also conferring on all other creeds and races in this country the inestimable benefits of good government.

"But it is not only to the official servants of the Crown that India is indebted for the wise application of the principles of Western civilisation to the steady development of her vast resources : and I should ill represent the feelings of my August Mistress if, on this occasion, I failed to assure Her non-official European subjects in India of the cordial satisfaction with which Her Majesty recognises and appreciates, not only their loyalty to Her Throne and Person, but also the benefits which Her Indian Empire derives from their industry, their enterprise, their social energy, and civic virtue.

"Wishing to increase Her opportunities of distinguishing the public services, or private worth, of Her subjects throughout this important portion of Her Dominions, Her Majesty has been pleased not only to sanction a certain enlargement of the Most Exalted Order of the Star of India, and of the Order of British India, but also to institute for this purpose an entirely new Order, which will be called the Order of the Indian Empire.

"Officers and Soldiers of the Army of India, British and Native,—The Queen recalls with pride your heroic achievements on every occasion, when, fighting side by side, you have upheld the honour of Her arms. Confident that all future occasions will find you no less efficiently united in the faithful performance of that high duty, it is to you that Her Majesty entrusts the great charge of maintaining the peace, and protecting the prosperity, of Her Indian dominions.

"Volunteer Soldiers,—Your loyal and successful endeavours to render yourselves capable of acting, if necessary, with the Regular Forces, claim cordial recognition on this occasion.

"Princes and Chiefs of this Empire,—which finds in your loyalty a pledge of strength, in your prosperity a source of splendour,—Her Majesty thanks you for your readiness, on which She reckons, if its interests be attacked or menaced, to assist Her Government in the defence of them. In The Queen's name I cordially welcome you to Delhi; recognising in your presence, on this great occasion, conspicuous evidence of

H H THE MAHARAJA OF JODHPUR G C S I

those sentiments of attachment to the Crown of England which received from you such emphatic expression during the recent visit of the Prince of Wales to this country. Her Majesty regards Her interests as identified with yours; and it is with the wish to confirm the confidence and perpetuate the intimacy of the relations now so happily uniting the British Crown and its feudatories and allies, that Her Majesty has been graciously pleased to assume the Imperial Title we proclaim to-day.

"NATIVE SUBJECTS OF THE EMPRESS OF INDIA,—The present conditions and permanent interests of this Empire demand the supreme supervision and direction of their administration by English Officers trained in the principles of that polity whose assertion is necessary to preserve the continuity of Imperial rule. It is to the wise initiative of these Statesmen that India chiefly owes that steady progress in civilisation which is a condition of her political importance, and the secret of her growing strength; and it is they who must long continue to form the most important practical channel through which the arts, the sciences, and the culture of the West (which have given to Europe its present pre-eminence in peace and war), may freely flow towards the East for the common benefit of all its children.

"But you the Natives of India, whatever your race, and whatever your creed, have a recognised claim to share largely with your English fellow-subjects, according to your capacity for the task, in the administration of the country you inhabit. This claim is founded in the highest justice. It has been repeatedly affirmed by the greatest British and Indian Statesmen, and by the Legislation of the Imperial Parliament. It is recognised by the Government of India, as binding on its honour, and consonant with all the aims of its policy. The Government of India, therefore, notices with satisfaction the marked improvement during recent years in the character of the native public service, especially in its higher grades.

"The administration of this great Empire demands, from many of those to whom a share in it is entrusted, attributes not exclusively intellectual, qualifications to which moral and social superiority are essential. More especially, therefore, does it rest with those who, by birth, rank, and hereditary influence, are your natural leaders, to fit themselves and their children for the honourable duty which is open to them, by accepting the only education that can enable them to comprehend and practise the principles steadily maintained by the Government of The Queen, their Empress.

"You must all adopt as your own that highest standard of public virtue which comprises loyalty, incorruptibility, impartiality, truth, and courage. The Government of Her Majesty will then cordially welcome your co-operation in the work of administration. For in every quarter of the globe over which its dominion is established, that Government trusts less to the strength of armies than to the willing allegiance of a contented and united people, who rally round the throne, because they recognise therein the stable condition of their permanent welfare.

"It is on the gradual and enlightened participation of Her Indian subjects in the undisturbed exercise of this mild and just authority, and not upon the conquest of weaker States, or the annexation of neighbouring territories, that Her Majesty relies for the development of her Indian Empire. Her interests and duties, however, are not confined to Her own dominions. She sincerely desires to maintain the most frank and friendly relations with the rulers of those territories which, adjoining the frontiers of this Empire, have so long owed their independence to the sheltering shadow of its power. But should the repose of that power be at any time threatened from without, the Empress of India will know how to defend her great inheritance. No foreign enemy can now attack the British Empire in India without thereby assailing the whole civilisation of the East, and the unlimited resources of Her dominions, the courageous fidelity of Her allies and feudatories, and the loyal affection of Her subjects, have provided Her Majesty with ample power to repel and punish every assailant.

"The presence, on this occasion, of the representatives of Sovereigns who, from the remotest parts of the East, have addressed to The Queen their congratulations on the event we celebrate to-day, significantly attests the pacific policy of the Government of India, and the cordiality of its relations with all neighbouring States. To his Highness the Khan of Khelat, and to those Ambassadors who have travelled so far to represent on British territory the Asiatic allies of the Empress of India, as also to our honoured guest his Excellency the Governor-General of Goa, and to the Foreign Consular Body, I desire to offer, on behalf of Her Majesty's Indian Government, welcome to this Imperial Assemblage.

"PRINCES AND PEOPLE OF INDIA,—It is now my pleasing duty to communicate to you the gracious message which The Queen, your Empress, has to-day addressed to you in her own Royal and Imperial name. These are the words of the telegraphic message which I have this morning received from Her Majesty.

"'We, Victoria by the Grace of God, of the United

Kingdom, Queen, Empress of India, send through our Viceroy to all our Officers, Civil and Military, and to all Princes, Chiefs, and Peoples now at Delhi assembled, our Royal and Imperial Greeting, and assure them of the deep interest and earnest affection with which we regard the people of our Indian Empire. We witnessed with heartfelt satisfaction the reception which they have accorded to our beloved son, and have been touched by the evidence of their loyalty and attachment to Our House and Throne. We trust that the present occasion may tend to unite in bonds of yet closer affection ourselves and our subjects; that from the highest to the humblest all may feel that under our rule the great principles of liberty, equity, and justice are secured to them; and that to promote their happiness, to add to their prosperity, and advance their welfare, are the ever present aims and objects of our Empire.'

"You will, I am confident, appreciate these gracious words.

"God save VICTORIA, Queen of the United Kingdom and Empress of India."

After the Viceroy's address was delivered, the whole of the Assembly spontaneously rose up and joined the troops in hearty cheers.

His Highness the Maharaja Sindia spoke to the following effect :—

"Shah-in-Shah Padishah. May God bless you. The princes of India bless you, and pray that your sovereignty and power may remain steadfast for ever."

THE DEWAN-I-KHAS, OR HALL OF AUDIENCE

Her Highness the Begum of Bhopal spoke in a similar sense.

His Excellency Sir Salar Jung rose on behalf of the Nizam and spoke as follows :—

"I am desired by his Highness the Nizam to request your Excellency to convey to her Majesty, on the part of himself and the chiefs of India, the expression of their hearty congratulations upon her assumption of the title of Empress of India, and to assure her that they pray for her long life and for the enduring prosperity of her empire both in India and England."

Their Highnesses the Maharajas of Udaipur and Jaipur rose and said that the united chiefs of Rajputana desired that a telegram might be sent to the Queen offering their dutiful and loyal congratulations to her Majesty on her assumption of the Imperial title.

The Maharaja of Kashmir expressed to the Lieutenant-Governor of the Punjab, who was sitting near him, his great satisfaction at the tenor of the Viceroy's speech, adding that the day would never be forgotten by him, or his children; that it will ever be regarded as an auspicious one; and that the shadow of her Majesty's gracious Empire will be his chief protection.

Several other chiefs endeavoured to speak, but were prevented doing so by the breaking up of the Assemblage.

It is impossible to estimate the whole effect of the Imperial Assemblage. Indeed, the extension of European rule over Asiatic nations is attended with a thousand problems which none can solve. It has been lamented and denounced, but history proves that it is inevitable, and that Asia profits largely by the change. But if the British empire in Asia is a political necessity, there is no reason to make it unpalatable; and no people in the world are so susceptible of sympathy as the natives of India. Roman simplicity may be intelligible to Europeans; it is hateful to Orientals. By yielding something to native ideas, it is possible to elicit corresponding concessions. Such was one result of the Imperial Assemblage. The ruling chiefs and notables at Delhi strove to accommodate themselves to the new era. They were profuse in their professions of gratification at British supremacy; they were lavish in their expressions of good-will towards each other. Hereditary feuds were forgotten; the Imperial Assemblage made them friends. Throughout the days which followed the Proclamation, the air was filled with the salutes which announced their visits to each other. Many gave large sums towards the relief of the famine districts; others initiated badges in their respective territories. All attempted to associate the occasion with some public act, which should perpetuate its memory in the hearts of their people.

W.H. Sleeman

'Thugs and Poisoners'. Rambles and Recollections of an Indian Official.

Westminster, A. Constable and Co., 1893.

CHAPTER XIII

Thugs and Poisoners.

LIEUTENANT BROWN had come on to Damoh chiefly with a view to investigate a case of murder, which had taken place at the village of Sujaina, about ten miles from Damoh, on the road to Hattā.[1] A gang of two hundred Thugs were encamped in the grove at Hindoria in the cold season of 1814, when, early in the morning, seven men well armed with swords and matchlocks passed them, bearing treasure from the bank of Motī Kochia at Jubbulpore to their correspondents at Bānda,[2] to the value of four thousand five hundred rupees.[3] The value of their burthen was immediately perceived by these *keen-eyed sportsmen*, and Kosarī, Drigpāl, and Faringia, three of the leaders, with forty of their fleetest and stoutest followers, were immediately selected for the pursuit. They followed seven miles unperceived; and, coming up with the treasure-bearers in a water-course half a mile from the village of Sujaina, they rushed in upon them and put them all to death with their swords.[4] While they were doing so a tanner from Sujaina

[1] A town on the Allahabad and Sāgar road, 61 miles N.E. of Sāgar. It was the headquarters of the Damoh district from 1818 to 1835.

[2] The chief town of the district of the same name in Bundēlkhand, situated on the Kēn river, 95 miles S.W. from Allahabad.

[3] Worth at that time £450 sterling, or a little more.

[4] An unusual mode of procedure for professed Thugs to adopt, who usually strangle their victims with a cloth. Faringia Brahman was one of the most noted Thug leaders. He is frequently mentioned in the author's *Report on the Depredations committed by the Thug Gangs* (1840), and the story of the Sujaina crime is fully told in the Introduction to that volume. Faringia became a valuable approver.

approached with his buffalo, and to prevent him giving the alarm they put him to death also, and made off with the treasure, leaving the bodies unburied. A heavy shower of rain fell, and none of the village people came to the place till the next morning early; when some females, passing it on their way to Hattā, saw the bodies, and returning to Sujaina, reported the circumstance to their friends. The whole village thereupon flocked to the spot, and the body of the tanner was burned by his relations with the usual ceremonies, while all the rest were left to be eaten by jackals, dogs and vultures, who make short work of such things in India.[1]

[1] Lieutenant Brown was suddenly called back to Jubbulpore, and could not himself go to Sujaina. He sent, however, an intelligent native officer to the place, but no man could be induced to acknowledge that he had ever seen the bodies or heard of the affair, though Faringia pointed out to them exactly where they all lay. They said it must be quite a mistake—that such a thing could not have taken place and they know nothing of it. Lieutenant Brown was aware that all this affected ignorance arose entirely from the dread these people have of being summoned to give evidence to any of our district courts of justice; and wrote to the officer in the civil charge of the district to request that he would assure them that their presence would not be required. Mr. Doolan, the assistant magistrate, happened to be going through Sujaina from Sāgar on deputation at the time; and, sending for all the respectable old men of the place, he requested that they would be under no apprehension, but tell him the real truth, as he would pledge himself that not one of them should ever be summoned to any district court to give evidence. They then took him to the spot and pointed out to him where the bodies had been found, and mentioned that the body of the tanner had been burned by his friends. The banker, whose treasure they had been carrying, had an equal dislike to be summoned to court to give evidence, now that he could no longer hope to recover any portion of his lost money; and it was not till after Lieutenant Brown had given him a similar assurance, that he would consent to have his books examined. The loss of the four thousand five hundred rupees was then found entered, with the names of the men who had been killed at Sujaina in carrying it. These are specimens of some of the minor difficulties we had to contend with in our efforts to put down the most dreadful of all crimes. All the prisoners accused of these murders had just been tried for others, or

We had occasion to examine a very respectable old gentleman at Damoh upon the case, Gobind Dās, a revenue officer under the former government,[1] and now about seventy years of age. He told us that he had no knowledge whatever of the murder of the eight men at Sujaina; but he well remembered another which took place seven years before the time we mentioned at Abhāna, a stage or two back, on the road to Jubbulpore. Seventeen treasure-bearers lodged in the grove near that town on their way from Jubbulpore to Sāgar. At night they were set upon by a large gang of Thugs, and sixteen of them strangled; but the seventeenth laid hold of the noose before it could be brought to bear upon his throat, pulled down the villain who held it, and made his way good to the town. The Rājā, Dharak Singh, went to the spot with all the followers he could collect; but he found there nothing but the sixteen naked bodies lying in the grove, with their eyes apparently starting out of their sockets. The Thugs had all gone off with the treasure and their clothes, and the Rājā searched for them in vain.

A native commissioned officer of a regiment of native infantry one day told me that, while he was on duty over some Thugs at Lucknow, one of them related with great seeming pleasure the following case, which seemed to him one of the most remarkable that he had heard them speak of during the time they were under his charge.

"A stout Mogul[2] officer of noble bearing and singularly handsome countenance, on his way from the Punjab to Oudh, crossed the Ganges at Garhmuktesar Ghāt, near

Lieutenant Brown would not have been able to give the pledge he did. [W. H. S.] Difficulties of the same kind beset the administration of criminal justice in India to this day.

[1] Of the Marāthās. The district was ceded in 1818.

[2] More correctly written Mughal. The term is properly applied to Muhammadans of Turk (Mongol) descent. Such persons commonly affix the title Beg to their names, and often prefix the Persian title Mirzā.

Meerut, to pass through Murādābād and Bareilly.[1] He was mounted on a fine Tūrkī horse, and attended by his "khidmatgār" (butler) and groom. Soon after crossing the river, he fell in with a small party of well-dressed and modest-looking men going the same road. They accosted him in a respectful manner, and attempted to enter into conversation with him. He had heard of Thugs, and told them to be off. They smiled at his idle suspicions, and tried to remove them, but in vain. The Mogul was determined; they saw his nostrils swelling with indignation, took their leave, and followed slowly. The next morning he overtook the same number of men, but of a different appearance, all Musalmāns. They accosted him in the same respectful manner; talked of the danger of the road, and the necessity of their keeping together, and taking advantage of the protection of any mounted gentleman that happened to be going the same way. The Mogul officer said not a word in reply, resolved to have no companions on the road. They persisted—his nostrils began again to swell, and putting his hand to his sword, he bid them all be off, or he would have their heads from their shoulders. He had a bow and quiver full of arrows over his shoulders,[2] a brace of loaded pistols in his waist-belt, and a sword by his side, and was altogether a very formidable-looking cavalier. In the evening another party that lodged in the same "sarāi"[3] became very intimate with the butler and groom. They were going the same road; and, as the Mogul overtook them in the morning,

[1] Meerut, the well-known cantonment, in the district of the same name. The name is written Meeruth by the author, and may be also written Mīrath. Ghāt (ghaut) means a ferry, or crossing-place. Murādābād and Bareilly (Barelī) are in Rohilkhand. The latter has a considerable garrison. Both places are large cities, and the head-quarters of districts.

[2] The bow and quiver are now never seen, except, possibly, in remote parts of Rājputāna.

[3] An inn of the Oriental pattern, often called caravanserai in books of travel.

they made their bows respectfully, and began to enter into conversation with their two friends, the groom and butler, who were coming up behind. The Mogul's nostrils began again to swell, and he bid the strangers be off. The groom and butler interceded, for their master was a grave, sedate man, and they wanted companions. All would not do, and the strangers fell in the rear. The next day, when they had got to the middle of an extensive and uninhabited plain, the Mogul in advance, and his two servants a few hundred yards behind, he came up to a party of six poor Musalmāns, sitting weeping by the side of a dead companion. They were soldiers from Lahore,[1] on their way to Lucknow, worn down by fatigue in their anxiety to see their wives and children once more, after a long and painful service. Their companion, the hope and prop of his family, had sunk under the fatigue, and they had made a grave for him; but they were poor unlettered men, and unable to repeat the funeral service from the holy Korān—would his highness but perform this last office for them, he would, no doubt, find his reward in this world and the next. The Mogul dismounted—the body had been placed in its proper position, with its head towards Mecca. A carpet was spread—the Mogul took off his bow and quiver, then his pistols and sword, and placed them on the ground near the body—called for water, and washed his feet, hands, and face, that he might not pronounce the holy words in an unclean state. He then knelt down and began to repeat the funeral service, in a clear, loud voice. Two of the poor soldiers knelt by him, one on each side in silence. The other four went off a few paces to beg that the butler and groom would not come so near as to interrupt the good Samaritan at his devotions.

All being ready, one of the four, in a low undertone, gave the "jhirnī" (signal),[2] the handkerchiefs were thrown

[1] Then the capital of Ranjīt Singh, the great Sikh chief.

[2] "This is commonly given either by the leader of the gang, or the *belhā*, who has chosen the place for the murder." It was

over their necks, and in a few minutes all three—the Mogul and his servants—were dead, and lying in the grave in the usual manner, the head of one at the feet of the one below him. All the parties they had met on the road belonged to a gang of Jamāldehī Thugs, of the kingdom of Oudh.[1] In despair of being able to win the Mogul's confidence in the usual way, and determined to have the money and jewels, which they knew he carried with him, they had adopted this plan of disarming him; dug the grave by the side of the road, in the open plain, and made a handsome young Musalmān of the party the dead soldier. The Mogul, being a very stout man, died almost without a struggle, as is usually the case with such; and his two servants made no resistance."

People of great sensibility, with hearts overcharged with sorrow, often appear cold and callous to those who seem to them to feel no interest in their afflictions. An instance of this kind I will here mention; it is one of thousands that I have met with in my Indian rambles. It was mentioned to me one day that an old "fakīr,"[2] who lived in a small hut close by a little shrine on the side of the road near the town of Morādābād, had lately lost his son, poisoned by a party of "datūriās," or professional poisoners,[3] that now infest every road throughout India. I sent for him, and requested him to tell me his story, as I might perhaps be able to trace the murderers. He did so,

usually some commonplace order, such as "Bring the tobacco." (*Ramaseeana*, p. 99, etc.)

[1] The Jamāldehī Thugs resided "in Oude and some other parts east of the Ganges. They are considered very clever and expert, and more staunch to their oath of secrecy than most other classes." (*Ibid.* p. 97.)

[2] Fakīr (fakeer), a religious mendicant. The word properly applies to Muhammadans only, but is often laxly used to include Hindoo ascetics.

[3] So called because the poison they use is made of the seeds of the "datūra" plant (*Datura alba*), and other species of the same genus. It is a powerful narcotic.

and a Persian writer took it down while I listened with all the coldness of a magistrate, who wanted merely to learn facts, and have nothing whatever to do with feelings. This is his story literally :—

"I reside in my hut by the side of the road a mile and [a] half from the town, and live upon the bounty of travellers, and the people of the surrounding villages. About six weeks ago, I was sitting by the side of my shrine after saying prayers, with my only son, about ten years of age, when a man came up with his wife, his son, and his daughter, the one a little older, and the other a little younger than my boy. They baked and ate their bread near my shrine, and gave me flour enough to make two cakes. This I prepared and baked. My boy was hungry, and ate one cake and a half. I ate only half a one, for I was not hungry. I had a few days before purchased a new blanket for my boy, and it was hanging in a branch of the tree that shaded the shrine, when these people came. My son and I soon became stupefied. I saw him fall asleep, and I soon followed. I awoke again in the evening, and found myself in a pool of water. I had sense enough to crawl towards my boy. I found him still breathing, and I sat by him with his head in my lap, where he soon died. It was now evening, and I got up, and wandered about all night picking straws—I know not why. I was not yet quite sensible. During the night the wolves ate my poor boy. I heard this from travellers, and went and gathered up his bones and buried them in the shrine. I did not quite recover till the third day, when I found that some washer-women had put me into the pool, and left me there with my head out, in hopes that this would revive me; but they had no hope of my son. I was then taken to the police of the town; but the landholders had begged me to say nothing about the poisoners, lest it might get them and their village community into trouble. The man was tall and fair, and about thirty-five; the woman short, stout, and fair, and about thirty; two of her teeth projected a good deal; the boy's eyelids were much diseased."

All this he told me without the slightest appearance of emotion, for he had not seen any appearance of it in me, or my Persian writer; and a casual European observer would perhaps have exclaimed, "What brutes these natives are! This fellow feels no more for the loss of his only son than he would for that of a goat." But I knew the feeling was there. The Persian writer put up his paper, and closed his inkstand, and the following dialogue, word for word, took place between me and the old man :—

Question.—What made you conceal the real cause of your boy's death, and tell the police that he had been killed, as well as eaten, by wolves?

Answer.—The landholders told me that they could never bring back my boy to life, and the whole village would be worried to death by them if I made any mention of the poison.

Question.—And if they were to be punished for this they would annoy you?

Answer.– Certainly. But I believed they advised me for my own good as well as their own.

Question.—And if they should turn you away from that place, could you not make another?

Answer.—Are not the bones of my poor boy there, and the trees that he and I planted and watched together for ten years?

Question.—Have you no other relations? What became of your boy's mother?

Answer.—She died at that place when my boy was only three months old. I have brought him up myself from that age; he was my only child, and he has been poisoned for the sake of the blanket! (Here the poor old man sobbed as if his heartstrings would break; and I was obliged to make him sit down on the floor while I walked up and down the room.)

Question.—Had you any children before ?

Answer.—Yes, sir, we had several, but they all died before their mother. We had been reduced to beggary by misfortunes, and I had become too weak and ill to work. I buried my poor wife's bones by the side of the road where she died ; raised the little shrine over them, planted the trees, and there have I sat ever since by her side, with our poor boy in my bosom. It is a sad place for wolves, and we used often to hear them howling outside ; but my poor boy was never afraid of them when he knew I was near him. God preserved him to me, till the sight of the new blanket, for I had nothing else in the world, made these people poison us. I bought it for him only a few days before, when the rains were coming on, out of my savings—it was all I had. (The poor old man sobbed again, and sat down while I paced the room, lest I should sob also ; my heart was becoming a little too large for its apartment.) " I will never," continued he, " quit the bones of my wife and child, and the tree that he and I watered for so many years. I have not many years to live ; there I will spend them, whatever the landholders may do—they advised me for my own good, and will never turn me out."

I found all the poor man stated to be true ; the man and his wife had mixed poison with the flour to destroy the poor old man and his son for the sake of the new blanket which they saw hanging in the branch of the tree, and carried away with them. The poison used on such occasions is commonly the datura, and it is sometimes given in the hookah to be smoked, and at others in food. When they require to poison children as well as grown-up people, or women who do not smoke, they mix up the poison in food. The intention is almost always to destroy life, as " dead men tell no tales " ; but the poisoned people sometimes recover, as in the present case, and lead to the detection of the poisoners. The cases in which they recover are, however, rare, and of those who recover few are ever able to trace the poisoners ; and, of those who recover and trace them, very few will ever undertake to prosecute them through the several courts of the magistrate, the sessions, and that of last instance in a distant district, to which the proceedings must be sent for final orders.

The impunity with which this crime is everywhere perpetrated, and its consequent increase in every part of India, are among the greatest evils with which the country is at this time affected. These poisoners are spread all over India, and are as numerous over the Bombay and Madras Presidencies as over that of Bengal. There is no road free from them, and throughout India there must be many hundreds who gain their subsistence by this trade alone. They put on all manner of disguises to suit their purpose; and, as they prey chiefly upon the poorer sort of travellers, they require to destroy the greater number of lives to make up their incomes. A party of two or three poisoners have very often succeeded in destroying another of eight or ten travellers with whom they have journeyed for some days, by pretending to give them a feast on the celebration of the anniversary of some family event. Sometimes an old woman or man will manage the thing alone, by gaining the confidence of travellers, and getting near the cooking-pots while they go aside; or when employed to bring the flour for the meal from the bazaar. The poison is put into the flour or the pot, as opportunity offers.

People of all castes and callings take to this trade, some casually, others for life, and others derive it from their parents or teachers. They assume all manner of disguises to suit their purposes; and the habits of cooking, eating, and sleeping on the side of the road, and smoking with strangers of seemingly the same caste, greatly facilitate their designs upon travellers. The small parties are unconnected with each other, and two parties never unite in the same cruise. The members of one party may be sometimes convicted and punished, but their conviction is accidental, for the system which has enabled us to put down the Thug associations cannot be applied, with any fair prospect of success, to the suppression of these pests to society.[1]

The Thugs went on their adventures in large gangs, and two or more were commonly united in the course of an expedition in the perpetration of many murders. Every man shared in the booty according to the rank he held in the gang, or the part he took in the murders ; and the rank of every man and the part he took generally, or in any particular murder, were generally well known to all. From among these gangs, when arrested, we found the evidence we required for their conviction—or the means of tracing it—among the families and friends of their victims, or with persons to whom the property taken had been disposed of, and in the graves to which the victims had been consigned.

To give an idea of the system by which the government of India has been enabled to effect so great a good for the people as the suppression of these associations, I will suppose that two sporting gentlemen, A at Delhi, and B in Calcutta, had both described the killing of a tiger in an island in the Ganges, near Hardwār,[2] and mentioned the names of the persons engaged with them. Amon the persons thus named were C, who had since returned to America, D, who had retired to New South Wales, E to England, and F to Scotland. There were four other persons named who were still in India, but they are deeply interested in A and B's story not being believed. A says that B got the skin of the tiger, and B states that he gave it to C, who cut out two of the claws. Application is made to C, D, E, and F, and without the possi-

[1] The crime of poisoning travellers is still prevalent, and its detection is still attended by the difficulties described in the text. The poisoning of cattle by arsenic, for the sake of their hides, was very prevalent twenty years ago, especially in the districts near Benares, but is now little heard of. It was checked under the ordinary law by numerous convictions and severe sentences.

[2] In the Sahāranpur district, where the Ganges issues from the hills.

bility of any collusion, or even communication between them, their statements correspond precisely with those of A and B, as to the time, place, circumstances, and persons engaged. Their statements are sworn to before magistrates in presence of witnesses, and duly attested. C states that he got the skin from B, and gave it to the Nawāb of Rāmpur[1] for a hookah carpet, but that he took from the left forefoot two of the claws, and gave them to the minister of the King of Oudh for a charm for his sick child.

The Nawāb of Rāmpur, being applied to, states that he received the skin from C, at the time and place mentioned, and that he still smokes his hookah upon it; and that it had lost the two claws upon the left forefoot. The minister of the King of Oudh states that he received the two claws nicely set in gold; that they had cured his boy, who still wore them round his neck to guard him from the evil eye. The goldsmith states that he set the two claws in gold for C, who paid him handsomely for his work. The peasantry, whose cattle graze on the island, declare that certain gentlemen did kill a tiger there about the time mentioned, and that they saw the body after the skin had been taken off, and the vultures had begun to descend upon it.

To prove that what A and B had stated could not possibly be true, the other party appeal to some of their townsmen, who are said to be well acquainted with their characters. They state that they really know nothing about the matter in dispute; that their friends, who are opposed to A and B, are much liked by their townspeople and neighbours, as they have plenty of money, which they spend freely, but that they are certainly very much addicted to field-sports, and generally absent in pursuit of wild beasts for three or four months every year; but, whether they were or were not present at the killing of the great Garhmuktesar tiger, they could not say.

Most persons would, after examining this evidence, be

[1] A small principality in Rohilkhand, between Murādābād and Bareilly (Barēlī).

tolerably well satisfied that the said tiger had really been killed at the time and place, and by the persons mentioned by A and B; but, to establish the fact judicially, it would be necessary to bring A, B, C, D, E, and F, the Nawāb of Rāmpur, the minister of the King of Oudh, and the goldsmith to the criminal court at Meerut, to be confronted with the person whose interest it was that A and B should not be believed. They would all, perhaps, come to the said court from the different quarters of the world in which they had thought themselves snugly settled; but the thing would annoy them so much, and be so much talked of, that sporting gentlemen, nawābs, ministers, and goldsmiths would in future take good care to have "forgotten" everything connected with the matter in dispute, should another similar reference be made to them, and so A and B would never again have any chance.

Thug approvers, whose evidence we required, were employed in all parts of India, under the officers appointed to put down these associations; and it was difficult to bring all whose evidence was necessary at the trials to the court of the district in which the particular murder was perpetrated. The victims were, for the most part, money-carriers, whose masters and families resided hundreds of miles from the place where they were murdered, or people on their way to their distant homes from foreign service. There was no chance of recovering any of the property taken from the victims, as Thugs were known to spend what they got freely, and never to have money by them; and the friends of the victims, and the bankers whose money they carried, were everywhere found exceedingly averse to take share in the prosecution.

To obviate all these difficulties separate courts were formed, with permission to receive whatever evidence they might think likely to prove valuable, attaching to each portion, whether documentary or oral, whatever weight it might seem to deserve. Such courts were formed at Hyderabad, Mysore, Indore, Lucknow, Gwālior, and were presided over by our highest diplomatic functionaries, in concurrence with the princes at whose courts they were accredited; and who, at Jubbulpore, were under the direction of the representative of the Governor-General of India.[1] By this means we had a most valuable species of unpaid agency; and I believe there is no part of their public life on which these high functionaries look back with more pride than that spent in presiding over such courts, and assisting the supreme government in relieving the people of India from this fearful evil.[2]

[1] The special laws on the subject, namely:—Acts xxx. of 1836; xviii. of 1837; xix. of 1837; xviii. of 1839; xviii. of 1843; xxiv. of 1843; xiv. of 1844; v. of 1847; x. of 1847; iii. of 1848; and xi. of 1848, are printed in p.p. 353-357 of the author's *Report on Budhuk alias Bagree Decoits, etc.* (1849).

[2] I may here mention the names of a few diplomatic officers of distinction who have aided in the good cause. *Of the Civil Service*—Mr. F. C. Smith, Mr. Martin, Mr. George Stockwell, Mr. Charles Fraser, the Hon. Mr. Wellesley, the Hon. Mr. Shore, the Hon. Mr. Cavendish, Mr. George Clerk, Mr. L. Wilkinson, Mr. Bax; *Majors-General*—Cubbon and Fraser; *Colonels*—Low, Stewart, Alves, Spiers, Caulfield, Sutherland, and Wade; Major Wilkinson; and, among the foremost, Major Borthwick and Captain Paton. [W. H. S.]

The author's characteristic modesty has prevented him from dwelling upon his own services, which were greater than those of any other officer. Some idea of them may be gathered from the collection of papers entitled *Ramaseeana*, the contents of which are enumerated in the Bibliographical Note, *ante*. Colonel Meadows Taylor has given a more popular account of the measures taken for the suppression of Thuggee (thagī) in his *Confessions of a Thug*, written in 1837, and published originally in 1839. The Thug organization dated from ancient times, but attracted little notice from the East India Company's government until the author, then Captain Sleeman, submitted his reports on the subject while employed in the Sāgar and Nerbudda Territories, where he had been posted in 1820. He proved that the Thug crimes were committed by a numerous and highly organized fraternity operating in all parts of India. In consequence of these reports, Mr. F. C. Smith, Agent to the Governor-General in the Sāgar and Nerbudda Territories, was invested, in the year 1829, with special powers, and the author, then Major Sleeman, was employed, in addition to his district duties, as Mr. Smith's coadjutor and assistant. In 1835 the author was relieved from district work, and appointed

General Superintendent of the operations for the suppression of the Thug gangs. He went on leave to the hills in 1836, and on resuming duty in February, 1839, was appointed Commissioner for the suppression of Thuggee and Dacoity, which office he continued to hold in addition to his other appointments. Between 1826 and 1835, 1,562 prisoners were tried for the crime of Thuggee, of whom 1,404 were hanged or transported for life. Some individuals are said to have confessed to over 200 murders, and one confesssd to 719. The Thug approvers, whose lives were spared, were detained in a special prison at Jubbulpore, where the remnant of them, with their families, are still kept under *surveillance*. They are employed in a tent and carpet factory, known as the School of Industry, which was founded in 1838 by the author and Captain Charles Brown. If released, they would probably resume their hereditary occupation, which exercised an awful fascination over its votaries. Most of the Thug gangs had been broken up by 1860, but cases of Thuggee have occurred occasionally since that date. A gang of Kahārs (palanquin bearers) committed a series of Thug murders in, I think, 1877, at Etāwa, in the North-Western Provinces. The office of Superintendent of Thuggee and Dacoity is still kept up, but the officer in charge is more concerned with Dacoity (that is to say, organized gang-robbery with violence) in the Native States than with the secret crime of Thuggee. It is never safe to assume in India that any ancient practice has been suppressed, and I have little doubt that, if administrative pressure were relaxed, the old form of Thuggee would again be heard of. The occasional discovery of murdered beggars, who could not have been killed for the sake of their property, leads me to suppose that the Megpunnia variety of Thuggee, that is to say, murder of poor persons in order to kidnap and sell their children, is still sometimes practised.

Among the officers named by the author the best known is Sir Mark Cubbon, who came to India in 1800, and died at Suez in 1861. During the interval he had never quitted India. He ruled over Mysore for nearly thirty years with almost despotic power, and reorganized the administration of that country with conspicuous success. (*Men whom India has Known*, Second Edition, By J. J. Higginbotham, Madras, 1874.)

The Hon. Frederick John Shore, of the Bengal Civil Service, officiated in 1836 as Civil Commissioner and Political Agent of the Sāgar and Nerbudda Territories. In 1837 he pubished his *Notes on Indian Affairs* (London, 2 vols. 8vo), a series of articles dealing in the most outspoken way with the abuses and weaknesses of Anglo-Indian administration at that time.

Mr. F. C. Smith was Agent to the Governor-General at Jubbulpore in 1830 and subsequent years. The author was then immediately subordinate to him. Messrs. Martin and Wellesley were Residents at Holkar's court at Indore. Mr. Stockwell tried some of the Thug prisoners at Cawnpore and Allahabad as Special Commissioner. This duty was in addition to his ordinary duties. Correspondence between him and the author is printed in *Ramaseeana*. Mr. Charles Fraser preceded the author in charge of the Sāgar district, and in January, 1832, resumed charge of the revenue and civil duties of that district, leaving the criminal work to the author. The Hon. Mr. Cavendish was Resident at Sindhia's court at Gwālior ; Mr. George Clerk became Sir George Clerk and Lieutenant-Governor of the North-Western Provinces, and ultimately Governor of Bombay. Mr. Lancelot Wilkinson was Political Agent in Bhopāl, and considered by the author to be "one of the most able and estimable members of the India Civil Service" (*Journey*, ii, 403). Mr. Bax was Resident at Indore; Colonel, afterwards Sir John Low was Resident at Lucknow, and had served at Jubbulpore ; Colonel Stewart and Major-General Fraser were Residents at Hyderabad ; Major (Colonel) Alves was Political Agent in Bhopāl and Agent in Rājputāna ; Colonel Spiers was Agent at Nīmach, and officiated as Agent in Rājputāna ; Colonel Caulfield had been Political Agent at Harautī ; Colonel Sutherland was Resident at Gwālior, and afterwards Agent in Rajputāna. Colonel Wade (Sir C. M. Wade) had been Political Agent at Lūdiāna ; Major Borthwick was employed at Indore ; and Captain Paton was Assistant Resident at Lucknow. (See *Journey through Kingdom of Oudh*, vol. ii, pp. 152-169.)

Besides the officers above named, others are specified in *Ramaseeana* as having done good service.

W.H.R. Rivers

'Introduction'. *The Todas*.

London: Macmillan, 1906.

THE TODAS

CHAPTER I

INTRODUCTION

THE people whose manners and customs I am about to describe live on the undulating plateau of the Nilgiri Hills in Southern India. The hills were visited by a Portuguese missionary in 1602, and have been invaded by Indian tribes on various occasions, but, at the beginning of the last century, the plateau and its inhabitants were absolutely unknown to Europeans. The earliest definite information about the hills at this time is given in a letter from William Keys, an assistant revenue surveyor, written in 1812, but it was not till several years later that further information about the people began to be published.

Of the various tribes inhabiting the hills, the Todas excited the greatest interest, and this interest has continued, partly because the people are so different from any other of the races by which they are surrounded, but still more because both they and their customs are so picturesque and, in many ways, so unique.

A very large literature[1] has accumulated about the Todas and their customs. This literature is so extensive that when I determined to go to the Nilgiri Hills, I was reproached by more than one anthropologist for going to people about whom we already knew so much; and one even said that, so far as his department of knowledge was concerned, he was sure that we had all the information we could expect to get.

[1] The bibliography of this literature is given in Appendix II.

A review of the literature, however, showed me that there were certain subjects about which our information was of the scantiest. This was especially the case in matters connected with the social organisation. Little was known of the system of kinship, and it was not known whether there was any definite system of exogamy. The Todas furnish one of the best existing examples of the custom of polyandry, but scarcely anything was known about the various social regulations which must be associated with such a practice.

I had not worked long among the Todas before I discovered the existence of many customs and ceremonies previously undescribed, and I was able to obtain much more detailed accounts of others which had already been repeatedly recorded. I found that there was so much to be done that I gave up an intention of working with several different tribes, and devoted the whole of my time to the Todas.

This book is not intended to be a complete account of all that is known about the Toda people. Their physical anthropology has been so ably dealt with by Mr. Edgar Thurston that I leave this subject almost untouched, and I omit all but a brief mention of my own psychological observations which I have published in detail elsewhere.[1] The book deals almost exclusively with the religion and sociology of the people. Even here, however, the account will be far from complete. After several months' work among a people about whom "we knew all there was to be known," I came away knowing that there were subjects of which I had barely touched the fringe, and many others on which my information could have been made far more complete with greater opportunity. About certain subjects the Todas are extremely reticent, and my information is in consequence very defective. There are many points on which I know my information to be far from complete, and doubtless there are far more numerous examples of deficiency of which I am not aware.

Some deficiencies of the record are due to certain untoward events which occurred during my visit. After I had been working among the Todas for about four months, various misfortunes befell some of those who had

[1] See *British Journal of Psychology*, 1905, vol. i., p. 321.

been my chief guides to Toda lore. One man who had pointed out to me certain sacred places fell ill and made up his mind that he was going to die. Another man lost his wife a few days after he had shown me the method of performing one of the most sacred of Toda ceremonies. A third man who had revealed to me the details of the ceremonial of the most sacred Toda dairy, suffered the loss of his own village dairy by fire.

The Todas consulted their diviners, who ascribed these events to the anger of the gods because their secrets had been revealed to the stranger. In consequence my sources of information ran dry to a large extent, and the difficulties in the way of the investigation of the more sacred topics were greatly increased. By the time it was settled that I was to blame I was nearly at the end of my visit, but it was in the last two or three weeks that I had hoped to overcome the scruples of the people and to obtain information on many doubtful points about which I had to come away unsatisfied.

One of the subjects on which my material is defective is the folk-lore. I have a number of tales, but they are only a small part of the store of Toda legend. I regret especially the incompleteness of my work in this respect because I believe that the Todas are rapidly forgetting their folk-tales and the legends of their gods, while their ceremonial remains to a large extent intact, and seems likely to continue so for some time.

I was especially struck by this because, in previous anthropological experience in the islands of Torres Straits with Dr. Haddon, we had found the exact opposite to be the case. In these islands, the ceremonial had disappeared, and the only record of it to be obtained was that derived from the memories of the oldest inhabitants. Nevertheless in Torres Straits the store of legend was still ample, and the agreement of the stories obtained from different individuals was so great that it was evident that the people had preserved their folk-lore with fidelity.

The difference between the two communities is easily explained. In Torres Straits missionary influence is strong, and missionary effort is always directed to break down the practices associated with belief. The ceremonial in Torres Straits had been swept away, while the stories of the legendary heroes were almost all that remained to the people of the old life and were in consequence still cherished.

Among the Todas missionary influence, whether of Christian or Hindu, has had little effect, and the ritual of the Todas in some parts of the hills is almost, if not quite, untouched by outside influences.[1] The effect of intercourse with other peoples seems to be showing itself largely in the form of loss of interest in the stories of the past.

One of the most striking aspects of the customs and ceremonies of the Todas is that these have in many cases no exact parallels in other places. Perhaps the most definite result which modern research in anthropology has brought out is the extraordinary similarity of custom throughout the world. Customs apparently identical are found in races so widely separated geographically and so diverse ethnologically that it seems certain the customs must have developed in total independence of one another. There seems to be an identity of idea actuating custom in peoples very different from one another in their surroundings and conditions of life.

The nearest parallels to Toda custom and ceremonial are undoubtedly to be found in the Indian peninsula, but even here, though there is often a general resemblance, this breaks down on going into detail. Even when the resemblance is so close as to suggest a common origin, the differences in detail are often very great.[2]

One clue to this exceptional nature of Toda custom and belief is to be found in the geographical position of the people, which has to a large extent isolated them from the world in general.

The plateau on which they live, broken by numerous hills and valleys, is the top of a scarp formed by the meeting of the Eastern and Western Ghats. Some of the hills project

[1] As we shall see later, this is only true of some parts of the hills and some institutions.

[2] With more exact knowledge of Indian customs and ceremonies which have lingered on side by side with, though often obscured by Brahmanism, it is possible that these differences would be found to be much slighter than the evidence at present available suggests.

more than the rest above the general level of the plateau, which ranges from 6,000 to 7,500 feet above the sea, and the loftiest of these hills reaches the height of 8,760 feet. The plateau is so high that, though it is situated only about eleven degrees from the equator, the thermometer rarely rises above 70° F., and in the nights of the cold season may touch the freezing point.

In every direction the sides of the hills leading up to the plateau are steep and often precipitous. To the south-east, east, and north-east there is a rapid fall of about 5,000 feet to the plains of the Coimbatore district, though to the south this plain only forms a gap about twenty miles in breadth between the Nilgiri and the Anaimalai Hills. On the north-west the slope is more gradual and is broken by the Wainad district about 3,000 feet above the sea. To the north there is a steep fall, but only for about 4,000 feet, to the plateau of Mysore, which is about 3,000 feet above the sea.

The south-western part of the hills is known as the Kundahs and may be regarded as a range separate from the greater part of the plateau, from which it is divided by a wide valley, the Avalanche Valley. From the Kundahs there is an extremely precipitous fall to the Malabar district.

The steep sides leading up to the plateau on which the Todas live are clothed with thick, almost impenetrable jungle, which is extremely malarious, so that a night spent on the way to the summit is very likely to produce fever.

The hills appear to have been for long an object of reverence to Hindus on account of their height and inaccessibility. Dubois states that "as it is very difficult to reach the top of this mountain, a view of the summit alone (and it is visible a long way off) is considered sufficient to remove the burden of sin from the conscience of any person who looks at it."[1]

When the hills were first visited by Europeans, their use as a sanatorium was long delayed owing to the difficulty of making roads, and it was not till after many years that the hills became a regular resort of the European population. We shall see later that the isolation of the Todas has certainly

[1] *Hindu Manners, Customs, and Ceremonies*, part ii., chap. v.

not been complete, and that the hills have been invaded by strangers, especially from the side of the Wainad; but the isolation has probably been considerable, and, for long periods, it may have been complete.

In their isolation from the world in general, however, the Todas have not been alone. Two other tribes, the Kotas and the Badagas, occupy the plateau with them, and the peculiar relations between the three tribes are among the most interesting features of the social life of the Nilgiris. The Todas are a purely pastoral people, limiting their activities almost entirely to the care of their buffaloes and to the complicated ritual which has grown up in association with these animals. The Badagas are chiefly agriculturists; the Kotas are artisans and mechanics; and both supply the Todas with part of their produce. There is here a well-marked instance of division of labour, in which the labour of the Todas is reduced to a minimum. Their privileged position is usually held to be due to the tradition that they are the "lords of the soil," and the produce which the Todas receive from the other tribes is supposed to be of the nature of tribute.

The jungle on the slopes of the hills is inhabited by two wild, dwarfish tribes, the Kurumbas and Irulas, who have a general resemblance to the many other jungle tribes of Southern India. These people are much feared by the tribes of the plateau for their supposed magical powers, but they have little to do with the complex social life of the others.

The district in which the three tribes live is not extensive. The extreme length of the plateau, from east to west, is about forty-two miles, and its average breadth, from north to south, about ten miles, the maximum breadth being fifteen miles in the centre of the district. The total area of the plateau is less than 500 square miles. In this district there live about 800 Todas, 1,200 Kotas, and 34,000 Badagas. In addition, there are now extensive European settlements, the largest of which is Ootacamund, the seat of the Madras Government for six months of the year. The other large European settlements are Coonoor and Kotagiri, while Wellington, near Coonoor, is a military station.

The plateau of the Nilgiris is divided into four districts,

ordinarily known by the names, Todanad, Mekanad, Peranganad, and Kundanad, and these districts are recognised by the Todas. The Todanad is the largest district, and is the part where the majority of the Todas live. Their own name for it is Marsâdr.

The Mekanad is called by the Todas Karâdr, and is now very sparsely inhabited, though there are many old villages in the district.

The Peranganad is the eastern part of the hills, and is called by the Todas Purgòdr, and is the chief seat of a few of their clans.

The fourth district, or Kundanad, is that already mentioned as the Kundahs in the south-west part of the hills. It is the chief seat of one Toda clan, but it also contains villages belonging to others. It is especially visited in the dry season, since its large rainfall often provides ample pasturage when this is burnt up on other parts of the hills. The Toda name of the district is Mêdr.

A few Todas live near Gudalur in the Wainad, some 3,000 feet lower than the main plateau.

METHODS

The description of Toda life to be given in this book is the outcome of an attempt to apply rigorous methods in the investigation of sociology and religion. In the brief time which was at my disposal, it was essential to employ methods of investigation which would enable me to tell with some certainty whether I was obtaining accurate and trustworthy information. Two great sources of error in anthropological investigation are the dependence on the evidence of only a few individuals and the necessity of paying for information.

The first source of error was easily avoided, and I was able to obtain my information from a large body of witnesses, usually independently of one another. As regards the second source, the Todas are inveterate beggars, and are now thoroughly accustomed to receive payment for every service rendered to the European, even of the most trivial kind. Payment for information was inevitable, but I minimised the danger by arranging that every man who came to me for work should receive a definite stipulated sum as a recompense for his time and trouble. I paid, not for the information, but for the trouble taken in giving a day or half a day to my service. As a general rule, anything like payment by results was carefully avoided. The sum paid was for coming to me, and if anyone was reluctant to talk about one subject, we passed on to another. Only at the end of my visit did I depart from this rule on a few occasions, and offered rewards to one or two individuals for certain items of information; but by this time I was in a position to judge the value of the information I received, and I only employed this procedure in cases where I knew the degree of trustworthiness of my informant.

Definite methods for the verification of the evidence obtained were the more necessary in my work among the Todas, in that I was obliged throughout to depend on interpreters. I was, however, very fortunate in my assistants. I first worked with a forest ranger, Albert Urrilla, who knew the Todas very well, though he had no special knowledge of their customs. He translated faithfully, and, owing to his wide knowledge of the hills, he was extremely useful in helping me to become familiar with the names and positions of the many Toda villages. After about six weeks' work, Albert had to return to his forest duties, and, except for a week towards the end of my visit, the interpreter for the rest of my work was P. Samuel, a catechist who had been endeavouring for ten years to convert the Todas to Christianity, under the auspices of the Church of England Zenana Missionary Society. When he began to work with me, Samuel had a very limited acquaintance with Toda ceremonies, but he was very familiar with the general life of the people, and was especially acquainted with the actual working of many of their social customs. Some of the Todas at first objected strongly to his helping me, probably on account of his missionary efforts, but he soon overcame this initial difficulty and gained the general confidence of the people. He was well acquainted with the Toda language, and soon became a very careful inquirer into customs and beliefs; and I owe much to his help. He often obtained independent information about customs, and I was put by him on the track of much that might otherwise have escaped me. I had hoped that he would have continued to make inquiries for me after I had left the hills, and soon after my departure, he forwarded to me a very valuable account of a ceremony which I had not been able to witness and other important material. While with me he had discovered, however, how little progress he had made with the people during his ten years' work among them, and how little he had known of their beliefs, and, soon after my departure, he asked to be given a new sphere of work and was removed to the Wainad, so that I have not had the opportunity for which I hoped, of making further inquiries into the many doubtful points which always arise in working up the notes of anthropological investigation.

One of the chief dangers arising from the use of interpreters is that they will often transmit, not what they are told, but their own versions of what they are told. They interpret the meaning as well as the words of the informants. I think I can be certain that this danger was avoided with both my interpreters, and that they gave me as accurate an account as possible of what the Todas told them. We always used the Toda names for all specific objects, individuals, and places, so that the information transmitted to me by the interpreters was often in such a form that nearly every noun was Toda in a setting of English verbs, adverbs, and pronouns. Thus, referring to one of my notebooks at random, I find the following: "After cleansing the *poh* in this manner, each *palol* puts salt in the *ponmukeri*, and takes it and the *karpun* to the *upunkudi*, taking also five pieces of *tudrpül*, five sprigs of *puthimul*, and a bundle of *taf*." In fact, we habitually used so many Toda words that the Todas sometimes obviously knew the general drift of my questions before they were interpreted to them, and, similarly, I could often understand the general drift of the answer.

The first principle of my investigation was to obtain independent accounts from different people ; I then compared these independent accounts and cross-examined into any discrepancies. The general result of this method was highly satisfactory from the point of view of Toda veracity. The general agreement of the accounts obtained from different individuals was very striking, and, whenever discrepancies occurred, it was nearly always found that they were due either to misunderstanding or to differences in the practices of different sections of the Toda people. These differences are so great that in many cases it made a rigorous application of the method of direct corroboration impossible. There are distinct differences in the ceremonial and social customs of the two chief divisions of the Todas and some differences in the practices of different clans. In the investigation of the dairy ritual, there were found to be great differences in the practices of different dairies, and, for the practice of any one dairy, I had sometimes to be content with the information of one native only; but I did not content myself with such independent accounts till I had satisfied myself of the trustworthiness of the witness, and had learnt enough of the customs in question to be in a position to weigh the evidence. As regards the differences in the customs of different sections of the community, many of my informants were able to describe the practices not only of their own section but also of others.

After a time I managed to put myself on such terms with my chief informants that they were always ready to confess any deficiencies in their knowledge and would refer me to others whose special experience would make them more satisfactory informants. Occasionally, however, they carried this a little too far and pleaded ignorance of a subject when they were really only reluctant to reveal the more esoteric knowledge.

Still more important than this method of direct corroboration of independent accounts is what I may call the method of indirect corroboration. By this I mean the method of obtaining the same information in different ways. Often this indirect corroboration occurred accidentally. The whole of Toda ceremonial and social life forms such an intricate web of closely related practices that I rarely set out to investigate some one aspect of the life of the people without obtaining information bearing on many other wholly different aspects, and the information so gained often afforded valuable corroboration of what I had been told on other occasions and by other individuals. Thus, in obtaining a prayer, various matters would arise which would confirm the accuracy of a legend obtained weeks earlier, or the investigation of a funeral custom would lead to the indirect corroboration of evidence concerning the regulation of marriage.

The most important way in which this method of indirect corroboration may be intentionally applied is by obtaining the same information first in an abstract form and then by means of a number of concrete instances. As an example of what I mean I may cite the method by which I inquired into the laws of inheritance of property. I first obtained an account of what was done in the abstract—of the laws governing the inheritance of houses, the division of the buffaloes and other property among the children, &c. Next I gave a number of hypothetical concrete instances; I took cases of men with so many children and so many buffaloes, and repeating the cases I found that my informant gave answers which were consistent not only with one another but also with the abstract regulations previously given. Finally I took real persons and inquired into what had actually happened when A or B died, and again obtained a body of information consistent in itself and agreeing with that already obtained.

By far my most valuable instrument of inquiry was that provided by the genealogical method.[1] The Todas preserve in their memories the names of all their ancestors and relatives extending back for several generations. In the tables given at the end of this book, I have recorded the pedigrees of seventy-two families, including the whole of the Toda community. Whenever the name of a man was mentioned in connexion with ceremony or social custom, his name was found in the genealogical record and the relation was ascertained in which he stood towards others participating in the ceremony or custom. By this means a concrete element was brought into the work which greatly facilitated inquiry.

[1] See chapter XX and *Journ. Anthrop. Inst.*, 1900, vol. xxx., p. 74.

Customs and rites were investigated by means of concrete examples in which the people taking part were real people to me as well as to my informants. In a later chapter I shall consider more fully the *rôle* of the genealogies in anthropological investigation. I mention them here to give a preliminary indication of the extensive part they played in my investigations. In order to give my readers the opportunity of following my method in some measure for themselves, I have given after the name of any individual mentioned in the book the number of the genealogical table in which his name occurs; thus "Kòdrner (7)" means that Kòdrner is a member of the family of which the pedigree is recorded in Table 7.

I have already referred to the trustworthiness of the evidence given by the Todas. I must now speak of the great differences in this respect shown by different individuals. Some would give full and elaborate accounts of ceremonial which close investigation showed to be, so far as one could tell, thoroughly accurate. Others gave careless and slovenly accounts, full of omissions and inaccuracies of detail, though they rarely said anything which was distinctly untrue.

After some experience had been gained, one day's work was usually sufficient to enable me to make up my mind whether a man was a careful witness, and if he did not seem to be so, he was not again called upon for help. Different men were known to have especial acquaintance with certain branches of knowledge, and I always endeavoured to obtain such people. In the case of the religious ritual, it was not practicable to make use, to any great extent, of men actually holding any of the sacred offices, but I always had recourse to people who had held these offices and were personally familiar with the ceremonial.

Among the many aspects of social life and religion, I soon found that there were some about which there was no reticence, and these could be discussed in public with men, women, or children standing by and perhaps taking part. There were others which were of a more sacred nature, and, if they were approached in public, it was immediately obvious that the people were ill at ease and their answers became hesitating and unsatisfactory. After a short time I adopted the practice of devoting the mornings to my psychological work and to the discussion of affairs of a non-sacred character. In the afternoons I had private interviews with one individual at a time, or occasionally two. If I approached any dangerous topic during the morning, my guide made me a sign and I changed the subject, to return to it at an afternoon sitting.

In the investigation of all the more sacred ceremonies, it was found to be best that the narrator should be alone. He knew that he was telling what should not be told and was embarrassed if any other Todas were there to hear him.

One of the difficulties of anthropological inquiry is that the good and trustworthy narrators are often the most reticent. They are trustworthy because they are honest and pious members of their community, and are therefore naturally reluctant to offend against the sanctity of their religious customs by talking of them to a stranger. Some of my best informants were such men, who were gradually led on to tell me far more than they had ever intended, and then, having told me so much about a given subject, they would sometimes throw reticence to the winds and tell me all. It was very instructive in such a case to start a fresh topic which I knew to be forbidden ground and observe the complete change of attitude. One old man who had entirely lost his scruples in our absorption in the details of dairy ritual absolutely refused to speak a word when I turned to the subject of animal sacrifice, and for this and some other topics I had to be content with less scrupulous but at the same time less trustworthy witnesses.

I only found one Toda who was deliberately untruthful, and yet he was so much less reticent and less scrupulous than others that I often had to have recourse to his services. After I had been able to convict him more than once of having given unsatisfactory evidence, he was more accurate, but I was especially careful to check and obtain independent accounts of everything he told me, and I have only made use of so much of his evidence as I believe to be trustworthy. His knowledge was not deep or accurate, but he often told me enough to enable me to extract the full account from others, who, seeing I knew something, thought they might as well tell me all. On one or two subjects, the whole of my information is derived from this man, but whenever this is the case I mention the fact, so that my readers may know the doubtful nature of the evidence. I only give such information, however, when I believe it to be correct. The informant in question was one of the cleverest of the Todas, and his usual fault was not that he deliberately deceived, but that he supplied the lacunæ in his knowledge by having recourse to his imagination. In the matter of folk-tales, where the difficulties of checking an account are especially great, I was obliged wholly to reject his assistance.

An altogether different type of witness was my constant attendant, Kòdrner. His special business was to bring me people as the subjects for my psychological work and to act as my guide in visiting various parts of the hills. He did not profess to any wide knowledge of custom or ceremonial, and was always diffident about the information he gave; but he was a good observer, and could give an excellent account of any ceremony which he had witnessed or of any procedure in which he had been involved.

Except in a few cases the Todas were quite unable to give any explanations of their customs; the answer to nearly every inquiry being that the custom in question was ordained by the goddess Teikirzi. In the few cases in which an explanation was forthcoming, it seemed to me that it was usually a recent invention. The explanations of customs given in this book are therefore almost invariably those arrived at by myself from the study of the available evidence.

While I was working I had by me the books or papers of Harkness, Marshall, Breeks, and Thurston, the chief previous writers on the Todas, and I inquired into most of the details mentioned by them; but I have not attempted any criticism or comment on the work of others except on special occasions when my own information is lacking or when I am uncertain as to the truth of their statements. Except in those cases in which I definitely refer to the work of others, every statement made in this book is the outcome of my own inquiry or observation. Whenever my account differs from those of others, it may be accepted that I have inquired into the discrepancy and that my account represents the result of a careful investigation.

As some of the accounts of the Todas were written many years ago, there is always the possibility that two dissimilar accounts may both be true and that the differences may represent changes in custom with lapse of time. There is one fact, however, which makes it probable that this explanation of discrepancies is not the true one. The accounts of the Todas which show the closest correspondence with my own are some of the earliest, especially the book of Captain Harkness, published in 1832, and the papers of Bernhard Schmid and C. F. Muzzy, published in 1837 and 1844 respectively. In many cases my work agrees more closely with these than with the accounts of later observers.

This is, perhaps, a suitable place to mention what I believe to be the chief source of error in previous accounts of the Todas. In their extensive intercourse with the Badagas, the Todas use the language of this people, with which they appear to be perfectly familiar. The Toda language is very difficult to understand, and the literature shows that from the first, most of those who have investigated Toda customs have used the Badaga language or Tamil as their means of communication. Every Toda village, every Toda institution or office, and nearly every object used by the Todas has its Badaga name as well as its proper Toda name, and, owing to intercourse through the intermediation of the Badagas, these names have come to be used not only by nearly all who have written on the Todas, but also in official documents connected with the people.

The names by which the Toda villages are known to Europeans are always the Badaga names and not those of the Todas, and similarly with the names of institutions such as clans, dairies, or ceremonies. The practice of giving Badaga names in their intercourse with Europeans has become so engrained that a Toda invariably uses these names when speaking to a European. During the first few weeks of my work, I received exclusively Badaga names, and to the end of my visit, whenever I visited a new district, the Badaga names would crop up till the people found that I wanted Toda and not Badaga. Kiunievan, who was the chief informant of Mr. Breeks in 1872, is still alive, and when I asked him why he gave Mr. Breeks the Badaga names in every case, he answered "He did not seem to want anything else," and this answer seems to me to give the clue to much of the error which has found its way into many of the accounts which have been given of the Todas.

One of the most serious errors which has arisen in this way is one connected with the Toda clans. Every account which has been given of the clan-system of the Todas is that of a system which is current among the Badagas as the Toda system, but has only a limited correspondence with the actual system as it is in use among the Todas themselves. Every Toda, if asked by a European to what clan or division he belongs, will promptly give his division according to the Badaga classification, and this has led to the incorporation of this classification in all the accounts of the Todas which deal with their social organisation.

Some words are necessary about the general plan of the book. I should have preferred to begin with the social organisation, and to approach the religious aspect of the life of the Todas through the ceremonies accompanying the chief incidents of life, including birth, marriage, and death. The ideas borrowed from the ritual of the dairy, however, so pervade the whole of Toda ceremonial, that I have been obliged to consider the ritual of the dairy at an early stage. After a preliminary chapter sketching the general character and life of the people, I have therefore given a full description of the elaborate ceremonial which centres round the dairy; and on this follow the accounts of other ceremonies and sacred institutions and a general discussion of the religion of the people. I then turn to the social aspect of life, and consider kinship, marriage, and the various factors upon which the social organisation depends. Then, after some chapters on diverse topics, I describe the relations of the Todas with the other tribes of the Nilgiris, and in the final chapters discuss certain special problems, including the origin and affinities of the Toda people.

H.H. Risley and E.A. Gait

'Introduction'. *The Census of India,* 1901. Calcutta: Office of Superintendent of Government Printing, 1903.

INTRODUCTION.

IN certain provinces such as Madras and the Punjab the custom of making periodic estimates of the population, founded on more or less accurate data, is of very old standing, but the first systematic attempt to obtain information regarding the population of the whole of India, based on an actual counting of heads, was made between the years 1867 and 1872. But even then, many of the Native States, including Hyderabad, Kashmir, the States of the Central India and Rajputana Agencies and those attached to the Punjab, were left out of the count. This Census, moreover, was non-synchronous; the arrangements were seldom very elaborate, and in some of the more remote tracts it was admittedly carried out in a very rough and imperfect manner. The experience gained, however, was very valuable and it paved the way for the first regular Census on the modern system, which was carried out on the 17th February 1881. On this occasion the operations were extended to all the provinces and states in India, as the term was then understood, except Kashmir and various small remote tracts. The count was a synchronous one, taken in the manner to be presently described, except in certain forest and desert tracts where counting by night was impracticable and the regular procedure was modified to a varying extent; in some places a simplified schedule was employed and the final count was carried out by day, while in others this process was dispensed with altogether and the Census officers recorded the ordinary resident population on the system followed until recently in some European countries. On the 26th February 1891 the second general Census was taken on lines very similar to those of the previous one, but more elaborate arrangements were made to ensure completeness, the non-synchronous area was smaller, and Upper Burma, which had meanwhile been acquired, was included in the operations, as well as the Native States of Kashmir and Sikkim.

Earlier Enumerations.

The third general Census of India, which is dealt with in these volumes, was taken on the night of the 1st March 1901, or ten years and three days after the previous enumeration. This date was chosen partly with reference to the age of the moon, which was at the full on the 5th March, and partly with the object of avoiding, as far as possible, the anniversaries of great religious festivals and fairs and the nights regarded as auspicious for marriage ceremonies or for bathing in the sacred rivers. The operations of this Census embraced for the first time the Baluchistan Agency, the Bhil country in Rajputana, the scattered island settlements of the wild Nicobarese and Andamanese and certain outlying tracts on the confines of Burma, the Punjab and Kashmir; they extended in fact to the whole of the Indian Empire, with the exception of a small disturbed tract in Burma and of a part of Baluchistan where tribal disputes and the possibility of disturbances rendered it inexpedient to attempt an enumeration. The non-synchronous area was again reduced, and even where it was not found practicable to effect a final revision, the enumeration was ordinarily carried out on the standard schedule. The arrangements for the operations were still further elaborated and a "Code of Census Procedure" was drawn up by the Census Commissioner for India, on the basis of which the Census Superintendents of the different provinces and states prepared their local codes with such

The Census of 1901.

modifications in matters of detail as were needed in order to meet local requirements.*

Outline of Procedure.

The general scheme provided for the division of the whole of India into blocks, each of which (except in the non-synchronous tracts where they were larger) contained from 30 to 50 houses and was in charge of an Enumerator. Above the block came the circle, a compact group of from 10 to 15 blocks, or about 500 houses, under a Supervisor, who was responsible for the work of all the Enumerators in his circle. Circles were grouped according to thanas, taluks, or other recognized administrative divisions, into charges under Charge Superintendents, who exercised general supervision over the Census operations and tested a large proportion of the work of their subordinates. Excluding Kashmir and two Districts in the Punjab, for which returns have not been received, the total staff of Census officers employed in the whole Empire included in round numbers 9,800 Charge Superintendents, 122,000 Supervisors, and 1,325,000 Enumerators.

During January and February—the precise period varied according to local conditions—the Enumerator wrote up the Census schedules for all the persons in his block; and this record was checked and corrected by the Supervisors and Superintendents and by officers of the district staff. On the 1st March, between 7 P.M. and midnight, the Enumerator went round his block and brought the entries up to date by striking out the names of people who had died or left the block, and filling up the papers for fresh arrivals and newly-born infants.

On the morning of the 2nd March the Enumerators of the various blocks met the circle Supervisor at a place previously arranged, and prepared the first totals of their blocks so as to show the number of occupied houses, males, females, and total population for each block. The Supervisor combined the block totals into a summary for the circle and sent this on to the Charge Superintendent, who did the same for his charge and reported the result to the District Officer. The charge Summaries were then combined into the district total, which was telegraphed to the Provincial Superintendent and the Census Commissioner for India. Careful arrangements were made for checking the additions at each stage and for preventing the omission of the figures for any block or circle.

The First Totals.

The arrangements for the preparation of these first totals were so complete that the results were received in time to be published by the Government of India on the 15th March, or exactly a fortnight after the date of the Census, and the figure then given (294,266,701) differed by only 94,355 or ·03 per cent. from that subsequently arrived at after detailed compilation. The figures for the Central Provinces were received complete on the 7th March; for the Punjab and United Provinces on the 9th; for Bengal and Madras on the 10th; and for Bombay and Assam on the 12th idem. The nearest approximation to the final results was obtained in Madras, where, in a population e ceeding 38 millions the net difference was only 827.

---

* It may be mentioned as an interesting, though very extreme, instance of the efforts which were made to secure as complete a Census as possible, that in the wild and sparsely inhabited Lushai hills which were incorporated in British territory as recently as 1890, a synchronous Census was taken by the officer in charge, Major J. Shakespear, C.I.E., but in order to do so it was found necessary in about ten circles to begin by teaching the men selected as Enumerators how to read and write.

At previous enumerations, the information contained in the schedules was extracted on "abstraction sheets" (one for each final table), which were divided by rules into spaces corresponding to the headings of the table concerned. A separate sheet was used for each Enumerator's book of schedules, and a tick was made in the appropriate column corresponding to each entry therein. When the whole book had been abstracted the ticks were counted. The figures thus obtained were added up for the thana or other administrative unit (this was called tabulation), and the figures for the latter were compiled into a total for the district. **Preparation of final tables.**

On the present occasion, under Mr. Risley's orders, this method was abandoned in favour of what is known as the slip, or card, system, which was invented by Herr Von Mayr in connection with the Bavarian Census of 1871 and has since been adopted in many European countries. A slip containing all the necessary particulars (in some provinces two slips were used) was prepared for each person enumerated, and these slips were sorted for all the final tables in turn into pigeon holes or other receptacles, *e.g.*, for the religion table there was one pigeon hole for Hindu males, another for Hindu females, another for Muhammadan males, and so on. When the sorting for a table had been completed, the slips in each hole were counted and the result was entered on a form prescribed for the purpose. The figures in these forms were posted in tabulation registers and totals were then struck for the district. This system has many obvious advantages. It is much less complicated than the old method; the work is more easily tested, and by putting together and sorting at one time the slips for a large number of persons the operation previously known as tabulation was almost entirely dispensed with. In order to reduce the labour of filling in the slips various devices were resorted to; slips of different colours were used for the different religions; sex and civil condition were indicated by the shape of, or symbols printed on, the slips, and abbreviations or conventional marks were prescribed for a certain number of the other entries most commonly met with. **The slip system.**

The copying of the slips was taken in hand immediately after the Census and within the next ten weeks the great bulk of the work had been completed over the whole of India. **Progress of the work.**

Sorting followed immediately and was, for the most part, completed by the end of September 1901. As soon as the sorting for a table was over it was compiled for the district and province, and, generally speaking, all but the tedious caste and occupation tables had been finished before the close of the year. The first of the more important provincial reports to be received in print complete was that for the Bombay Presidency, which reached the Census Commissioner's Office on the 3rd June 1902. Then followed Assam and the Central Provinces (in July) and Madras (in August) and then (in the first week of October) Bengal, the United Provinces, the Punjab, and Burma. The only reports which had not by this time come to hand were those for Hyderabad, Mysore, Cochin, and Travancore.

The total actual cost of the operations was R20,65,105, or R21,93,984 if we include charges which were not debited against the Census budget in the public accounts. In 1891 the actual cost was R26,09,587 exclusive of certain tracts which have contributed about a *lakh* and a half towards the total **The cost of the Census.**

outlay on the present occasion. Practically the whole of this great reduction in the expenditure may be attributed to the savings effected in the three larges provinces, Bengal, Madras and the United Provinces, and it is due to a very large extent to the introduction of the slip system. In Bengal (excluding Calcutta) and in the United Provinces the total cost of operations was only R5 per thousand; and in Madras R6·4.

Comparison with the Hollerith machine.

In America and a few other countries the Census results are now tabulated with the aid of the Hollerith machine, a very ingenious contrivance, by means of which the totals for the various tables are obtained mechanically. All possible answers to the questions in the enumeration schedule are printed on cards; one such card is taken for each person, and holes to indicate his age, sex, civil condition, etc., are punched in the appropriate places with the aid of a punching machine; these cards are then passed through the tabulating machine and, an electric current being established through the different holes, the necessary additions are made automatically. The initial cost of these machines, which I believe is about £400, would in any case render it impossible to use them in India, and they could not be employed for the more complicated tables such as caste and language, which involve many more entries than it would be feasible to provide for on the cards and punching machines; but apart from this, in a country where the lower class of clerical labour is as cheap and plentiful as it is here, it is clear that the machine could never compete successfully with hand labour. The tabulation of the results in Cuba with the aid of this machine was done by contract at the rate of 3½ cents per head or about R105 per thousand of the population, which is about fifteen times as great as the rate of expenditure in India on the whole of the Census Operations taken together. In point of speed also the Indian system has the advantage, and in one country where twelve of these machines were employed the tabulation of 24 millions of the people took over two years to complete.

The control of the operations.

Province or State.	Name of Superintendent of Census.
Ajmer-Merwara	Mr. R. C. Bramley.
Andamans	Colonel Sir R. Temple, Bart. C.I.E.
Assam	Mr. B. C. Allen, I.C.S.
Baluchistan	Mr. R. Hughes-Buller, I.C.S.
Bengal	Mr. E. A. Gait, I.C.S.
Berar	Mr. A. D. Chinoy.
Bombay	Mr. R. E. Enthoven, I.C.S.
Bombay City	Mr. S. M. Edwardes, I.C.S.
Burma	Mr. C. C. Lowis, I.C.S.
Calcutta City	Mr. J. R. Blackwood, I.C.S.
Central Provinces	Mr. R. V. Russell, I.C.S.
Madras and Coorg	Mr. W. Francis, I.C.S.
Punjab	Mr. H. A. Rose, I.C.S.
United Provinces	Mr. R. Burn, I.C.S.
Baroda State	Mr. J. A. Dalal.
Central India Agency	Captain C. E. Luard, I.A.
Cochin State	Mr. M. Sankara Menon.
Gwalior State	Mr. J. W. D. Johnstone.
Hyderabad State	Mirza Medhi Khan.
Kashmir State	Khan Bahadur Munshi Ghulam Ahmed Khan.
Mysore State	Mr. T. Ananda Row.
Rajputana Agency	Captain A. D. Bannerman, C.I.E., I.A.
Travancore State	Mr. N. Subramhanya Aiyar.

The Officers in charge of the Census Operations in the different Provinces and States who were immediately responsible for the conduct of the work in their respective charges and who wrote the Provincial Reports on the results were, for the most part, appointed early in April 1900 or about ten months before the date of the census. The intervening period was occupied in making the various arrangements required, such as the partition of the country into blocks, circles and charges, the elaboration of the necessary instructions, the preparation, translation and supply of forms, tours undertaken to supervise the local arrangements and the training of the Census staff, and the elaboration of the procedure for the subsequent stages of the work. The Office of Census Commissioner for India was held by Mr. H. H. Risley, C.I.E., from its creation in October 1899 until September 1902, when, unfortunately for the Census, his services were required for a higher appointment and his immediate connection with the operations came to an end. At that time the reports for a number of Provinces and States still remained to be received, and it had thus been impossible to make much progress with the General Report for the whole of India. Mr. W. S. Meyer, C.I.E., took charge of the office temporarily, in addition to his duties as Editor of the Imperial Gazetteer, and I succeeded him as Census Commissioner on the 23rd January 1903. In spite of the pressure of other work, Mr. Risley has himself completed the Chapter on Caste and the portions of four other Chapters, as noted in the margin, are also from his pen. The Chapter on Language has been contributed by Dr. G. A. Grierson, C.I.E., Ph.D., D. Litt., who is in charge of the Linguistic Survey which is now being conducted under the orders of the Government of India and who, as is well known, possesses very special qualifications for dealing with this subject. For the rest of the Report I am responsible, and also for the tables dealing with Caste and Occupation, and, in part, for the Language table, which was carefully revised in consultation with Dr. Grierson. So far as my share of the Report is concerned, I am painfully conscious of the difficulties under which it has been prepared, owing to the want of time for adequate preparation and to my ignorance of actual local conditions beyond the borders of Bengal and Assam. At the stage when I took up the work, it had become imperative that the Report should be completed without any avoidable delay, and there was no time to travel or to discuss matters locally with the late Provincial Superintendents. I sent them for examination my drafts on the "Movement of Population" in their respective charges and I am indebted to several of them, especially to Mr. Burn, for valuable hints and criticism. In other respects I have had to rely solely on the published reports of the present and previous Censuses and on such publications, official and otherwise, bearing on the subjects dealt with, as I have been able to obtain and peruse in the limited time at my disposal and, although all must regret that Mr. Risley was unable to complete the work which he so ably began, I can only hope that my own disqualifications for the task have not made themselves too apparent and that I have not too often fallen into the error of thinking that the conclusions drawn from personal experience in the Provinces where I have served are necessarily applicable to other parts of India.

Chapter I, paras. 1 to 72.
Chapter II, paras. 93 to 108 and 121 to 129.
Chapter VIII, paras. 614 to 633.
Chapter IX, paras. 692 to 718.

Acknowledgments.

In conclusion I have to express my obligations to Mr. Ross, the Superintendent of Government Printing, for the expedition with which he has carried through the printing of the Report and Tables, to Babu Srinath Chakravarti, my Personal Assistant, who successfully controlled the Calcutta Office for the last few months of the operations, and to Babu Pramatha Nath Sen who was in charge of the compilation of the tables from the very beginning and performed his duties most efficiently.

E. A. GAIT.

I welcome the opportunity afforded me by Mr. Gait's courtesy of adding a few words to his concise and lucid account of the administration of the last Census of India, and of making some of the acknowledgments that are due, for work faithfully done, to my colleagues the Provincial Superintendents, to the district and departmental officers both Civil and Military, and more than all perhaps to the people themselves, to all sorts and conditions of men from one end of the Empire to another, who gave their unpaid services for an object which most of them understood but imperfectly and many must have regarded with positive suspicion. An Indian Census is pre-eminently the work of the people of India. If they held aloof, or even demanded the most trifling remuneration for their trouble the whole undertaking would be financially impracticable. As it is, the greater part of the enumeration is done for nothing by an army of private individuals, numbering on this occasion more than a million and a quarter, who bring to their troublesome task a spirit of pains-taking and occasionally grotesque accuracy which is unequalled anywhere in the world. Mr. Burn, the Superintendent of Census in the United Provinces, tells us how the zeal of one volunteer enumerator impelled him to turn into verse the Census instructions and to suggest that the weaker brethren should be required to learn his production by heart. Other Census officials, with the subtle ingenuity characteristic of the Oriental mind, were insistent in demanding a solution of the problem how the sixteen columns of the schedule were to be filled up for a deaf and dumb lunatic found wandering about by himself on the Census night. With equally Oriental incapacity to appreciate questions of fact, they met the suggestion that the case was an unlikely one with the rejoinder that such unfortunates were extremely numerous. Curiously enough, in the same Province an assemblage of ascetics under vows of silence gave rise to a very similar difficulty, for which special arrangements had to be made. But perhaps the most remarkable instance of voluntary exertion in the public interest occurred in Bombay City where the teaching staff and the senior students of the Elphinstone High School came forward spontaneously and offered to conduct the entire operations of the Census for the quarter in which the school is situated. There was plague in Bombay at the time, the Census enumerators were especially exposed to infection, and several of them fell victims to the disease.

Co-operation of the people.

Extension of operations.

Each successive Census represents an advance on the methods of its predecessor and the Census of 1901 was no exception to this rule. It covered for the first time the whole of the Indian Empire with the exception of the Wa country in Burma and certain tracts in Baluchistan where there was a risk of kindling tribal disputes. The magnitude of the operations may be gathered from the fact that the area dealt with on this occasion extends from the Persian frontier to the confines of China, and from the snow-passes which look down upon Tibet to the tropical forests where Burma touches Siam. Within these wide limits, subject to a few exceptions of minor numerical importance, a uniform schedule of particulars was employed, and a synchronous Census was taken on the night of the 1st March 1901. The exceptions include the greater portion of Baluchistan, the Shan States, the Chin Hills, and other outlying tracts in Burma, the Bhil country of Rajputana, and the scattered villages of the Andamanese and Nicobarese. All of these areas were enumerated for the first time in 1901 and all demanded the application of special methods adapted to the character of the country and the temper of the people. We owe the Census of Baluchistan, with the remarkably interesting results that it has disclosed, to the unrivalled knowledge of the Agency and its races which enabled Sir Hugh Barnes to devise a new and original mode of procedure based upon the organization of the principal tribes and employing the machinery for collecting the grazing tax levied in the pastoral tracts as a means of carrying out and testing the enumeration of the large body of nomadic herdsmen. In Rajputana the Bhils' experience of the liberal help given to them during the famine combined with Captain Bannerman's tact and energy to allay their suspicions, and they were induced to abandon their ancient claims to be exempt from Census and to submit to enumeration by a special system which recognised their prejudice against outsiders entering their villages and required the headmen to muster their people and have them counted at convenient places in the neighbourhood. They were, I believe, duly impressed by the practical argument that for people who were not enumerated there would be no food at the next famine, and there appears to have been no desire on their part to evade the operation. The proceedings in the non-synchronous areas of Burma were of interest by reason of the use made in a portion of them of a system of estimating population by means of typical areas which had been suggested to me by Mr. Scott Keltie's paper on 'The Population of Uncivilized Countries.' In the Andaman and Nicobar islands the admirable arrangements made by the Chief Commissioner, Sir Richard Temple, rendered it possible to effect the first enumeration of the aborigines. The Census was conducted by special parties of the Settlement officials, at some risk to themselves, in a series of tours by steamer and boat in imperfectly charted waters. At Port Campbell they were attacked by the implacably hostile Jarawas of South Andaman and were obliged to fire on their assailants, one Jarawa being killed. The enumeration brought to light a tribe hitherto unknown, the Tābō of North Andaman, concerning whom it is stated, in explanation of their small numbers, that when a contagious disease appeared recently among them they proceeded to kill off all those who were attacked until very few of the tribe were left. Sir Richard Temple's report on the Census contains a mass of interesting information regarding the history and ethnography of the islands.

The attempt to accelerate the publication of the first totals of the census and to bring these figures into closer relation with the final statistics imposed upon the Provincial Superintendents and upon all ranks of district and census officials an amount of labour that can be realised only by those who are familiar with the administrative machinery employed and have seen portions of the voluminous correspondence involved. In order to secure the concerted action which resulted in the publication, within a fortnight from the census, of provincial and district totals for nearly three hundred millions of people differing by only ·03 per cent. from the final figures, the most careful and minute instructions had to be issued to 9,872 Charge Superintendents, 122,053 Supervisors, and 1,325,478 Enumerators. For every one of these persons special meeting places had to be arranged for working out the totals, first of the Enumerators' blocks, then of the Supervisors' circles, and finally of the Superintendents' charges. This last set of figures had in their turn to be conveyed to the head-quarters of the district and combined into the district total which was telegraphed to the Provincial Superintendent and to the Census Commissioner for India. On paper it all looks simple enough, but in practice the execution of the scheme involved a series of problems in transport and the mobilization of an army of volunteers, most of whom had been recruited some six weeks

The first totals.

before, while none had been exercised in this particular evolution. The idea of breaking the record (already held by India) for rapid publication was taken up with much enthusiasm, especially in the Native States, and the distinction of being first in the field belongs to Sheikh Abdul Ghafur, Minister of the small State of Rampur in the United Provinces, who despatched his totals to me at 9-20 on the morning of the 2nd March. The Rampur Census staff worked all night while the Imperial Service Cavalry rode round and collected the summaries. In British territory Mr. R. V. Russell, Superintendent of the Central Provinces, where communications are difficult and the area of jungle is large, was the first to send in his totals on the 7th March. The labour of compilation in the Census Commissioner's Office was considerable and involved the calculation against time of a large number of percentages of variation. For the benefit of statisticians who may have to do the same sort of thing in a hurry, I may mention that every percentage was first worked with a Thomas arithmometer and then checked by Crelle's *Rechen-Tafeln*. If the results differed the operation was repeated. On this system the machine and the tables exercise a reciprocal control which effectually guards against the liability to set up wrong figures on the one and to read the wrong line in the other. The combination of the two is practically infallible.

Tabulation of statistics. But the most distinctive feature of Census administration in 1901 was the introduction of the 'slip system' of compilation briefly described above. This process has never been applied on so large a scale before, and it resulted in a reduction of cost which Mr. Gait elsewhere estimates at over £45,000. As the special literature of the subject is mostly in French or German, and is not readily accessible, it seems worth while to give a somewhat fuller account of it here.

The books of schedules containing the various particulars recorded by the enumerators for each individual may be described as the raw material of the Census, and the final tables as the manufactured product. The transformation of the one into the other involves three processes,—abstraction, tabulation, and compilation,—of which the first is by far the most difficult and complicated. Abstraction is the process which groups individual entries by classes, such as sex, religion, occupation and the like, and gives totals of these classes for small territorial units, such as blocks or villages. Tabulation brings together the abstraction-totals by larger units, such as towns, thanas or tahsils. Compilation arranges the tabulation-totals by districts or provinces.

The old 'tick' system. Abstraction had hitherto been conducted in India by means of abstraction-sheets, which practically reproduced the final tables on a greatly enlarged scale. If, for example, one of the final tables was to show the population grouped according to sex, age, religion, and civil condition, the abstraction-sheet, in which the requisite data were entered, would contain, assuming three religions to be dealt with, 836 distinct compartments, each representing a separate combination of the factors exhibited in the table, or a total relating to such combination. The entries in the sheet consisted of strokes or 'ticks,' each representing an individual. Thus, if a male Hindu, who was married and was 35 years old, had to be recorded, the abstractor looked first to the general heading "Males," and under that to the division "Hindus," which was sub-divided into "Married, Single and Widowed." He then ran his eye down the side-column till he found the age-period 35—39. In the compartment thus marked off he made a tick.

Further ticks were added for other persons falling into the same category, every fifth tick being made diagonally through the four preceding it, so as to enable the ticks to be totalled by fives. The unit of abstraction was the block, and for each block there were as many abstraction-sheets as there were final tables. The totals and cross-totals of the ticks on the abstraction-sheet gave the block-totals for religion, sex, civil condition, and age-periods. These, after undergoing certain tests, and in a certain proportion of cases being re-abstracted *ab initio*, were entered in the tabulation registers, where the block-totals were combined into village-totals, and the village-totals into totals for towns, taluks, thanas or tahsils—whichever was adopted as the unit of tabulation in any particular case.

This method of abstraction is open to the following objections :—

(1) However careful the abstractor may be, the difficulty of picking out the right compartment in a large sheet is very great, and even with expert abstractors, such as are employed on this work in Europe, mistakes are frequent. For some tables the sheets were enormous and one used in 1891 in the United Provinces is reported to have been thirteen feet long.

(2) With the class of abstractors available in India, carelessness and wilful fudging have also to be reckoned with, especially when the abstractor is paid by the month and has to do a certain task in order to earn his pay.

(3) No test of the correctness of any sheet can be applied while abstraction is proceeding; even when a sheet has been totalled, the accuracy of its totals can only be gauged by comparison with the corresponding totals as worked out on other sheets; and, when these totals do not correspond, as is usually the case, the only method of determining which of the discrepant totals is correct is re-abstraction; in other words, doing the work again from the beginning. In Bengal, in 1891, the cost of abstraction alone, apart from supervision and checking, was estimated at ₨3,200 per million, of which ₨800 was for re-abstraction; and the Superintendent, after remarking that the test slip prescribed for the purpose of comparing the different abstraction-sheets "became the cause of much fudging," went on to say that in practice "re-abstraction was permitted free of fines on the abstractors up to a sum equal to 33 per cent. of original abstraction." Mr. Stuart, in Madras, gave 33·04 as the percentage of re-abstraction, and observed that only 14·32 per cent. of the books were correctly abstracted at the first working.

(4) As it is usually impossible to abstract on a single working sheet more than one book of schedules, and there may be several books for a single block, the number of small totals to be entered in the tabulation registers is unduly multiplied, and the possibility of error very greatly increased.

In the Census of 1901, therefore, I substituted for the system of abstraction by strokes or ticks the method of abstraction by slips which had been successfully The Bavarian 'slip' system.

used by Dr. Georg von Mayr, now Professor of Statistics at the University of Munich, in the Bavarian Census of 1871, and which appeared to be admirably adapted for use in India. The Professor was good enough to send me a copy of his report, which gave a brief account of the working of his system.

For every person enumerated in Bavaria all the particulars recorded in the schedule were extracted on a separate slip. The slips were of eight different colours indicating sex and civil condition—as single, married, widowed, or divorced, and were filled up in the following manner :—

Specimen slip.	*Explanation of entries.*
6. I. 1	Serial number of village, block, and schedule.
V	Symbol for head of family.
✓	Symbol for born in the place where enumerated.
29	Age.
K	Roman Catholic.
Badereibesitzer. S.	Proprietor of bathing establishment: independent.
B	Bavarian subject.
M {2, 4} — 6	Symbol denoting that the person enumerated is the head of a household of 6 persons—2 males and 4 females.

The slips were arranged in the order of the schedules and tied into bundles by villages. They were then sorted (also by villages) into heaps corresponding to the columns of the final tables which were to be filled up.

The Indian 'slip' system.

The Bavarian system, while employing colour to denote sex combined with civil condition, did not vary the shape of the slip so as to express any other general attribute, such as religion, literacy, or illiteracy. In India the system was modified in three particulars—

(1) by using colour to indicate religion ;

(2) by varying the shape or size of the slip or by printing on it special symbols, to express sex and civil condition ;

(3) by filling up for each individual two slips instead of one, so as to expedite the completion of the heavier tables.

The selection of colour was of course determined by the price of the paper ; the cheapest paper of a suitable kind being used for Hindus, as the most numerous religion ; the next cheapest for Muhammadans ; and so on. The number of colours that could be employed depended on the number that the average abstractor could be got to manipulate with accuracy. In Mysore the artistic instincts of the Superintendent, Mr. T. Ananda Row, led him to print on the slips pictorial busts indicating for each sex the states of celibacy, marriage, and widowhood. I quote his own description of this quaint device :—"The busts represent male faces and emale faces, and are designed to picture their respective civil conditions. They are self-explanatory to persons familiar with South Indian life. To others the following notes may be interesting :—

Male, Bachelor is represented by the face of a male youth with a caste "*Bottu*" (dot) on his forehead, and a cap and a buttoned jacket indicative of student life.

Male, Married is represented by an elderly face with moustaches, caste dot on the forehead, turban on the head, a coat and upper cloth in Indian style—all characteristic of what is known by the term "*Grihasthāsrama.*"

Male, Widower is represented by an elderly face with moustaches, head bare indicating grief or mourning, and body also bare but for its being partially covered with a loose upper garment commonly called "*Angavasthra.*" The absence of any caste mark on the forehead is an additional sign of grief or mourning.

Female, Unmarried.—A young face with combed hair on the head and "*Bottu*" (caste mark) on the forehead, a simple close fitting necklet and earring.

NOTE.—The "*Bottu*" is a small circular mark placed in the centre of the forehead by most Indian females. It is practically an ornamental non-sectarian mark.

Female, Married.—A face of mature age with caste mark on the forehead and ornaments on the ears, nose and neck, such as are given at wedding to a bride by the bridegroom, and particularly a gold band (called "*Bandi*") sitting loose and low round the neck with a medallion (called "*Tāli*") indicative of married life with husband living.

Female, Widow.—Face indicating advanced age, no caste mark on the forehead, no ornaments, head periodically shaved and therefore with short or no hair, and covered by one end of the cloth worn round the person—all illustrating widowhood as it is manifested mostly among Brahmans."

It will be seen that each slip denoted religion by its colour, and sex and civil condition by its shape, size, symbol, or picture. These data, therefore, had not to be written down. In copying the remaining particulars certain standard abbreviations were made use of in order to economise time. When the slips had been written up for the unit-area—village, police-station or *tahsil*—of a given table, they were sorted according to the headings of the table, counted, and the results entered in the prescribed form. The system is in fact an adaptation to Census purposes of the familiar 'card catalogue,' and its principle is so simple that there is really nothing to describe. When applied to the production of statistics relating to 294 millions of people in the form of eighteen major and several minor tables the mere bulk of the operation demands considerable organization. As the system was a new one and the procedure for sorting the slips admitted of indefinite variation, I contented myself with suggesting two alternative methods by which this might be done, and left it to Superintendents to adopt one or other of my schemes, or to devise improvements of their own, as they thought fit. Into these details it is the less necessary for me to enter as the subject has recently been examined by Professor Von Mayr* himself with Teutonic industry and parental interest in the application of his own methods to the largest Census in the world. The results attained speak for themselves in the large saving effected and in the reduction of the time spent on compilation of the statistics. In Madras, for example, Mr. Francis completed in 7 months tables, which on the system in force in 1891 had taken 21 months

* Die Verwendung des Zählblättchens bei der Volkszählung in Britisch-Indien vom 1 März 1901. *Allgemeines Statistiches Archiv.*

to compile, and a similar acceleration of processes took place in almost every Province of India.

Among the Provincial Superintendents Mr. Gait stands in a class by himself. His charge was the largest and the most populous and embraced the most varied physical conditions and the most heterogeneous races. To carry out successfully the census of more than seventy-eight millions of people comprising the quick-witted and adaptive Bengali of the deltaic rice swamps, the sluggish and depressed peasantry of Bihar, the conservative priest-ridden Oriya, and the primitive but excitable tribes of the Chota Nagpur plateau and the Orissa hills, is a task demanding in itself no mean administrative capacity. To describe effectively the results of the operations requires a grasp of statistics, philology, history, and ethnography which few officials possess. Mr. Gait's report is of permanent value for the light which it throws on these subjects and for the comprehensive account which it gives not only of the Bengal of to-day but of the changes which have passed over the Province since the first Census of 1872. It forms a worthy companion to Mr. Beverley's well-known report of thirty years ago.

The United Provinces of Agra and Oudh present fewer difficulties than Bengal. Their population, though large, is fairly homogeneous, and the Superintendent has at his disposal the invaluable village agency which the Permanent Settlement has denied to Bengal. Mr. Burn has done ample justice to his charge and his report is of special interest for its account of linguistic developments in the Province and its study of the working religion of the ordinary Hindu and of the curious quasi-Vedic revival known as the Ārya Samāj.

Census work in Bombay was greatly impeded by administrative difficulties connected with famine and plague. The effects of these calamities on the population are vividly depicted in Mr. Enthoven's report which has the further merit of being eminently readable and of bringing out both the pathetic and the humorous aspects of an Indian Census.

In the Central Provinces the succession of bad seasons which preceded the two great famines and the successful efforts made by the administration to combat the second and more widespread calamity have been carefully recorded by Mr. Russell, who himself took part in the famine campaign.

For Madras Mr. Francis has produced a concise and business-like report, illustrated by admirable maps and diagrams, and containing an instructive notice of the causes which have promoted the spread of Christianity in the South of India, and a useful glossary of the obscure and intricate caste system which has developed there.

The Burma report treats of a fascinating people concerning whom much has been written. Mr. Lowis has given us an interesting sketch of the animism, thinly veneered with Buddhism, that makes up the religion of the Burman, and has entered upon a lucid exposition of the obscure question of tonic languages.

In the Assam Report Mr. Allen has made a careful study of an obscure subject—the decline of the indigenous population of the Brahmaputra valley.

He shows by means of certain caste statistics that the decrease among the Assamese coincides with the prevalence of the severe form of malaria known as ***Kālā āzār*** or the black sickness, and is not due to any lack of vitality on the part of the people themselves.

The first Census of Baluchistan offered Mr. Hughes-Buller an opportunity of which he has made admirable use. His report discloses remarkable insight into the origin and mutual relations of the characteristic races of the Agency; it is full of local colour and it gives a vivid picture of a strange un-Indian country, of parts of which a native proverb says "Oh, God! when thou hadst created Sibi and Dādhar, what object was there in conceiving hell?" Central India and Rajputana were also completely enumerated for the first time. Both Agencies present exceptional difficulties and my thanks are due to Captain Luard and Captain Bannerman for the excellent results attained.

In all Provinces much attention was paid to religion and ethnography, and the reports contain a considerable amount of material which has not been published before. Mr. Gait's treatment of these subjects is perhaps the most complete and systematic, but Mr. Russell has dealt very fully with the interesting tribes and castes of the Central Provinces; Mr. Enthoven has done much to elucidate the complicated structure of native society in Bombay; Mr. Rose gave much attention to religious development in the Punjab and to the multifarious considerations which affect intermarriage between different groups within the same caste or tribe; and the Superintendents of Census in the Native States have brought out a variety of details which add substantially to our knowledge. I may mention in particular Mr. M. Sankara Menon's careful account of the rise and spread of Christianity in Cochin; Mr. Dalal's analysis of the caste system in Baroda; Mr. Ananda Row's examination of the marriage systems of Mysore; and Mr. Subrahmania Aiyar's chapter on religion and description of the castes of Travancore. Students who wander in the by-paths of ethnography will find much curious information in the notes on tattooing and diagrams of standard designs which are given in the Baroda and Mysore reports. Finally, I commend to all who are interested in the rise and growth of our Empire in the East Mr. Edwardes' picturesque sketch of the various stages of development by which an obscure fishing village has been transformed into the stately City of Bombay.

H. H. RISLEY.

Herbert Risley

'Social Types'. *The People of India*. Calcutta: Thacker, Spink & Co.,1908.

CHAPTER II.

SOCIAL TYPES.

κρῖν' ἄνδρας κατὰ φῦλα, κατὰ φρήτρας, Ἀγάμεμνον,
ὡς φρήτρη φρήτρηφιν ἀρήγῃ, φῦλα δὲ φύλοις.

Il. II. 362.

Social divisions: the tribe.

Up to this point I have been dealing with the racial divisions of the people of India, with ethnology properly so called. I now turn to their social divisions, to the ethnographic data as distinguished from the ethnological. These divisions are either tribes or castes, which in their turn are further subdivided with reference usually to matrimonial considerations. A tribe as we find it in India is a collection of families or groups of families bearing a common name which as a rule does not denote any specific occupation; generally claiming common descent from a mythical or historical ancestor, and occasionally from an animal, but in some parts of the country held together rather by the obligations of blood feud than by the tradition of kinship; usually speaking the same language and occupying, professing, or claiming to occupy a definite tract of country. A tribe is not necessarily endogamous; that is to say, it is not an invariable rule that a man of a particular tribe must marry a woman of that tribe and cannot marry a woman of a different tribe.

Types of tribes.

We may distinguish several kinds of tribes in various parts of India, and although it cannot be said that each of the seven racial types has its own distinctive form of tribe, nevertheless the correspondence between the two sets of groupings is sufficiently close to warrant the conjecture, that each type was originally organized on a characteristic tribal basis and that, where tribes have disappeared, their disappearance has been effected by caste insensibly absorbing and transforming the tribal divisions which it found in possession of particular localities. In describing the varieties of tribes I shall therefore follow the ethnic types already determined by physical characters.

The Dravidian tribe.

The *Dravidian* tribe exists in its most compact and vigorous form among the people of Chutia Nāgpur. Descriptions of two typical instances are given in the appendix under the heads of Munda and Santāl. Such a tribe is generally divided into a number of exogamous groups, each of which bears the name of an animal or plant common in the locality. Usually also there is a distinct village organization comprising in its most developed forms a headman with his assistant and a priest with various acolytes whose business it is to propitiate the various undefined powers from whom physical ills are to be apprehended. Another remarkable instance of the tribal organization of the Dravidians is to be found among the Kandhs or Kondhs of the Orissa Kandh Māls, once infamous for the human sacrifices which they offered to the earth goddess with the object of ensuring good crops and immunity from disease and accidents. A grim memorial of these forgotten horrors is to be seen in the Madras Museum in the form of a rude representation in wood of the head and trunk of an elephant pivoted on a stout post. To this the victim was bound head downwards and the machine was slowly turned round in the centre of a crowd of worshippers who hacked and tore away scraps of flesh to bury in their fields, chanting the while a ghastly hymn an extract from which illustrates very clearly the theory of sympathetic magic underlying the ritual—

> As the tears stream from thine eyes,
> So may the rain pour down in August ;
> As the mucus trickles from thy nostrils,
> So may it drizzle at intervals ;
> As thy blood gushes forth,
> So may the vegetation sprout :
> As thy gore falls in drops,
> So may the grains of rice form.

A number of these wooden elephants, which had been used at sacrifices, were found and burnt by the British officers who put down human sacrifice in the Kandh country. The worm-eaten specimen at Madras is probably unique. The Kandhs are divided into 50 *gochis* or exogamous sects, each of which bears the name of a *muta* or village, believes all its members to be descended from a common ancestor, and as a rule dwells as a body of blood-relations in the commune or group of villages after which it is called. The Kandh *gochi* appears, therefore, to represent the nearest approach that has yet been discovered to the local exogamous tribe believed by Mr. McLennan to be the primitive unit of human society.

The Mongoloid tribe.

The *Mongoloid* type of tribe as found in the Naga Hills is divided somewhat on the same pattern as the Kandhs into a number of *khels*, each of which is in theory an exogamous group of blood relations dwelling apart in its own territory and more or less at war with the rest of the world. Each *khel* fortifies the locality which it inhabits with a stockade, a deep ditch full of bamboo caltrops, and a craftily devised ladder, and raids are constantly made by one upon the other for the purpose of capturing wives. So far as our present researches have gone no very clear traces have been found of totemism among the Mongoloid races of India, but the Mongoloid people of the Eastern Himalayas and the Chittagong Hills have a singular system of exogamous groups based upon their real or mythical ancestors. Instances of this grotesque variant of eponymy are the Chakma clans *Ichāpochā*, 'the man who ate rotten shrimps,' *Pirā bhāngā* 'the fat man who broke the stool,' *Aruya*, 'the skeleton,' and so forth.

The Turko-Iranian tribes: the Afghan type.

Among the *Turko-Iranians* there seem to be two distinct types of tribe :—

The Baloch and Brahui type.

(*a*) Tribes based upon kinship like the Afghan group of tribes, otherwise known as Pathāns or speakers of the Pashtu language, who trace their lineage to one Qais Abdul Rashid who lived in the country immediately to the west of the Takht-i-Suliman and was thirty-seventh in descent from Malik Talut (King Saul). In theory, says Mr. Hughes-Buller in his admirable account of the tribal systems of Baluchistan, "an Afghan tribe is constituted from a number of kindred groups of agnates; that is to say, descent is through the father, and the son inherits the blood of his father. Affiliated with a good many tribes, however, are to be found a certain number of alien groups known as *Mindun* or *Hamsayah*. The latter term means 'living in the same shade.' These groups are admittedly not united to the tribe by kinship." They do not, indeed, even claim descent from the common ancestor, and the nature of the tie that binds them to the tribe is best expressed in the picturesque phrase which describes them as *Neki aur badimen sharik*, 'partners for better or worse'; in other words, active participators in any blood-feud that the tribe may have on their hands. Yet such is the influence of the idea of kinship upon which the tribe is based that the alien origin of the *Hamsayah* is admitted with reluctance, and although for matrimonial purposes they are looked upon as inferior, the tendency is continually to merge the fact of common vendetta in the fiction of common blood. These are the two leading principles which go to the making of an Afghan tribe. There are also—Mr. Hughes-Buller explains—"two other ties which unite the smaller groups: common pasture, or, more important still, common land and water, and common inheritance. The area occupied by each section can be pretty easily localised, and a group which separates itself permanently from the parent stock and makes its way to a remote locality, where it either sets up for itself or joins some other tribe, ceases to have any part or portion with the parent stock. Here the test question is: 'Has the individual or group on separating from the parent stock, departed only temporarily or permanently?' For, among a population largely composed of graziers, there must be constant fission, groups leaving the locality of the majority for other places as pasture or water are required for the flocks. Where the change is only temporary, groups retain as a matter of course their union with the group to which they belong. There are others, however, who wish to sever their connection with the parent group permanently, and, once this has been done, the idea of participation in the common good and ill of the parent stock disappears. Common inheritance can, in the nature of things, only be shared by the more minute groups, and this, in the absence of blood-feud, is the bond of unity in the family or *Kahol*. And this leads me to explain that all the four principles which I have mentioned do not affect every group equally. Thus, the smaller groups or *Kahols*, which in most cases correspond with the family, are united by kinship and common inheritance, but within the family group there can be no blood-feud. For blood-feud can only be carried on when help is given from outside, and no one will help the murderer within the family. Leaving the lowest group, we find that common good and ill, merging in the fiction of kinship, is the influence affecting all the groups, even the largest unit, of the tribe. Common land and water are only shared by comparatively minute groups, *i.e.*, by the *Khel* or *Zai*, but the groups united by common locality, and possibly by common grazing, are both numerous and large."

(*b*) The second type of Turko-Iranian tribe is based, primarily, not upon agnatic kinship, but upon common good and ill; in other words, it is cemented together by the obligations arising from the blood-feud. There is no eponymous ancestor, and the tribe itself does not profess to be composed of homogeneous elements. In the case of the Marri tribe of Baloch Mr. Hughes-Buller has shown that 'Brāhuis. Baloch from the Punjab, Baloch from other parts of Afghanistan, Khetrans, Afghans, Jāts, all gained easy admission to the tribe. As soon as a man joined the tribe permanently he became a participator in good and ill. Then, having shown his worth, he was given a vested interest in the tribal welfare by acquiring a portion of the tribal lands at the decennial division, and his admission was sealed with blood by women from the tribe being given to him or his sons in marriage. Starting, therefore, with the principle of participation in common good and common ill, participation in the tribal land came to be the essence of tribesmanship among the Marris. The process is easy to follow: Admission to participation in common blood-feud; then admission to participation in tribal land; and lastly admission to kinship with the tribe. It was not until after a man or group had been given a share of tribal land at the decennial distribution that women were given to him or them in marriage.' The same principles hold good in the case of the Brāhui, who like the Baloch, appear both by their history and by their physique to be of Central Asian or Scythian origin, though their numbers have been recruited from among Afghans, Kurds, Jāgdals, Baloch, and other elements, all probably belonging to the same ethnic stock.

Both Baloch and Brāhui possess an elaborate organization for offensive and defensive purposes, based in each case on the principle that the clan or section must provide for the service of the tribe a number of armed men proportioned to the share of the tribal land which it holds. The Brāhui system, introduced by Nasir Khān about the end of the seventeenth century, is somewhat the more complete of the two, and binds together all the Brāhui tribes in a regular confederacy which is now, according to Mr. Hughes-Buller, beginning to regard the British Government as its effective suzerain. A full account of the Brāhui taken from Mr. Hughes-Buller's report on the first census of Baluchistan will be found in the ethnographic volume of the Imperial Census Report.

Marriage in Baluchistan.

None of the numerous tribes comprised in the names Afghan, Brāhui, Baloch are strictly endogamous, and stalwart aliens, whose services are considered worth having, are admitted into the tribe by the gift of a wife, or perhaps one should rather say the loan, for, in the absence of stipulations to the contrary, a woman so given goes back to her own family on the death of her husband. Among the Baloch and Brāhui however, a distinct tendency towards endogamy results from the practice of marrying a woman of the same group, a near kinswoman, or, if possible, a first cousin. This seems to be due partly to the feeling that a woman's marriage to an outsider deprives the tribe of the accession of strength that may accrue to it from her offspring; and partly also to the belief that "while among animals heredity follows the father, among human beings it follows the mother. It is argued, therefore, that there is more hope of the stock remaining pure if a man marries a woman who is nearly related to him." In marked contrast to the Baloch and Brāhui, the business instincts of the Afghan lead him to regard women as a marketable commodity, and under the system of *walwar* or payment for wives "girls are sold to the highest bidder, no matter what his social status." It is possible, however, that in a tribe of comparatively homogeneous descent the sentiment in favour of purity of blood may operate less strongly than in a tribe of admittedly composite structure.

The word 'caste.'

We shall see in a later chapter how the word *fetish*, which has had a great vogue in the history of religion, owes its origin to the Portuguese navigators who were brought into contact with the strange religious observances of the natives of west Africa. In the same way *caste*, which has obtained an equally wide currency in the literature of sociology, comes from the Portuguese adventurers who followed Vasco de Gama to the west coast of India. The word itself is derived from the Latin *castus* and implies purity of breed. In his article on caste in Hobson-Jobson, Sir Henry Yule quotes a decree of the sacred council of Goa dated 1567, which recites how in some parts of that province "the Gentoos divide themselves into distinct races or castes (*castas*) of greater or less dignity, holding the Christians as of lower degree, and keep these so superstitiously that no one of a higher caste can eat or drink with those of a lower." From that time to this it has been assumed without much critical examination that the essential principle of caste is mainly concerned with matters of eating and drinking. It need not surprise us to find foreign observers laying stress upon the superficial aspects of a social system which they understood but imperfectly, and overlooking the material fact that the regulations affecting food and drink are comparatively fluid and transitory, while those relating to marriage are remarkably stable and absolute.

Definition of caste.

A caste may be defined as a collection of families or groups of families bearing a common name; claiming common descent from a mythical ancestor, human or divine; professing to follow the same hereditary calling; and regarded by those who are competent to give an opinion as forming a single homogeneous community. The name generally denotes or is associated with a specific occupation. A caste is almost invariably endogamous in the sense that a member of the large circle denoted by the common name may not marry outside that circle, but within the circle there are usually a number of smaller circles each of which is also endogamous. Thus it is not enough to say that a Brahman at the present day cannot marry any woman who is not a Brahman; his wife must not only be a Brahman, she must also belong to the same endogamous division of the Brahman caste.

M. Senart's description.

By the side of this rigid definition I may place the general description of caste which is given by M. Emile Senart in his fascinating study of the caste system of India. After reminding his readers that no statement that can be made on the subject of caste can be considered as absolutely true, that the apparent relations of the facts admit of numerous shades of distinction, and that only the most general characteristics cover the whole of the subject, M. Senart goes on to describe a caste as a close corporation, in theory at any rate rigorously hereditary; equipped with a certain traditional and independent organization, including a chief and a council; meeting on occasion in assemblies of more or less plenary authority, and joining in the celebration of certain festivals; bound together by a common occupation; observing certain common usages which relate more particularly to marriage, to food and to questions of ceremonial pollution; and ruling its members by the exercise of a jurisdiction the extent of which varies, but which succeeds, by the sanction of certain penalties and above all by the power of final or revocable exclusion from the group, in making the authority of the community effectively felt.

An English parallel.

These, in the view of one of the most distinguished of French scholars, are the leading features of Indian caste. For my own part I have always been much impressed by the difficulty of conveying to European readers who have no experience of India even an approximate idea of the extraordinary complexity of the social system which is involved in the word caste. At the risk of being charged with frivolity I shall, therefore, venture on an illustration, based on one which I published in *Blackwood's Magazine* a good many years ago, of a caste expressed in terms of an English social group. Let us take an instance, and, in order to avoid the fumes of bewilderment that are thrown off by uncouth names, let us frame it on English lines. Let us imagine the great tribe of Smith, the 'noun of multitude,' as a famous headmaster used to call it, to be transformed by art magic into a caste organized on the Indian model, in which all the subtle *nuances* of social merit and demerit which *Punch* and the society papers love to chronicle should have been set and hardened into positive regulations affecting the intermarriage of families. The caste thus formed would trace its origin back to a mythical eponymous ancestor, the first Smith who converted the rough stone hatchet into the bronze battle-axe and took his name from the "smooth"* weapons that he wrought for his tribe. Bound together by this tie of common descent, they would recognize as the cardinal doctrine of their community the rule that a Smith must always marry a Smith, and could by no possibility marry a Brown, a Jones, or a Robinson. But over and above this general canon three other modes or principles of grouping within the caste would be conspicuous. First of all, the entire caste of Smith would be split up into an indefinite number of "in-marrying" clans based upon all sorts of trivial distinctions. Brewing Smiths and baking Smiths, hunting Smiths and shooting Smiths, temperance Smiths and licensed-victualler Smiths, Smiths with double-barrelled names and hyphens, Smiths with double-barrelled names without hyphens, Conservative Smiths, Radical Smiths, tinker Smiths, tailor Smiths, Smiths of Mercia, Smiths of Wessex—all these and all other imaginable varieties of the tribe Smith would be as it were crystallised by an inexorable law forbidding the members of any of these groups to marry beyond the circle marked out by the clan name. Thus the Unionist Mr. Smith could only marry a Unionist Miss Smith, and might not think of a Home Rule damsel; the free trade Smiths would have nothing to say to the tariff reformers; a hyphen-Smith could only marry a hyphen-Smith and so on. Secondly, within each class enquiry would disclose a number of 'out-marrying'

* Skeat, *Etymological Dictionary s. v.* Smith.

groups, bearing distinctive names, and governed by the rule that a man of one group could in no circumstances marry a girl of the same group. In theory each group would be regarded as a circle of blood-kindred and would trace its descent from a mythical or historical ancestor like the Wayland-Smith of the Berkshire hills, the Captain Smith who married Pocahontas, or the Mr. W. H. Smith of the railway bookstalls. The name of each would usually suggest its origin, and marriages within the limits defined by the group-name would be deemed incestuous, however remote the actual relationship between the parties concerned. A Wayland could not marry a Wayland, though the two might come from opposite ends of the kingdom and be in no way related, but must seek his bride in the Pocahontas or book-stall circle, and so on. Thus the system, the converse of that just described, would effect in a cumbrous and imperfect fashion what is done for ourselves by the table of prohibited degrees at the end of the prayer-book—cumbrous because it would forbid marriage between people who are in no sense relations, and imperfect because the group-name would descend in the male line and would of itself present no obstacle to a man marrying his grandmother. Thirdly, running through the entire series of clans we should find yet another principle at work breaking up each in-marrying clan into three or four smaller groups which would form a sort of ascending scale of social distinction. Thus the clan of hyphen-Smiths, which we take to be the cream of the caste—the Smiths who have attained to the crowning glory of double names securely welded together by hyphens—would be again divided into, let us say, Anglican, Dissenting, and Salvationist hyphen-Smiths, taking regular rank in that order. Now the rule of this series of groups would be that a man of the highest or Anglican group might marry a girl of his own group or of the two lower groups, that a man of the second or Dissenting group might take a Dissenting or Salvationist wife, while a Salvationist man would be restricted to his own group. A woman, it will be observed, could under no circumstances marry down into a group below her, and it would be thought eminently desirable for her to marry into a higher group. Other things being equal it is clear that two-thirds of the Anglican girls would get no husbands, and two-thirds of the Salvationist men no wives. These are some of the restrictions which would control the process of match-making among the Smiths if they were organized in a caste of the Indian type. There would also be restrictions as to food. The different in-marrying clans would be precluded from dining together, and their possibilities of reciprocal entertainment would be limited to those products of the confectioner's shop into the composition of which water, the most fatal and effective vehicle of ceremonial impurity, had not entered. Water pollutes wholesale, but its power as a conductor of malign influence admits of being neutralised by a sufficient admixture of milk, curds, whey, or clarified butter—in fact of anything that comes from the sacred cow. It would follow from this that the members of our imaginary caste could eat chocolates and other forms of sweetmeats together, but could not drink tea or coffee, and could only partake of ices if they were made with cream and were served on metal, not porcelain, plates. I am sensible of having trenched on the limits of literary and scientific propriety in attempting to describe an ancient and famous institution in unduly vivacious language, but the parallel is as accurate as any parallel drawn from the other end of the world can well be, and it has the advantage of being presented in terms familiar to European readers. The illustration, indeed, may be carried a step further. If we suppose the various aggregates of persons bearing the two or three thousand commonest English surnames to be formed into separate castes and organized on the lines described above, so that no one could marry outside the caste-name and could only marry within that limit subject to the restrictions imposed by differences of residence, occupation, religion, custom, social status and the like—the mental picture thus formed will give a fairly adequate idea of the bewildering complexity of the Indian caste system.

Conversion of tribes into castes.

All over India at the present moment tribes are gradually and insensibly being transformed into castes. The stages of this operation are in themselves difficult to trace. The main agency at work is fiction, which in this instance takes the form of the pretence that whatever usage prevails to-day did not come into existence yesterday, but has been so from the beginning of time. It may be hoped that the Ethnographic Survey now in progress will throw some light upon the singular course of evolution by which large masses of people surrender a condition of comparative freedom and take in exchange a condition which becomes more burdensome in proportion as its status is higher. So far as my own observation goes several distinct processes are involved in the movement, and these proceed independently in different places and at different times.

(I) The leading men of an aboriginal tribe, having somehow got on in the world and become independent landed proprietors, manage to enrol themselves in one of the more distinguished castes. They usually set up as Rajputs, their first step being to start a Brahman priest who invents for them a mythical ancestor, supplies them with a family miracle connected with the locality where the tribe is settled, and discovers that they belong to some hitherto unheard-of clan of the great Rajput community. In the earlier stages of their advancement they generally find great difficulty in getting their daughters married, as they will not take husbands from their original tribe and Rajputs of their adopted caste will, of course, not condescend to alliances with them. But after a generation or two their persistency obtains its reward and they intermarry, if not with pure Rajputs, at least with a superior order of manufactured Rajputs whose promotion into Brahmanical society dates far enough back for the steps by which it was gained to have been forgotten. Thus a real change of blood may take place, as indeed one is on occasion in a position to observe, while in any case the tribal name is completely lost and with it all possibility of correctly separating this class of people from the Hindus of purer blood and of tracing them to any particular Dravidian or Mongoloid tribe. They have been absorbed in the fullest sense of the word, and henceforth pass and are locally accepted as high-class Hindus. All stages of the process, family miracle and all, can be illustrated by actual instances taken from the leading families in various parts of India. The most picturesque instance of the class of legend to which I refer is that associated with the family of the Maharajas of Chutia Nāgpur, who call themselves Nāgbansi Rajputs, and on the strength of their mythical pedigree have probably succeeded in occasionally procuring wives of reputed Rajput blood. The story itself is a variant of the well-known Lohengrin legend. It tells how a king of the Nāgas or snakes, the strange pre-historic race which figures so largely in Indian mythology, took upon himself human form and married a beautiful Brahman girl of Benares. His incarnation, however, was in two respects incomplete, for he could not get rid of his forked tongue and his evil-smelling breath. Consequently, as the story goes, in order to conceal these disagreeable peculiarities he always slept with his back to his wife. His precautions, however, were unsuccessful, for she discovered what he sought to conceal and her curiosity was greatly inflamed. But the snake king, being bound by the same condition as his Teutonic prototype, could only disclose his origin at the cost of separation from his wife. Accordingly, by a device familiar to Indian husbands, he diverted her attention by proposing to take her on a pilgrimage to the shrine of Jagannath at Puri in Orissa. The couple started by the direct route through the hills and forests of Chutia Nāgpur, and when they reached the neighbourhood of the present station of Rānchi the wife was seized by the pains of childbirth. Her curiosity revived, and she began to ask questions. By folk-lore etiquette questions asked on such an occasion must be answered, and her husband was compelled to explain that he was really the Takshak Raja, the king of the snakes. Having divulged this fatal secret he did not, like Lohengrin, make a dignified exit to the strains of slow music. He straightway turned into a gigantic cobra, whereupon his wife was delivered of a male child and died. The poor snake made the best of the trying position in which he found himself; he spread his hood and sheltered the infant from the rays of the mid-day sun. While he was thus occupied, some wood-cutters of the Munda tribe appeared upon the scene and decided that a child discovered in such remarkable circumstances must be destined to a great future and should at once be adopted as their chief. That is the family legend of the Nāgbansi Rajas of Chutia Nāgpur. It was received with derisive merriment by a number of genuine Rajputs who attended a conference which I held at Mount Abu in 1900 for the purpose of organizing the census of Rajputana. They had never heard of such a thing as a Nāgbansi Rajput, but they entirely appreciated the point of the story. Similar tales, associated sometimes with a peacock, sometimes with a cow, sometimes with other animals or trees, are told of various land-owning families which have attained brevet rank as local Rajputs. Anyone who has the curiosity to inquire into the distribution of tenures on the estates of these manufactured Rajputs will usually find that a number of the best villages lying round the residence of the Chief are held on peppercorn rents by the descendants of the Brahmans who helped him to his miraculous pedigree.

(2) A number of aborigines, as we may conveniently call them, though the term begs an insoluble question, embrace the tenets of a Hindu religious sect, losing thereby their tribal name and becoming Vaishnavas, Lingayats, Rāmāyats, or the like. Whether there is any mixture of blood or not will depend upon local circumstances and the rules of the sect regarding intermarriage. Anyhow, the

identity of the converts as aborigines is usually, though not invariably, lost, and this also may, therefore, be regarded as a case of true absorption.

(3) A whole tribe of aborigines, or a large section of a tribe, enrol themselves in the ranks of Hinduism under the style of a new caste, which, though claiming an origin of remote antiquity, is readily distinguishable by its name from any of the standard and recognized castes. Thus the great majority of the Kochh inhabitants of Jalpaiguri, Rangpur, and part of Dinājpur now invariably describe themselves as Rājbansis or Bhanga Kshatriyas—a designation which enables them to represent themselves as an outlying branch of the Kshatriyas of Hindu tradition who fled to north-eastern Bengal in order to escape from the wrath of Parasu-Rāma. They claim descent from Raja Dasaratha, the father of Rāma, they keep Brahmans, imitate the orthodox ritual in their marriage ceremony, and have begun to adopt the Brahmanical system of *gotras*. In respect of this last point they are now in a curious state of transition, as they have all hit upon the same *gotra* (Kāsyapa) and thus habitually transgress the primary rule of the Brahmanical system, which absolutely prohibits marriage within the *gotra*. But for this defect in their connubial arrangements—a defect which will probably be corrected in course of time as they and their priests rise in intelligence—there would be nothing in their customs to distinguish them from Indo-Aryan Hindus; although there has been no mixture of blood and they remain thoroughly Kochh under the name of Rājbansi. It is right to add that, however baseless the tradition must be in the case of the tribe as a whole, it does not follow that it may not enshrine a grain of fact as applied to their Chief. The Rajputs in India, like the Normans in Europe, travelled far afield in their conquering excursions. In a country where history masquerades in the garb of legend there is nothing *prima facie* improbable in the conjecture that the story of the Bhanga-Kshatriyas may be really a mythological version of the true origin of the reigning family of Cooch Bihar. A Chief of the higher race ruling a people of the lower is a phenomenon too common to require explanation.

(4) A whole tribe of aborigines, or a section of a tribe, become gradually converted to Hinduism without, like the Rājbansis, abandoning their tribal designation. This is what has happened among the Bhumij of Western Bengal. Here a pure Dravidian race have lost their original language and now speak only Bengali; they

worship Hindu gods in addition to their own (the tendency being to relegate the tribal gods to the women) and the more advanced among them employ Brahmans as family priests. They still retain a set of totemistic exogamous sub-divisions closely resembling those of the Mundas and the Santāls. But they are beginning to forget the totems which the names of the sub-divisions denote, and the names themselves will probably soon be abandoned in favour of more aristocratic designations. The tribe will then have become a caste in the full sense of the word, and will go on stripping itself of all customs likely to betray its true descent. The physical characteristics of its members will alone survive. With their transformation into a caste the Bhumij will be more strictly endogamous than they were as a tribe, and even less likely to modify their physical type by intermarriage with other races.

Types of Caste.

By such processes as these, and by a variety of complex social influences whose working cannot be precisely traced, a number of types or varieties of caste have been formed which admit of being grouped as follows :—

(1) Tribal castes.

(*i*) *The tribal type*, where a tribe like the Bhumij referred to above has insensibly been converted into a caste, preserving its original name and many of its characteristic customs, but modifying its animistic practices more and more in the direction of orthodox Hinduism and ordering its manner of life in accordance with the same model. Numerous instances of this process are to be found all over India ; it has been at work for centuries and it has even been supposed that the Sudras of Indo-Aryan tradition were originally a Dravidian tribe which was thus incorporated into the social system of the conquering race. Considerations of space preclude me from attempting an exhaustive enumeration of the castes which may plausibly be described as tribes absorbed into Hinduism, but I may mention as illustrations of the transformation that has taken place, the Ahir, Dom, and Dosādh of the United Provinces and Bihar ; the Gujar, Jāt, Meo, and Rajput of Rajputana and the Punjab ; the Koli, Mahār, and Marātha of Bombay ; the Bagdi, Bāuri, Chandāl (Nāmasudra), Kaibartta, Pod, and Rājbansi-Kochh of Bengal ; and in Madras the Māl, 'Nāyar, Vellāla, and Paraiyan or Pariah, of whom the last retain traditions of a time when they possessed an independent organisation of their own and had not been relegated to a low place in the Hindu social system.

(ii) Functional castes

(*ii*) *The functional or occupational type* of caste is so numerous and so widely diffused and its characteristics are so prominent that community of function is ordinarily regarded as the chief factor in the evolution of caste. Whatever the original impulse may have been, it is a matter of observation at the present day not only that almost every caste professes to have a traditional occupation, though many of its members have abandoned it, but that the adoption of new occupations or of changes in the original occupation may give rise to sub-divisions of the caste which ultimately develop into entirely distinct castes. Thus among the large castes shown in the maps at the end of this chapter the Ahirs are by tradition herdsmen ; the Brahmans priests ; the Chamārs and Mochis workers in leather ; the Chuhras, Bhangis, and Doms scavengers ; the Dosādhs village watchmen and messengers ; the Goālas milkmen ; the Kaibarttas and Kewats fishermen and cultivators ; the Kāyasths writers ; the Koiri and Kāchhi market gardeners ; the Kumhārs potters ; the Pods fishermen ; and the Teli and Tili oil-pressers and traders. But the proportion of a caste that actually follows the traditional occupation may vary greatly. It is shown in the Bengal Census Report that 80 per cent of the Ahirs in Bihar are engaged in agriculture ; that of the Bengal Brahmans only 17 per cent and of the Bihar Brahmans only 8 per cent are engaged in religious functions ; that not more than 8 per cent of the Chamārs in Bihar live by working in leather, the remainder being cultivators or general labourers ; that two-thirds of the Kāyasths in Bengal are agriculturists, and that only thirty-five per cent of the Telis follow their traditional profession. A remarkable instance of the formation of a caste on the basis of distinctive occupation is supplied by the Garpagāri or hail-averter in the Maratha districts of the Central Provinces, a village servant whose duty it is to control the elements and protect the crops from the destructive hail storms which are frequent in that part of India. For this, says Mr. Russell, 'he receives a contribution from the cultivators ; but in recent years an unavoidable scepticism as to his efficiency has tended to reduce his earnings. Mr. Fuller told me that on one occasion when he was hastening through the Chanda District on tour and pressed for time, the weather at one of his halting places looked threatening, and he feared that it would rain and delay the march. Among the villagers who came to see him was the local Garpagāri, and not wishing to neglect any chance he ordered him to take up his position outside the camp and keep off the rain. This the Garpagāri did, and watched through the night. In the event the rain held off, the camp moved, and that Garpagāri's reputation was established for life.'* Changes of occupation in their turn, more especially among the lower castes, tend to bring about the formation of separate castes. The Sadgops of Bengal have within recent times taken to agriculture and broken away from the pastoral caste to which they originally belonged; the educated Kaibarttas and Pods are in course of separating themselves from their brethren who have not learnt English; the Madhunāpit are barbers who became confectioners; the Chāsadhobas washermen who took to agriculture. But perhaps the best illustration of the contagious influence of the fiction that differences of occupation imply a difference of blood is to be found in the list of Musalman castes enumerated by Mr. Gait in the Bengal Census Report of 1901. This motley company includes the Abdāl of Northern and Eastern Bengal, who circumcise Muhammadan boys and castrate animals, while their women act as midwives; the Bhatiyāra or inn-keepers of Bihar; the butchers (Chik and Kasāi); the drummers (Nāgarchi and Dafāli), of whom the latter exorcise evil spirits and avert the evil eye by beating a drum (*daf*) and also officiate as priests at the marriages and funerals of people who are too poor to pay the regular Qāzi; the cotton-carders (Dhunia or Nadāf) numbering 200,000 in Bengal; the barbers (Hajjām or Turk-Nāia); the Jolāha weavers, cultivators, bookbinders, tailors, and dyers numbering nearly a quarter of a million in Bengal and nearly three millions in India; the oil-pressers (Kalu); the green-grocers (Kunjra); the embroiderers (Patwa) and a number of minor groups. All of these bodies are castes of the standard Hindu type with governing committees (*panchāyats* or *mātbars*) of their own who organize strikes and see that no member of the caste engages in a degrading occupation, works for lower wages than his brethren, eats forbidden food, or marries a woman of another caste. Breaches of these and various other unwritten ordinances are visited in the last resort by the extreme penalty of excommunication. This means that no one will eat or smoke with the offender, visit at his house, or marry his daughter, while in extreme cases he is deprived of the services of the barber and the washerman.

---

*Census Report of the Central Provinces, 1901

(iii) Sectarian castes.

(*iii*) *The sectarian type* comprises a small number of castes which commenced life as religious sects founded by philanthropic enthusiasts who, having evolved some metaphysical formula offering a speedier release from the *tædium vitæ* which oppresses the East, had further persuaded themselves that all men were equal, or at any rate that all believers in their teaching ought to be equal. As time went on the practical difficulties of realizing this ideal forced themselves upon the members of the sect; they found their company becoming unduly mixed; and they proceeded to re-organize themselves on the lines of an ordinary caste. A notable instance of this tendency to revert to the normal type of Hindu society is to be found in the present condition of the Lingāyat or Virshaiv caste of Bombay and Southern India, which numbers 2,600,000 adherents. Founded as a sect in the twelfth century by a reformer who proclaimed the doctrine of the equality of all who received the eightfold sacrament ordained by him and wore on their persons the mystic *phallus* emblematic of the god Siva, the Lingāyat community had begun by the close of the seventeenth century to develop endogamous sub-castes based upon the social distinctions which their founder had expressly abjured. At the recent Census the process of transforming the sect into a caste had advanced still further. In a petition presented to the Government of India the members of the Lingāyat community protested against the "most offensive and mischievous order" that all of them should be entered in the Census papers as belonging to the same caste, and asked that they might be recorded as Virshaiv Brahmans, Kshatriyas, Vaisyas, or Sudras, as the case might be. It would be difficult to find a better illustration of the essentially particularist instinct of the Indian people, of the aversion with which they regard the doctrine that all men are equal, and of the growing attraction exercised by the aristocratic scheme of society which their ancient traditions enshrine. The legend of the four original castes may have no historical foundation, but there can be no question as to the spread of its influence or the strength of the sentiment which it inspires.

A somewhat similar case is that of the Sarāks of western Bengal, Chutia Nāgpur, and Orissa, who seem to be a Hinduised remnant of the early Jain people to whom local legends ascribe the ruined temples, the defaced images, and even the abandoned copper mines of that part of Bengal. Their name is a variant of

Srāvaka (Sanskrit 'hearer'), the designation of the Jain laity; they are strict vegetarians, never eating flesh, and on no account taking life, and if in preparing their food any mention is made of the word 'cutting,' the omen is deemed so disastrous that everything must be thrown away. In Orissa they call themselves Buddhists and assemble once a year at the famous cave temples of Khandagiri near Cuttack to make offerings to the Buddhist images there and to confer on religious matters. But these survivals of their ancient faith have not saved them from the all-pervading influence of caste. They have split up into endogamous groups based partly on locality and partly on the fact that some of them have taken to the degraded occupation of weaving, and they now form a Hindu caste of the ordinary type. The same fate has befallen the Gharbāri Atiths, the Sānnyāsi, the Jugis, the Jāti-Baishtams of Bengal, the Bānhra of Nepal—Newārs who were originally Buddhist priests but abandoned celibacy and crystallized into a caste—and the Bishnois and Sadhs of the United Provinces. The Bishnois of Rohilkhand, says Mr. Burn,* are divided into nine endogamous groups or sub-castes 'called after the castes from which they were recruited. New converts take their place in the appropriate sub-castes.' In the case of the Sādhs 'recruits are no longer admitted, and it is peculiar that no endogamous or exogamous divisions exist, the only restriction on marriage being that intermarriage is forbidden between two families as long as the recollection of a former marriage connexion between them remains. The instance is of special interest as the equality maintained by the tenets of the sect, which has developed into a caste, has not yet been destroyed, as is usual in such cases.' A still more remarkable, because a more modern, case is mentioned by Sir Henry Cotton, who states that 'the more self-assertive portion of the Brahmo community' appears to be 'in the course of forming' a new caste. All these curious developments serve to illustrate the comparatively insignificant part that religion has played in the shaping of the caste system, and the strength of the tendency to *morcellement*, to splitting up into fractional groups, that is characteristic of Hindu society. So long as the sectarian instinct confines itself to expressing a mere predilection for one god rather than another, or simply develops a new cult, however fantastic, which permits men to indulge in the luxury of religious eccentricity without quitting the

---

* Census Report of the United Provinces, 1901.

narrow circle of their social environment, its operations are undisturbed and the sects which it forms may flourish and endure. But directly it invades the social sphere and seeks to unify and amalgamate groups of theoretically different origin it comes in contact with a force too strong for it and has to give way. Race dominates religion ; sect is weaker than caste.

Even Christianity has not altogether escaped the subtle contagion of caste. Almost everywhere in India a tendency has been observed on the part of converts from Hinduism to group themselves according to the castes to which they originally belonged. This sometimes assumes the form of a division into two groups, the higher restricted to those who were members of the 'clean' castes from whom Brahmans can take water, while the lower comprises all those of inferior rank. On the west coast the retention of caste distinctions was deliberately recognised by the Portuguese missionaries, and the results of this policy have survived down to the present day. The Indian Roman Catholic Christians of the Konkan, the low-lying strip of coast between the Western Ghats and the sea, are divided into Bambans or Bammans (Brahmans), Charodas or Chardos (Kshatriyas or Chhatris), Sudirs (Sudras), Renders (drawers of palm-juice), Gavids or Gavdas (salt-makers), Modvals (washermen), Kumbārs (potters), and Kāphris or Sidis (labourers), whose thick lips, slanting foreheads and curly beards suggest an infusion of Somali blood. Intermarriages among these groups, while not absolutely forbidden, are said to be rare, though in South Kanara such unions 'are gradually becoming more frequent in cases in which members of castes other than the Bammans have succeeded in obtaining a good position in the official, legal, or commercial community.'* Infant marriage is forbidden among the Konkani Christians, but girls are married as soon as they are twelve years old, and sometimes even before that age under a special dispensation from the Bishop. Widow marriage, though not forbidden, 'is as much condemned as among the pagans.' Many of them, especially the women, cannot bear the idea of eating beef, and they observe the characteristic Hindu prohibition against a wife addressing or speaking of her husband by his name. The marriage ceremony is performed in Church according to Christian rites, but it is preceded and followed by observances which are palpable

---

* *Manual of South Kanara.* J. Sturrock, I.C.S., 1894. *Vide* also *Bombay Gazetteer,* Vol. XV, Part I, 1883; and *Indian Caste,* by Mr. J. A. Saldanha, 1904.

survivals from the Hindu customs of betrothal and marriage. These include the formal bathing of the betrothed couple, the giving of a dinner to the poor for the benefit of the deceased ancestors of the family, the tying of a *tāli* or lucky necklace (which sometimes has a cross or a figure of the infant Jesus as a pendant) round the bride's neck, the exchange of presents, and the formal transfer of the bride to her husband's family.

Further south in the little State of Cochin on the Malabar coast, where Christianity has been established for many centuries and is believed by some authorities to date from apostolic times, a different principle has asserted itself. In the course of ages, disputes as to theological doctrine, ecclesiastical ritual, or spiritual supremacy have led to the formation among the non-Protestant Christians in Cochin of a number of sects—the Roman Catholics of the Latin rite, who use the Liturgy of the Romish Church in Latin, and are further sub-divided into the Three Hundred, the Five Hundred, and the Seven Hundred, obscure schisms possibly derived merely from the number of families that were converted by the Portuguese missionaries on successive occasions ; the Roman Catholics of the Syrian rite, who use the Romish Liturgy in ancient Syriac ; the Chaldean Syrians, who are under the Patriarch of Babylon and differ in several minute points of ritual from the Romo-Syrians ; the Jacobite Syrians, who are under the Patriarch of Antioch ; and the Reformed or St. Thomas Syrians, an offshoot of the Jacobites who recognise the supremacy neither of the Pope nor of the Patriarch of Antioch and obey a Bishop of their own. These last have come to some extent under Protestant influence, and they insist upon the title of St. Thomas Syrians as marking their close adherence to the teaching and ritual of the apostolic age. They deny that the Bible should be interpreted by the traditions of the Church ; they reject confession, absolution, fasting, the invocation of Saints, and the veneration of relics ; they object to masses for the dead and dispute the doctrine of baptismal regeneration. Of these seven sects the first five appear to have crystallised into regular castes between the members of which no intermarriage is possible. The two branches of the Jacobite Syrians still intermarry, subject to a further distinction between residents of the northern and southern divisions of the State, the former of whom claim to be superior to the latter on the ground of their descent from the first colonists from Syria.

(*iv*) *Castes formed by crossing.*—Modern criticism has been especially active in its attacks on that portion of the traditional theory which derives the multitude of mixed or inferior castes from an intricate series of crosses between members of the original four. No one can examine the long lists which purport to illustrate the working of this process without being struck by much that is absurd and inconsistent. But in India it does not necessarily follow that, because the individual applications of a principle are ridiculous, the principle itself can have no foundation in fact. The last thing that would occur to the literary theorists of those times, or to their successors the *pandits* of to-day, would be to go back upon actual facts, and to seek by analysis and comparison to work out the true stages of evolution. They found, as I infer from plentiful experience of my own, the *a priori* method simpler and more congenial. That at least did not compel them to pollute their souls by the study of plebeian usage. Having once got hold of a formula, they insisted, like Thales and his contemporaries, on making it account for the entire order of things. Thus, castes which were compact tribes, castes which had been developed out of corporations like the mediæval trade guilds, and castes which expressed the distinction between fishing and hunting, agriculture and handicrafts, were all supposed to have been evolved by interbreeding.

(iv) Castes formed by crossing.

But the initial principle, though it could not be stretched to explain everything, nevertheless rests upon a residuum of historical fact. It happens that we can still observe its workings among a number of Dravidian tribes, which, though not yet drawn into the vortex of Brahmanism, have been in some degree affected by the example of Hindu organization. As regards inter-tribal marriages, they seem to be in a stage of development through which the Hindus themselves may have passed. A man may marry a woman of another tribe, but the offspring of such unions do not become members of either the paternal or maternal groups, but belong to a distinct endogamous aggregate, the name of which often denotes the precise cross by which it was started. Among the large tribe of Mundās we find, for instance, nine such groups—Khangar-Mundā, Kharia-Mundā, Konkpat-Mundā, Karanga-Mundā, Mahili-Mundā, Nāgbansi-Mundā, Orāon-Mundā, Sad-Mundā, Savar-Mundā—descended from intermarriages between Mundā men and women of other tribes. The Mahilis again have five sub-tribes of this kind, and themselves trace their descent to the union of a Mundā with a Santāl woman. Illustrations of this sort might be multiplied almost indefinitely. The point to be observed is that the sub-tribes formed by inter-tribal crossing are from an early stage complete endogamous units, and that they tend continually to sever their slender connection with the parent group, and stand forth as independent tribes. As soon as this comes to pass, and a functional or territorial name disguises their mixed descent, the process by which they have been formed is seen to resemble closely that by which the standard Indian tradition seeks to explain the appearance of other castes alongside of the classical four.

Within the limits of the regular caste system Mr. Gait mentions the Shāgirdpeshās of Bengal as a true caste "which takes its origin from miscegenation, and which is still adding to its numbers in the same way. Amongst the members of the higher castes of Orissa who do not allow widow remarriage, and also amongst the Kāyasth immigrants from Bengal it is a common practice to take as maid-servants and concubines women belonging to the lower clean castes, such as Chāsa and Bhandāri. The offspring of these maid-servants are known as Shāgirdpeshā. They form a regular caste of the usual type and are divided into endogamous groups with reference to the caste of the male parent. Kāyasth Shāgirdpeshās will not intermarry with Karan Shāgirdpeshās, nor Rajput Shāgirdpeshās (their number is very small) with those of Kāyasth origin, but intermarriage between the Shāgirdpeshās of Karan and of Khandāit descent sometimes takes place, just as such marriages sometimes occur between persons belonging to the castes to which they owe their origin. The caste of the mother makes no difference in the rank of the children, but those who can count several generations from their original progenitor rank higher than those in whose case the stigma of illegitimacy is more recent.

The word Shāgirdpeshā, which is commonly pronounced Sāgarpeshā, means servant, and is applied with reference to the traditional occupation, which is domestic service. It is said that the word should properly be confined to the offspring of Bengali Kāyasths, and that the illegitimate children of Karans and other castes of Orissa should be called Krishnapakshi, or Antarpua, or, again, Antarkaran, Antarkhandāit, etc. This distinction, however, is not observed in practice. The relationship between the legitimate children of a man of good caste and their bastard brothers and sisters is recognised, but the latter cannot eat with the former, hence they are called ***bhātāntar***, or separated by rice. They are entitled to maintenance, but cannot inherit their father's property so long as there are any legitimate heirs. They usually serve in their father's house until they grow up and marry; male children are then usually given a house and a few *bighas* of land for their support. The Shāgirdpeshās are also sometimes known as *Golām* (slave)—a term which is also applied to the Sudras of Eastern Bengal, who appear in several respects to be an analogous caste. Another appellation is *Kothā po* (own son), as distinguished from *Prajā po* (tenant son), which formerly denoted a purchased slave. Their family name is usually Singh or Dās. Some of them have taken to cultivation, but they will not themselves handle the plough. They usually live in great poverty. It is said to be impossible for a Shāgirdpeshā under any circumstances to obtain admission to his father's caste. If a man of that caste were to marry a Shāgirdpeshā woman he would be outcasted and his children would become Shāgirdpeshā. Persons of higher rank (usually outcasts) are admitted to the caste. A feast is given by the applicant for admission, and he is then formally acknowledged as a caste-fellow.

In their social observances the Shāgirdpeshās follow the practices of the higher castes. They forbid the remarriage of widows and do not allow divorce. Polygamy is only permitted when good cause is shown, *e.g.*, if the first wife is barren or diseased. They belong to the Vaishnava sect, worship the ordinary Hindu gods, and employ good Brahmans. The binding portion of the marriage ceremony is the joining of the hands of bride and bridegroom by the officiating priest. Shāgirdpeshās of the first generation, being illegitimate, cannot perform their father's *srādh*. They usually cremate their dead. In spite of their number (about 47,000) the caste is said to be of quite recent origin, and it is asserted that it did not exist a century and-a-half ago."

An older and more instructive illustration, dating possibly from before the Christian era, of the formation of a caste by crossing, is furnished by the Khas of Nepal, who are the offspring of mixed marriages between Rajputs or Brahman immigrants and the Mongolian women of the country. "The females,"* says Hodgson, "would indeed welcome the polished Brahmans to their embraces, but their offspring must not be stigmatised as the infamous progeny

* Essay on the Origin and Classification of the Military Tribes of Nepal, J. A. S. B., 1833, p. 217.

of a Brahman and a Mlechha—must, on the contrary, be raised to eminence in the new order of things proposed to be introduced by their fathers. To this progeny also, then, the Brahmans, in still greater defiance of their creed, communicated the rank of the second order of Hinduism ; and from these two roots, mainly, sprung the now numerous, predominant, and extensively ramified tribe of the Khas, originally the name of a small clan of creedless barbarians, now the proud title of the Kshatriyas, or military order of the kingdom of Nepal. The offspring of original Khas females and of Brahmans, with the honours and rank of the second order of Hinduism, got the patronymic titles of the first order, and hence the key to the anomalous nomenclature of so many *stirpes* of the military tribes of Nepal is to be sought in the nomenclature of the sacred order. It may be added, as remarkably illustrative of the lofty spirit of the *Parbattias*, that in spite of the yearly increasing sway of Hinduism in Nepal, and of the various attempts of the Brahmans in high office to procure the abolition of a custom so radically opposed to the creed both parties now profess, the Khas still insist that the fruit of commerce (marriage is out of the question) between their females and males of the sacred order shall be ranked as Kshatriyas, wear the thread, and assume the patronymic title." The Khas now call themselves Chattris or Kshatriyas—a practice which, according to Colonel Vansittart,* dates from Sir Jang Bahadur's visit to England in 1850. Allied to the Khas are the Ektharia and the Thākurs, both of Rajput parentage on the male side, the Thākur ranking higher because their ancestors are supposed to have been rulers of various petty States in Nepal. The Matwāla Khas, again, are the progeny of Khas men and Magar women, and the Uchai Thākurs are of the same lineage on the female side.

The Sudra caste of Eastern Bengal, the Rājbansi Baruas of Chittagong, believed to be the offspring of Burmese fathers and Bengali mothers, the Vidurs of the Central Provinces, who claim Brahman parentage on the male side and, though now marrying among themselves, still receive into their community the children of mixed unions between Brahmans and women of other castes, are minor instances of the same process. The Boria caste of Assam is said by Mr. Allen† to comprise the offspring of Brahman and Ganak widows and their descendants, and the children of Brahmans who

* Notes on Nepal, 1896, p. 89.

† Census Report of Assam, 1901.

attained puberty before marriage, and so had to be married to men of lower caste. The name Boria is popularly derived from *bari*, a widow, but the members of the caste prefer to call themselves *Sut* or *Suta*, the Shastric designation of the children of a Brahman woman by a Kshatriya, or Vaisya father. Borias are more numerous in Nowgong than in any other district of Assam, though the number of Brahmans there is comparatively small. On pointing this out to an educated Brahman of Nowgong, Mr. Allen received the singular explanation that "the Gosāins and Mohants of that district had put pressure upon householders to give away young Brahman widows in marriage to men of lower castes to prevent the society from becoming demoralized."

(v) National castes

(*v*) *Castes of the national type.*—Where there is neither nation nor national sentiment, it may seem paradoxical to talk about a national type of caste. There exist, however, certain groups, usually regarded as castes at the present day, which cherish traditions of bygone sovereignty and seem to preserve traces of an organization considerably more elaborate than that of an ordinary tribe. The Newārs, a mixed people of Mongoloid origin, who were the predominant race in Nepal proper until the country was conquered and annexed by the Gurkha Prithi Nārāyan in 1768, may be taken as an illustration of such a survival. The group comprises both Hindus and Buddhists. The latter are at present slightly more numerous, but the former are said to be gaining ground by more frequent conversions. The two communities are quite distinct, and each is divided into an elaborate series of castes. Thus, among the Hindu Newārs, we find at the top of the social scale the Devabhaja, who are Brahmans and spiritual teachers; the Surjyabansi Mal, members of the old royal family; the Sreshta, consisting of ministers and other officials; and the Japu, who are cultivators. Then comes an intermediate group including, among others, the Awā, masons; the Kawmi, carpenters and sweetmeat-makers, an odd combination of trades; the Chhipi, dyers of cloth; the Kāu, blacksmiths; and the Nāu, barbers. Lowest of all are the Pāsi, washermen; the Jugi, tailors and musicians; the Po, sweepers, burners of dead bodies, and executioners, and the Kulu, drum-makers and curriers.

If the Marāthas can be described as a caste, their history and traditions certainly stamp them as a caste of the national type. They number five millions at the present census, 3,650,000 in Bombay,

1,102,000 in Hyderabad, 81,000 in Madras, 53,000 in Mysore, 34,000 in the Central Provinces, the same number in Central India, and nearly 27,000 in Berar. According to Mr. Enthoven,* the Bombay Marāthas "may be classified as a tribe with two divisions, Marātha and Marātha Kunbi, of which the former are hypergamous to the latter, but were not originally distinct. It remains to be explained that the Kunbis also consist of two divisions, Desh Kunbis numbering 1,900,000, and Konkani Kunbis, of which there are 350,000 recorded. Intermarriage between these divisions is not usual. The barrier, however, seems to be purely geographical. It may not withstand the altered conditions due to improvements in communications, and it is not apparently based on any religious prohibition of intermarriages. The fact that the Kunbis consist of two branches must, however, be borne in mind in attempting to arrive at a correct description of the tribal configuration." The highest class of Marāthas is supposed to consist of ninety-six families, who profess to be of Rajput descent and to represent the Kshatriyas of the traditional system. They wear the sacred thread, marry their daughters before puberty, and forbid widows to marry again. But their claim to kinship with the Rajputs is effectually refuted by the anthropometric data now published, and by the survival among them of *kuldevaks* or totems, such as the sun-flower, the *kadamba* tree (*Nauclea Kadamba*), the mango, the conch-shell, the peacock's feather, and turmeric, which are worshipped at marriages and at the ceremony of dedicating a new house, while their close connection with the Kunbis is attested by the fact that they take Kunbi girls as wives, though they do not give their own daughters to Kunbi men. A wealthy Kunbi, however, occasionally gains promotion to and marries into the higher grade and claims brevet rank as a Kshatriya. The fact seems to be that the ninety-six superior families represent Kunbis who came to the front during the decline of the Moghal Empire, won for themselves princedoms or estates, claimed the rank of landed gentry, and asserted their dignity by refusing their daughters to their less distinguished brethren.

(vi) Castes formed by migration.

(*vi*) *Castes formed by migration.*—If members of a caste leave their original habitat and settle permanently in another part of India, the tendency is for them to be separated from the parent group and to develop into a distinct

---

* Census Report of Bombay, 1901.

caste. The stages of the process are readily traced. In the first instance it is assumed that people who go and live in foreign parts must of necessity eat forbidden food, worship alien gods, and enter into relations with strange women. Consequently, when they wish to take wives from among their own people, they find that their social status has been lowered, and that they have to pay for the privilege of marrying within the parent group. This luxury grows more and more expensive, and in course of time the emigrants marry only among themselves and thus become a sub-caste usually distinguished by a territorial name, such as Jaunpuria, Tirhutia, Bārendra, and the like. Mr. Gait has pointed out that "the prolonged residence of persons of Bihar castes in Bengal generally results in their being placed under a ban as regards marriage," and I had observed some years earlier that up-country barbers who settle in Bengal are called *khotta* and practically form a separate sub-caste, as Bengali barbers will not intermarry with them, while they are regarded as impure by the barbers of Upper India and Bihar by reason of their having taken up their residence in Bengal. If the process of differentiation is carried a step further (as indeed usually happened before the potent influence of railways had made itself felt), and the settlers assume a distinctive caste-name, all traces of their original affinities disappear and there remains only a dim tradition of their migration 'from the West,' the quarter whence, in Bengal at any rate, promotion is believed to come. Owing to this loss of identity the number of instances in which we can point with certainty to the formation of castes by migration is comparatively small. Mr. Russell, writing of the Central Provinces, tells us how a native gentleman said to him, in speaking of his people, that when a few families of Khedāwal Brahmans from Gujarat first settled in Damoh, they had the greatest difficulty in arranging their marriages. They could not marry with their caste-fellows in Gujarat, because their sons and daughters could not 'establish themselves,' that is, could not prove their identity as Khedāwal Brahmans; but since the railway has been opened, intermarriages take place freely with other Khedāwals in Gujarat and Benares. So the geographical isolation of Chhattisgarh, the country of the 'thirty-six forts' of the Haihaibansi dyanasty of Ratanpur, has led to the social isolation of the inhabitants. "The Chhattisgarhi Brahmans," says Mr. Russell, "form a class apart, and up-country Brahmans will have nothing to do with them." The contempt in which the people of this tract are held by their neighbours, finds expression in the following depreciatory verses :—

Wah hai Chhattisgarhi desh,
Jahān Gond hai naresh,
Niche bursi upar khāt,
Lagā hai chongi kā thāt,
Pahile jutā pichhe bāt,
Tab āwe Chhattisgarhi hāt.

which may be rendered thus :—

"This is Chhattisgarh, where the Gond is king of the jungle,
Under his bed is a fire, for he cannot pay for a blanket ;
Nor for a hookah indeed,—a leaf-pipe holds his tobacco.
Kick him soundly first and then he will do what you tell him."

The verses reflect the intolerant and domineering attitude of the Indo-Aryan towards the Dravidian, of the high-caste man towards the low, that has been characteristic of Indian society from the earliest times down to the present day.

A good illustration of the formation of a caste by migration is to be found in the traditions of the Nambudri or Namputiri Brahmans of Malabar. These Brahmans claim to have come to the west coast from various sacred localities in Kathiawar and the northern Deccan ; Mr. Fawcett describes them as "the truest Aryans in Southern India ;" and their complexion and features seem to lend some support to the tradition which assigns to them a foreign origin. Whatever their original stock may have been, they are now an entirely separate caste differing from the Brahmans of other parts of India by their systematic practice of polygamy ; by their rejection of infant marriage ; by their restriction of marriage to the eldest son, the other brothers entering into polyandrous relations with Nāyar women ; and by the curious custom of ceremonial fishing which forms part of their marriage ritual. Another instance of the same process is furnished by the Rārhi Brahmans of Bengal. The current legend is that early in the eleventh century A.D., Adisura or Adisvara, Raja of Bengal, finding the Brahmans then settled in his dominions too ignorant to perform for him certain Vedic ceremonies, applied to the Raja of Kanauj for priests conversant with the sacred ritual of the Aryans. In answer to his request there were sent to him five Brahmans of Kanauj, one of them a son of the Raja, who brought with them their wives, their sacred fire, and their sacrificial implements. It is said that Adisura was at first disposed to treat them with scanty respect, but he was soon compelled to acknowledge his mistake and to make terms with people who had a monopoly of the magical powers associated with the correct performance of ancient ritual. He then made over to them five populous villages, the number of which was subsequently increased to fifty-six. The tradition seems to chronicle an early *brahmottar* grant, the first perhaps of the long series of similar transactions that has played so important a part in the history of land tenures, in the development of caste influence and custom, and in promoting the spread of orthodox Hinduism throughout Bengal. Adisura did what the Rajas of outlying and unorthodox tracts of country (such as Bengal was in the eleventh century) have constantly done since and are doing still. A local chief, far removed from the great centres of Brahmanical lore, somehow becomes aware of his ceremonial shortcomings. In many cases, as indeed is narrated of Adisura himself, a wandering priest brings home to him that his outlandish ritual is not up to the orthodox standard. He sends for Brahmans, gives them grants of land near his own residence, and proceeds at their dictation to reform his ways on the model of the devout kings whom Brahmanical literature holds up as the ideal for a Raja to follow. The Brahmans find for him a pedigree of respectable antiquity and provide him with a family legend, and in course of time, by dint of money and diplomacy, he succeeds in getting himself recognized as a member of the local Rajput community. But that does not mean that the real Rajputs will acknowledge his pretensions; nor will the Brahmans who have attached themselves to his fortunes retain their status among the community from which they have broken off. It will be said of them, as is said of the Brahman immigrants into Bengal, that they have married local women, eaten forbidden food, adopted strange customs, and forgotten the endless details of the elaborate ritual which they set forth to teach. As priests *in partibus infidelium* they will be regarded with suspicion by the Brahmans of their original stock; they will have to pay high for brides from among their own people, and eventually will be cut off altogether from the *jus connubii*. When that stage has been reached they will have become to all intents and purposes a separate caste retaining the generic name of Brahman, but forming a new species and presenting a distinctive type. And this great change will have been brought about by the simple fact of their abandoning the habitat of their original community.

Occasionally it may happen that social promotion, rather than degradation, results from a change of residence. In Chanda, a remote district of the Central Provinces, a number of persons returned themselves as Barwaiks and the designation, being unknown in the Census office, was referred to the district officer for explanation. It was stated in reply that the Barwaiks were a clan of Rajputs from Orissa who had come to Nāgpur in the train of the Bhonsla Rajas and had taken military service under them. Now in Chutia Nāgpur the Baraiks or Chik-Baraiks are a sub-caste of the Pans—the helot weavers and basket-makers who perform a variety of servile functions for the organized Dravidian tribes and used to live in a kind of Ghetto in the villages of the Kandhs (Khonds) for whom they purveyed children destined for human sacrifice and, when they had failed to steal other people's children, sold their own for this ghastly purpose. Mr. Russell observes that "though it is possible that the coincidence may be accidental, still there seems good reason to fear that it is from these humble beginnings that the Barwaik sect of Rajputs in Chanda must trace its extraction. And it is clear that before the days of railways and the half-anna post an imposture of this sort must have been practically impossible of detection." The conjecture seems a plausible one, and the fact that Baraik is a title actually in use among the Jadubansi Rajputs may have helped the Pans to establish their fictitious rank.

(vii) Castes formed by changes of custom.

(*vii*) *Castes formed by changes of custom.*—The formation of new castes as a consequence of the neglect of established usage or the adoption of new ceremonial practices or secular occupations has been a familiar incident of the caste system from the earliest times. We are told in Manu how men of the three twice-born castes, who have not received the sacrament of initiation at the proper time, or who follow forbidden occupations, become Vrātyas or outcasts, intercourse with whom is punished with a double fine, and whose descendants are graded as distinct castes. Living as a Vrātya is a condition involving of itself exclusion from the original caste, and a Brahman who performs sacrifices for such persons has to do penance. The idea of such changes of status is inherent in the system, and illustrations of its application are plentiful. Sometimes it figures in the traditions of a caste under the form of a claim to a more distinguished origin than is admitted by current opinion. The Skanda Purana, for example, recounts an episode in Parasu Rāma's raid upon the Kshatriyas, the object of which is to show that the Kāyasths are by birth Kshatriyas of full blood, who by reason of their observing the ceremonies of the Sudras are called Vrātya or incomplete Kshatriyas. The Bābhans or Bhuinhārs of the United Provinces and

Bihar are supposed, according to some legends, to be Brahmans who lost status by taking to agriculture, and the Mongoloid Kochh of Northern Bengal describe themselves as Rājbansis, or as Vrātya or Bhanga (broken) Kshatriyas—a designation which enables them to pose as an outlying branch of that exalted community who fled to these remote districts before the wrath of Parasu Rāma, and there allowed their characteristic observances to fall into disuse. At the present day the most potent influence in bringing about elevations or depressions of social status which may result ultimately in the formation of new castes is the practice of widow marriage. With the advance of orthodox ideas that may plausibly be ascribed to the extension of railways and the diffusion of primary education it dawns upon some members of a particular caste that the custom of marrying widows is highly reprehensible, and with the assistance of their Brahmans they set to work to discourage it. The first step is to abstain from intermarriage with people who practise the forbidden thing, and thus to form a sub-caste which adopts a high-sounding name derived from some famous locality like Ajodhya or Kanauj, or describes itself as *Biyāhut* or *Behuta* 'the married ones,' by way of emphasising the orthodox character of their matrimonial arrangements. Thus the Awadhia or Ayodhya Kurmis of Bihar and the Kanaujia Kurmis of the United Provinces pride themselves on prohibiting the remarriage of widows and are endeavouring to establish a shadowy title to be recognized as some variety of Kshatriya, in pursuance of which, with singular ignorance of the humble origin of the great Marātha houses, they claim kinship with Sivaji, Sindhia and the Bhonsla family of Nāgpur. In Bihar they have succeeded in attaining a higher rank than ordinary Kurmis. Brahmans take water from their hands; the funeral ceremony is performed on the twelfth day after death, according to the custom of the higher castes; and *kachchi* food prepared by them is eaten by Kahārs, Bhāts, and other castes who would refuse to accept food of this kind from Sudras. They have abandoned domestic service, and the wealthier members of the group exchange presents with the higher castes and are invited by them to ceremonial functions. But although the Awadhias have achieved complete practical separation from the main body of Kurmis no one accepts them as Kshatriyas or Rajputs, nor are they recognized by Hindu public opinion as forming a distinct caste. In the Punjab Sir Denzil Ibbetson wrote in 1881 that the Gaurwa Rajputs of Gurgaon and Delhi, though retaining the title of Rajput in deference to the strength of caste-feeling and because the change in their customs was then too recent for the name to have fallen into disuse, yet had, for all purposes of equality, communion, or intermarriage, ceased to be Rajputs since they took to *karewa* or widow marriage. And the distinction between the Jāts and Rajputs, both sprung from a common Indo-Aryan stock, is marked by the fact that the former practise and the latter abstain from a usage which more than any other is regarded as a crucial test of relative social position. In allusion to this fact one of the rhyming proverbs of the Punjab makes a Jāt father say—'Come my daughter and be married; if this husband dies there are plenty more.' The same test applies in the Kāngra Hills, the most exclusive Hindu portion of the Punjab, where Musalman domination was never fully established, and the Brahman and Kshatriya occupy positions most nearly resembling those assigned to them by Manu. Here the line between the Thakkar and Rāthi castes, both belonging to the lower classes of Hill Rajputs, is said to consist in the fact that Rāthis do and Thakkars do not ordinarily practise widow marriage.

In Southern India movements of the same sort may be observed. Among the begging castes which form nearly one per cent of the population of the Tamil country in Madras, the Pandarams rank highest in virtue of their abstention from meat and alcohol and more especially of their prohibition of widow marriage. The Pancharamkatti division of the Idaiyan shepherd caste allow widow marriage but connect it with the peculiar neck ornament which their women wear, and say that "Krishna used to place a similar ornament round the necks of the Idaiyan widows of whom he was enamoured, to transform them from widows into married women to whom pleasure was not forbidden." The story seems to be an *ex post facto* apology for the practice. The Jatāpu again, a branch of the Kandh (Kondh) tribe which has developed into a separate caste, are beginning to discourage widow marriage by way of emphasising the distinction between themselves and their less civilised brethren. In Baroda, according to Mr. Dalāl, widow marriage is allowed by some degraded sub-castes of Brahmans, Tapodhan, Vyās Sārasvat, Rajgor, Bhojak, Tragala and Koligor, which are virtually distinct castes, and also by the Kāthis, Marāthas, Rajputs, Tāghers, and Vadhels. "The higher families, among castes allowing remarriage of widows, do not, as a rule, have recourse to it, as such a marriage is considered undignified for grown-up women.

It is this sense of honour and a desire to pass for superior people which has put a stop to widow remarriage among an influential section of the Lewa Kunbis and Sonis."

An account is given in the chapter on marriage and caste of what may be called the internal structure of tribes and caste in India—the various endogamous, exogamous, and hypergamous divisions which restrict and regulate matrimony and form the minor wheels of the vast and intricate machinery by which Hindu society is controlled. From the point of view of general ethnology considerable interest attaches to one particular kind of division, to those exogamous groups which are based upon totems. The existence

Totemism.

of totemism in India on a large scale has been brought to notice only in recent years; the enquiries instituted in connexion with the census have added materially to our knowledge of the subject; and special attention is being given to it in the ethnographic survey now being conducted in all British provinces and the more important Native States. No apology therefore is needed for mentioning it at length here, since it throws an important sidelight on the development of castes from tribes. At the bottom of the social system, as understood by the average Hindu, we find in the Dravidian region of India a large body of tribes and castes each of which is broken up into a number of totemistic septs. Each sept bears the name of an animal, a tree, a plant, or of some material object, natural or artificial, which the members of that sept are prohibited from killing, eating, cutting, burning, carrying, using, etc. Well-defined groups of this type are found among the Dravidian Santāls and Orāons, both of whom still retain their original language, worship non-Aryan gods, and have a fairly compact tribal organization. The following are specimens selected from among the seventy-three Orāon and the ninety-one Sāntal septs :—

ORAON.		SANTAL.	
Name of sept.	*Totem.*	*Name of sept.*	*Totem.*
Tirki.	Young mice.	Ergo.	Rat.
Ekka.	Tortoise.	Murmu.	Nilgāi.
Kispotta.	Pig's entrails.	Hānsdā.	Wild goose.
Lakra.	Hyena.	Mārudi.	A kind of grass.
Bāgh.	Tiger.	Besrā.	Hawk.
Kujrar.	Oil from *Kujrar* tree.	Hemron.	Betel palm.
		Saren.	The constellation Pleiades.
Gede.	Duck.		
Khoepa.	Wild dog.	Sankh.	Conch-shell.
Minji.	Eel.	Guā.	Areca nut
Chirra.	Squirrel.	Kārā.	Buffalo.

The Hos of Singhbhum and the Mundās of the Chutia Nāgpur plateau have also exogamous septs of the same type as the Orāons and Santāls, with similar rules as to the totem being taboo to the members of the group. The lists given in *The Tribes and Castes of Bengal* contain the names of 323 Mundā septs and 46 Ho septs. Six of the latter are found also among the Santāls. The other Ho septs appear to be mostly of the local or communal type, such as are in use among the Kandhs, but this is not quite certain, and the point needs looking into by some one well acquainted with the Ho dialect, who would probably find little difficulty in identifying the names, as the tribe is known to be in the habit of giving to places descriptive names having reference to their natural characteristics. Nearly all the Mundā sept names are of the totem type, and the characteristic taboos appear to be recognized. The Tarwār or Talwār sept, for example, may not touch a sword, the Udbāru may not use the oil of a particular tree, the Sindur may not use vermilion, the Baghela may not kill or eat a quail, and, strangest of all, rice is taboo to the Dhān sept, the members of which, though rice is grown all round them, must supply its place with *gondli* or millet. It is difficult not to be sceptical as to the rigid observance of this last prohibition.

In Chutia Nagpur.

A step higher in the social scale, according to Hindu estimation, the Bhumij of Mānbhum mark an early stage in the course of development by which a non-Aryan tribe transforms itself into a full-blown caste, claiming a definite rank in the Brahmanical system. With the exception of a few residents of outlying villages bordering on the Mundā country of the Chutia Nāgpur plateau, the Bhumij have lost their original language (Mundāri), and now speak only Bengali. They worship Hindu gods in addition to the fetishistic deities more or less common to them and other Dravidians, but the tendency is to keep the latter rather in the background and to relegate the less formidable among them to the women and children to be worshipped in a hole-and-corner kind of way, with the assistance of a tribal hedge-priest (*Lāyā*), who is supposed to be specially acquainted with their ways. Some of the leading men of the tribe, who call themselves Bhuinhārs, and hold large landed tenures on terms of police service, have set up as Rajputs, and keep a low class of Brahmans as their family priests. They have, as a rule, borrowed the Rajput class titles, but cannot conform with the Rajput rules of intermarriage, and marry within a narrow circle of pseudo-Rajputs like themselves.

The rest of the tribe, numbering at the last census 370,239, are divided into a number of exogamous groups, of which the following are examples. It is curious to observe in a tribe still in a state of transition, that one of the Brahmanical *gotras*, Sāndilya, has been borrowed from the higher castes, and in the process of borrowing has been transformed from a Vedic saint into a bird :—

BHUMIJ.

Name of sept	*Totem.*
Sālrisi.	*Sāl* fish.
Hānsda.	Wild goose.
Leng.	Mushroom.
Sāndilya.	A bird.
Hemron.	Betel palm.
Tumarung.	Pumpkin.
Nāg.	Snake.

At a further stage in the same process of evolution, and on a slightly superior social level, we find the Mahilis, Korās, and Kurmis, all of whom claim to be members of the Hindu community. They have totemistic exogamous sections, of which the following are fairly representative :—

MAHILI.

Name of section.	*Totem.*
Dungri.	*Dumur* fig
Turu.	*Turu* grass.
Kānti.	Ear of any animal.
Hānsda.	Wild goose.
Murmu.	Nilgāi.

KORA.

Name of section.	*Totem.*
Kasyab	Tortoise.
Saulā	*Sāl* fish.
Kāsibak.	Heron.
Hānsda.	Wild goose.
Butku.	Pig.
Sānpu.	Bull.

KURMI.

Name of section.	*Totem.*
Kesariā.	*Kesar* grass.
Tarār.	Buffalo.
Dumuriā.	*Dumur* fig.
Chonchmukruār.	Spider.
Hastowār.	Tortoise.
Jālbanuār.	Net.
Sankhowār.	Shell ornaments.
Bāghbanuār.	Tiger.
Katiār.	Silk cloth.

Of these three castes the Mahilis appear to have broken off most recently from the tribe. They still worship some of the Santāl gods in addition to the standard Hindu deities ; they will eat food cooked by a Santāl ; their caste organization is supervised, like that of the

Santāls, by an official bearing the title of Parganāit ; they permit the marriage of adults and tolerate sexual intercourse before marriage within the limits of the caste ; and they have not yet attained to the dignity of employing Brahmans for ceremonial purposes. If I may hazard a conjecture on so obscure a question, I should be inclined to class them as Santāls who took to the degraded occupation of basket-making, and thus lost the *jus connubii* within the tribe. In the case of the Korās there is no clue to warrant their affiliation to any particular tribe, but their traditions say that they came from the Chutia Nāgpur plateau, while their name suggests a Dravidian origin, and it seems possible that they may be an offshoot of the Mundās, who somehow sank from the status of independent cultivators to their present position of earth-cutting and tank-digging labourers. They allow adult marriage, their standard of feminine chastity is low, and they have not yet fitted themselves out with Brahmans. In the customary rules of inheritance which their *panchāyat* or caste council administers, it is curious to find the usage known in the Punjab as *chundavand*, by which the sons, however few, of one wife take a share equal to that of the sons, however many, of another. The Kurmis may perhaps be a Hinduised branch of the Santāls. The latter, who are more particular about food, or rather about whom they eat with, than is commonly supposed, will eat cooked rice with the Kurmis, and according to one tradition regard them as elder brothers of their own. However this may be, the totemism of the Kurmis of Western Bengal stamps them as of Dravidian descent, and clearly distinguishes them from the Kurmis of Bihar and the United Provinces. They show signs of a leaning towards orthodox Hinduism, and employ Brahmans for the worship of Hindu gods, but not in the propitiation of rural and family deities or in their marriage ceremonies.

In Orissa.

One more instance of totemism in Bengal deserves special notice here, as it shows the usage maintaining its ground among people of far higher social standing than any of the castes already mentioned. The Kumhārs of Orissa take rank immediately below the Karan or writer caste, and thus have only two or three large castes above them. They are divided into two endogamous sub-castes—Jagannāthi or Oriya Kumhārs, who work standing and make large earthen pots, and Khattya Kumhārs, who turn the wheel sitting and make small earthen pots, cups, toys, etc. The latter are immigrants from Upper India, whose number is comparatively insignificant. For matrimonial purposes the Jagannāthi Kumhārs are sub-divided into the following exogamous sections :—

JAGANNATHI KUMHAR.

Name of section.	*Totem.*
Kaundinya.	Tiger.
Sarpa.	Snake.
Neul.	Weasel.
Goru.	Cow.
Mudir.	Frog.
Bhadbhadria.	Sparrow.
Kurmā.	Tortoise.

The members of each section express their respect for the animal whose name the section bears by refraining from killing or injuring it, and by bowing when they meet it. The entire caste also abstain from eating, and even go so far as to worship the *sāl* fish, because the rings on its scales resemble the wheel which is the symbol of the potter's art. The Khattya Kumhārs have only one section (Kasyapa), and thus, like the Rājbansis of Rangpur, are really endogamous in spite of themselves. The reason, no doubt, is that there are too few of them in Orissa to fit up a proper exogamous system, and they content themselves with the pretence of one. Both sub-castes appear to be conscious that the names of their sections are open to misconception, and explain that they are really the names of certain saints who, being present at Daksha's horse sacrifice, transformed themselves into animals to escape the wrath of Siva, whom Daksha, like Peleus in the Greek myth, had neglected to invite.* It may well be that we owe the preservation of these interesting totemistic groups to the ingenuity of the person who devised this respectable means of accounting for a series of names so likely to compromise the reputation of the caste. In the case of the Khattya Kumhārs, the fact that their single section bears the name of Kasyapa, while they venerate the tortoise (*kachhap*), and tell an odd story by way of apology for the practice, may perhaps lend weight to the conjecture, in itself a fairly plausible one, that many of the lower castes in Bengal who are beginning to set up as pure Hindus have taken advantage of the resemblance in sound between *Kachhap* and *Kasyap* (*chh* and *s* both become *sh* in colloquial

* Muir, *Sanskrit Texts*, IV, p. 872

Bengali) to convert a totemistic title into an eponymous one, and have gone on to borrow such other Brahmanical *gotras* as seemed to them desirable. If, for example, we analyse the matrimonial arrangements of the Bhars of Mānbhum, many of whom are the hereditary personal servants of the pseudo-Rajput Raja of Pachete, we find the foregoing conjecture borne out by the fact that two out of the seven sections which they recognize are called after the peacock and the *bel* fruit, while the rest are eponymous. But this is an exceptionally clear case of survival, and I fear it is hardly possible to simplify the diagnosis of non-Aryan castes by laying down a general rule, that all castes with a section bearing the name Kasyapa who have not demonstrably borrowed that appellation from the Brahmans, are probably offshoots from some non-Aryan tribe.

In the Bombay Presidency the Kātkaris of the Konkan will not kill a red-faced monkey, the Vaidus, or herbalists of Poona will not kill a rabbit, and the Vadārs whose name is derived from the *Vaa* (*Ficus Indica*), will not fell the Indian fig tree. The totemistic character of the septs which regulate marriage is, however, most pronounced in the Kanara district which borders on the Dravidian tract of the South. The rice-growing caste of Halvakki Vakkal in Kanara have a number of exogamous septs or *bali* (lit. a creeper) which include the tortoise, the sambar, the monkey, the hog-deer, two sorts of fish, saffron, the acacia and several other trees, and the axe used for felling them. As we find them now, these groups are plainly totemistic. Thus the members of the screw-pine *bali* will neither cut the tree nor pluck its flowers, and those of the *Bargal bali* will not kill or eat the *barga* or mouse-deer. The followers of the *Shirin bali*, named after the *shirkal* tree (*Acacia speciosa*), will not sit in the shade of the tree, and refrain from injuring it in any way. But in Kanara, as in Orissa, there is a tendency to disguise or get rid of these compromising designations as the people who own them rise in the social scale. The Halepaik, once freebooters and now peaceful tappers of toddy trees, are divided into two endogamous groups, one dwelling on the coast and taking its name (*Tengina*) from the cocoanut tree, and the other living in the hills and calling itself *Bainu* after the sago-palm. Each of these again contains a number of exogamous *balis*. The *Tengina* have the wolf, the pig, the porcupine, the root of the pepper plant, turmeric, and the river; to which

In Bombay.

the *Bainu* add the snake, the sambar, and gold. The members o the *Nāgchampa* group will not wear the flower of that name in thei hair, nor will the *Kadave bali* kill a sāmbhar. Two of the *balis* ar called after the low castes Mahār and Hole, and it is curious to finc that the other groups, though they will take girls from these *balis*, wil not give them their own daughters to wife. Among the Halepaiks, unlike most of the Kanara castes, the *bali* descends through the female line, that is to say, the children belong to the *bali* of the mother, not of the father. Similar groups are found among the Suppalig (musicians), the Ager (salt workers and makers of palm-lea umbrellas), the Ahir (cowherds), and the Mukur (labourers and makers of shell-lime). Several of these have the elephant for a totem and may not wear ornaments of ivory.

Among the Bhils of the Sātpura hills, who may be taken to represent the furthest extension westward of the Dravidian type, Major Luard has discovered forty-one septs, all of which are exogamous. Where two distinct septs have the same totem intermarriage is prohibited. All the septs revere and refrain from injuring or using their totems, and make a formal obeisance when meeting or passing them, while the women veil their faces. Among the totems are moths (*ava*), snakes, tigers, bamboos, *pipal* and other trees, and a kind of creeper called *gaola* on which the members may not tread, and if they do so accidentally must apologise by making a *salaam*. The *Maoli* sept have as their totem a sort of basket (*kiliya*) for carrying grain which they are forbidden to use. The basket resembles in shape the shrine of the goddess of a certain hill where women may not worship. The *Mori* or peacock sept may not knowingly tread on the tracks of a peacock, and if a woman sees a peacock she must veil her face or look away. The cult of the totem consists in seeking for the footprint of a peacock in the jungle and

In Central India.

making a *salaam* to it. The ground is then made smooth round the footprint, a *svastika* is inscribed in the dust, and offerings of grain are deposited on a piece of red cloth. The *Sanyar* sept worship the cat, but consider it unlucky for their totem to enter their houses and usually keep a dog tied up at the door to frighten it away. The Khangar caste of Bundelkhand, which is cited by Major Luard as an illustration of the conversion of a tribe into a caste, have among their totems horses, iguanas, snakes, cows, elephants, alligators, rice, turmeric, various trees and shrubs, and bricks. The members of the *Ent* or brick sept may not use bricks in their houses and their domestic architecture is restricted to wattle and mud. The report on the census of Central India also contains a curious instance of the apparent degradation of a caste into a tribe accompanied by the adoption of totems. The Sondhiās or Sundhiās of Malwa are said to be descended from the survivors of a Rajput army who were defeated by Shah Jahan and were ashamed to return to their homes. They therefore stayed in Malwa, married Sondhiā women, borrowed some of the Sondhiā totems and the Sondhiā gods, and in course of time allowed widows to marry again. Ten of the twenty-four septs into which the tribe is divided still cherish traditions of their Rajput origin and, while taking wives from the other septs, refuse to give their daughters in return.

In the Central Provinces.

For the Central Provinces Mr. Russell gives a long list of totems found among sixteen castes and tribes, including not only the primitive Gonds, Korkus, and Orāons, and the leather-working Chamārs, but also the pastoral Ahirs, the respectable carpenter caste (Barhai) and the Dhimars, from all of whom Brahmans can take water, while the last named are commonly employed by them as personal servants. The list comprises elephants, lions, tigers, bears, wolves, jackals, buffaloes, goats, monkeys, peacocks, parrots, crocodiles, lizards, tortoises, porcupines, scorpions, snakes, also salt, rice, Indian corn, pumpkins, mangoes, cucumbers, lotus leaves, vermilion and a variety of trees. All of these are regarded with reverence, and members of the sept abstain from killing, using or naming them.

In Madras.

In Madras the Boya *shikāri* tribe of the Deccan is divided into 101 totemistic septs, among them *chimalu*, ants; *eddulu*, bulls; *jenneru*, sweet-scented oleander; *jerrabutula*, centipedes; *yenumalu*, buffaloes; and *kusa*, grass. The Jatapu, the civilised division of the Kandhs or Khonds, have among their totems *koaloka*, arrows; *kondacorri*, hill sheep; *kutraki*, wild goats; and *vinka*, white ants. The large agricultural caste of Kapu, numbering nearly three millions, have among their exogamous sections the cock (*kodi*), the sheep (*mekala*), and a shrub known as *tangedu* (*Cassia auriculata*). Of the 102 sections of the trading Komatis six are totemistic, the totems including the tamarind, the *tulsi* (*Ocymum Sanctum*), and the betel vine. The weaving Kurnis count among their totems saffron, gold, cummin, gram, pepper, buffaloes, and certain trees.

In Assam the Gāros have monkeys, horses, bears, mice, lizards, frogs, crows, pumpkins, and a number of trees among their totems; the Kachāris recognize as totems the tree snail, the *muga* insect, the sesamum plant, the *kumra* or giant gourd, and the tiger. Members of the tiger sept have to throw away their earthenware utensils by way of atonement when a tiger is killed. The louse and the buffalo are the only animal totems on record among the Khāsi; the Kuki have the dog; the Lalung eggs, fish, and pumpkins; the Mikir totems appear to be mainly vegetable. Our information, however, on totemism in Assam is extremely scanty, and the subject requires further investigation.

In Assam.

For Burma the facts, so far as they go, are thus stated by Mr. Lowis :—

"The question of endogamy naturally leads to that of totemism. Sir George Scott says in the *Upper Burma Gazetteer*: 'All the Indo-Chinese races have a predilection for totemistic birth stories. Some claim to be sprung from eggs, some from dogs, some from reptiles.' The Wās, like a tribe in North-West America cited by Mr. Andrew Lang in his *Custom and Myth*, state that their primæval ancestors were tadpoles. The Palaungs trace their beginnings back to a Nāga princess who laid three eggs, out of the first of which their early ancestor was hatched. An egg-laying Nāga princess figures in the early legendary history of the Mons or Talaings and points to an affinity between the Palaungs and the Talaings which the most recent linguistic research has done much to strengthen. Up to the present time all attempts to ascertain the original of the Kachin family names have failed. The totem of the Kachins should, if anything, be a pumpkin, for legend has it that the whole race is descended from a being who was made out of a pumpkin. So far as I can discover, however, their belief in this singular genesis does not deter Kachins from eating the vegetable to which they owe their origin. They do not even appear to be precluded from gathering it under certain circumstances or at a particular period of the year, as is the case with some of the Western Australian tribes." The Southern Chins, on the other hand, are forbidden to kill or eat the King-Crow which hatched "the original Chin egg." The bird is regarded in the light of a parent, but, as it is not used as a crest by the Chins, Mr. Houghton is of opinion that it cannot be looked upon as, properly speaking, a totem. The rising sun

In Burma.

of the Red Karens is something of the nature of a totemistic badge. Mr. Smeaton refers to it as follows in his *Loyal Karens of Burma* :—

'Every Red Karen has a rising sun—the crest of his nobility—tattooed on his back. In challenging to combat he does not slap his left folded arm with his right palm, as the rest of the Karens and the Burmans do, but, coiling his right arm round his left side, strikes the tattoo on his back. This action is supposed by him to rouse the magic power of the symbol.'

Sir George Scott, however, seems to detect no totemistic inwardness in this tattoo mark, for he sums up the matter under consideration in the following words :—

'Totemism also shows itself in the prescribed form of names for Shān and Kachin children and in the changing or concealing of personal names, but, so far as is yet known, there is no tribe which habitually takes its family name or has crests and badges taken from some natural object, plant or animal, though the limiting of marriages between the inhabitants of certain villages only practised both by tribes of Karens and Kachins is no doubt the outgrowth of this totem idea.'

Enough has been said to show that totemistic exogamy prevails in India on a fairly large scale, that it is still in active operation, and that it presents features which deserve further investigation in their bearing on the problems of general ethnology. On these grounds I venture to add a few comments on the striking explanation of the origin of totemism which was put forward by Mr. J. G. Frazer in the *Fortnightly Review* in 1899.* The subject is one of special interest in India because the Indian evidence seems not only to point to conclusions different from those arrived at by Mr. Frazer on the basis of the Australian data published by Messrs. Spencer and Gillen,† but to suggest a new canon for determining the historical value of ethnographic evidence in general.

Mr. Frazer's theory of totemism.

"A totem," says Mr. Frazer, "is a class of natural phenomena or material object—most commonly a species of animals or plants—between which and himself the savage believes that a certain intimate relation exists. The exact nature of the relation is not easy to ascertain; various explanations of it have been suggested, but none has as yet won general acceptance. Whatever it may be, it generally leads the savage to abstain from killing or eating his totem, if his totem happens to be a species of animals or plants. Further, the group of persons who are knit to any particular totem by this mysterious

---

* *Fortnightly Review*, N. S., LXV, pp. 647-665, 835-852.

† Spencer and Gillen, *Native Tribes of Central Australia.*

tie commonly bear the name of the totem, believe themselves to be of one blood, and strictly refuse to sanction the marriage or cohabitation of members of the group with each other. This prohibition to marry within the group is now generally called by the name of exogamy. Thus totemism has commonly been treated as a primitive system both of religion and of society. As a system of religion it embraces the mystic union of the savage with his totem ; as a system of society it comprises the relations in which men and women of the same totem stand to each other and to the members of other totemic groups. And corresponding to these two sides of the system are two rough and ready tests or canons of totemism : first, the rule that a man may not kill or eat his totem animal or plant ; and second, the rule that he may not marry or cohabit with a woman of the same totem. Whether the two sides—the religious and social—have always co-existed or are essentially independent, is a question which has been variously answered. Some writers—for example, Sir John Lubbock and Mr. Herbert Spencer—have held that totemism began as a system of society only, and that the superstitious regard for the totem developed later, through a simple process of misunderstanding. Others, including J. F. McLennan and Robertson Smith, were of opinion that the religious reverence for the totem is original, and must, at least, have preceded the introduction of exogamy."

The system of totems prevailing in Central Australia is so far parallel to that known in India that it includes, not only animals and plants, but also a number of objects, animate and inanimate. Thus while the Australians have "totems of the wind, the sun, the evening star, fire, water, cloud, and so on," we find among our Dravidians in India the month of June, Wednesday in every week, the moon, the rainbow, and the constellation Pleiades figuring as totems among a number of names which include pretty well the entire flora and fauna of the country where the tribe is settled. But while among the Australians the religious aspect of the totem is relatively more prominent than the social, in India the position is reversed ; the social side of the system is very much alive while the religious side has fallen into disuse. It is the religious side on which Mr. Frazer lays stress, and he explains totemism as "primarily an organized and co-operative system of magic designed to secure for the members of the community, on the one hand, a plentiful supply of all the commodities of which they stand in need, and, on the other hand, immunity from all the perils and dangers to which man is exposed in his struggle with nature." In other words, totemism is a primitive Commissariat and General Providence Department which at a later stage took over the business of regulating marriage. The evidence for this proposition is derived from the magical ceremonies called *intichiuma* in which the members of each totem solemnly mimic the animals and plants after which they are called, and eat a small portion of them with the object of ensuring a plentiful supply of the species. Thus the men of the totem called after the Witchetty grub, a succulent caterpillar of some kind which is esteemed a great luxury, paint their bodies in imitation of the grub, crawl through a structure of boughs supposed to represent its chrysalis, chant a song inviting the insect to go and lay eggs, and butt each other in the stomach with the remark "You have eaten much food." The Emu men dress themselves up to resemble Emus and imitate the movements and aimless gazing about of the birds; the Kangaroo men and the men of the Nakea flower totem go through similar mummeries. An admirable collection of the totemistic symbols of the Aranta, together with photographs of the ritual observed in the invocation of the totems themselves, may be seen in the Ethnological department of the Museum at Melbourne.

Now in the first place the doubt occurs to one whether small and moribund tribes, such as the Australians, can fairly be taken to be typical of primitive man. If they could, then man would be primitive still, and we should none of us have got to the point of vexing our souls about the origin of anything. The one distinctive feature of the Australian natives is their incapacity for any sort of progressive evolution. Surely an atrophied or, it may be, degenerate man of that type is not the sort of ancestor we want to discover; for it is difficult to see what we can learn from him. In Europe, on the other hand, primitive man, so far as we can judge from the traces he has left behind, seems to have been an animal of an entirely different type. He had, indeed, his weaknesses—does not his *vates sacer*, Mr. Andrew Lang, impute to him a diet of oysters and foes—but he fought a good fight with his environment and, as events show, he came out a winner. It seems then that the quest of primitive man ready made and only waiting to be observed and analysed may be nothing better than a tempting short-cut leading to delusion, and that what we must look to is not so much primitive man as primitive usage regarded in its bearing on evolution.

It is from this point of view that I wish to put in a plea for the consideration of the Indian data. Primitive usages may, I would suggest, be divided, as Mr. Bagehot divided political institutions, into the effective and the ineffective, in other words, into those which affect evolution and those which do not. In the case of totemism we can distinguish these two pretty clearly. The magical ritual of the Arunta tribe obviously belongs to the ineffective class. No one outside the Arunta—and even among them one would think there must be augurs—supposes that by performing the most elaborate parody of the demeanour of certain animals a man can really cause them to increase and multiply. In India, on the other hand, our totemistic people have got rid of all such antics, if, indeed, they ever practised them, and retain only the unquestionably effective factor in the system, the rule that a man may not marry a woman of his own totem. They have, it is true, also the rule that people may not eat, injure or make use of their totems, but this prohibition is relatively weak, and in some cases the totems are articles such as rice and salt, which the members of the totem-kin could hardly do without.

Totemism and Exogamy.

Given then a state of things such as this, that tribes which are in no way moribund or degenerate, but on the contrary extremely full of life, retain the effective part of an archaic usage along with traces of its ineffective parts, may we not reasonably conclude that this effective part, which has stood the wear and tear of ages and contributed to the evolution of the tribe, furnishes the clue to the real origin of the usage itself? Assume this to be so and totemism at once wheels into line and takes the place, which it appears clearly to occupy in India, of a form of exogamy. The particular form presents no great difficulty. Primitive men are like children: they are constantly saying to themselves "Let's pretend," and a favourite and wide-spread form of the game is to pretend to be animals. Only they play it in earnest, and very grim earnest it sometimes is, as any one will discover who has to administer a district where people believe that men can transform themselves into animals at will, or can be so transformed by the agency of witchcraft.

It will be asked, what then is the origin of exogamy? Here again I think the Indian evidence suggests an answer. Just as the special phenomenon of totemism may be explained by reference to the general law of exogamy, so exogamy itself may be traced to the still more general law of natural selection. Nor need we strain the law. We know that there is a tendency in individuals or groups of individuals to vary their habits; and that useful variations tend to be preserved and ultimately transmitted. Now suppose that in a primitive community, such as the Nāga *khel* or the Kandh *gochi*, the men happened to vary in the direction of taking their wives from some other community and that this infusion of fresh blood proved advantageous to the group. The original instinct would then be stimulated by heredity, and the element of sexual selection would, in course of time, come into play. For an exogamous group would have a larger choice of women than an endogamous one, and would thus get finer women, who again, in the course of the primitive struggle for wives, would be appropriated by the strongest and most warlike men. The exogamous groups so strengthened would tend, as time went on, to 'eat up,' in the expressive Zulu phrase, their endogamous neighbours, or at any rate to deprive them of the pick of their marriageable girls; and the custom of exogamy would spread, partly by imitation, and partly by the extinction of the groups which did not practise it.

The fact that we cannot say how people came to vary in this particular fashion is not necessarily fatal to the hypothesis put forward. In the case of animals other than man we do not call in question the doctrine of natural selection because we cannot trace the precise cause which gave rise to some beneficial variation. It is enough that variations do occur, and that the beneficial ones tend to be transmitted. If, however, an attempt must be made to pierce the veil which shuts off from our view the ages of pre-historic evolution, it does not seem unreasonable to suppose that here and there some half-accidental circumstance, such as the transmission of a physical defect or an hereditary disease, may have given primitive man a sort of warning, and thus have induced the particular kind of variation which his circumstances required. Conquest again may have produced the same effect by bringing about a beneficial mixture of stocks, though it is a little difficult to see, as Mr. Lang pointed out long ago, why the possession of foreign women should have disinclined people to marry the women of their own group. At the same time it is conceivable that the impulse may have been set going by some tribe from which all its marriageable women had been raided and which was thus driven by necessity to start raiding on its own account. I have elsewhere given instances, drawn from the Kandhs and Nāgas, which lend themselves to this view; but I am not sure that we need travel beyond the tendency to accidental variation which appears in all living organisms and may be assumed to have shaped the development of primitive man.

In a country where the accident of birth determines irrevocably the whole course of a man's social and domestic relations, and he must throughout life eat, drink, dress, marry, and give in marriage in accordance with the usages of the community into which he was born, one is tempted at first sight to assume that the one thing that he may be expected to know with certainty, and to disclose without much reluctance, is the name of the caste, tribe, or race to which he belongs. As a matter of fact no column in the Census schedule displays a more bewildering variety of entries, or gives so much trouble to the enumerating and testing staff and to the central offices which compile the results. If the person enumerated gives the name of a well-known tribe, such as Bhil or Santāl, or of a standard caste like Brahman or Kāyasth, all is well. But he may belong to an obscure caste from the other end of India; he may give the name of a religious sect, of a sub-caste, of an exogamous sept or section, of a hypergamous group; he may mention some titular designation which sounds finer than the name of his caste; he may describe himself by his occupation or by the province or tract of country from which he comes. These various alternatives, which are far from exhausting the possibilities of the situation, undergo a series of transformations at the hands of the more or less illiterate enumerator who writes them down in his own vernacular, and of the abstractor in the central office who transliterates them into English. Then begins a laborious and most difficult process of sorting, referencing, cross-referencing, and corresponding with local authorities, which ultimately results in the compilation of a table showing the distribution of the inhabitants of India by Caste, Tribe, Race, or Nationality. The arrangement of this table is alphabetical and it consists of two parts. The first is a general list of all the groups returned, with their distribution by religion; while the second shows the distribution by provinces and states of all groups with an aggregate strength of 10,000. An analysis of the table shows that it includes 2,378 main castes and tribes and 43 races or nationalities. With the latter we are not concerned here; as to the former, the question at once arises—on what principle should they be arranged? An alphabetical system is useful for reference, and essential for the purely statistical purposes of a census table. But it does not help us in the least towards

Classification of castes.

presenting an intelligible picture of the social grouping of that large proportion of the people of India which is organized, admittedly or tacitly, on the basis of caste. In this matter a new departure was taken at the last Census. The classification followed in 1891 was then described as "based on considerations partly ethnological, partly historical, and partly, again, functional. The second predominate, for instance, in the first caste group, and the last throughout the middle of the return; but wherever practicable, as it is in the latter portion of the scheme, ethnological distinctions have been maintained. Then, again, it must be mentioned that the functional grouping is based less on the occupation that prevails in each case in the present day than on that which is traditional with it, or which gave rise to its differentiation from the rest of the community." The main heads of the scheme embodying the application of these principles are given at page 188 of the Report on the Census of India for 1891, and its detailed application is shown in Imperial Table XVII.

Judged by its results this scheme is open to criticism in several respects. It accords neither with native tradition and practice, nor with any theory of caste that has ever been propounded by students of the subject. In different parts it proceeds on different principles, with the result that on the one hand it separates groups which are really allied, and on the other includes in the same category groups of widely different origin and status. It is in fact a patch-work classification in which occupation predominates, varied here and there by considerations of caste, history, tradition, ethnical affinity, and geographical position. Illustrations of these defects might be multiplied almost indefinitely, but it is sufficient to mention that the Dravidian Khandāits of Orissa are classed with Rajputs and Bābhans, Jāts, Marāthas, and Nāyars; that Brahman priests, Mirāsi musicians, and Bahurupia buffoons fall within the same general category; that the Mongoloid Koch, Kachāri, Thāru, and Mech are widely separated; and that more than half of the Musalmans, including the converted aborigines of Eastern Bengal and Assam, are shown as "Musalman Foreign Races," the rest being merged among a number of occupational groups purporting to be endogamous.

In organizing the Census of 1901 I suggested to my colleagues that an attempt should be made to arrange the various groups that had to be dealt with on some system which would command general acceptance, at any rate within the limits of the province to which it was applied. I did not expect that the same system would suit all provinces or even all divisions of the same province; and I was quite prepared to find the preparation of a combined table for the whole of India a task of insuperable difficulty. But I was confident that the provincial results would throw light upon a variety of social movements which at present escape notice; that they would add greatly to the interest of the reports; and that they would provide a sound statistical groundwork for the ethnographic survey of India which is now in progress.

Method adopted in Census of 1901.

The principle suggested as a basis was that of classification by social precedence as recognized by native public opinion at the present day, and manifesting itself in the facts that particular castes are supposed to be the modern representatives of one or other of the castes of the theoretical Hindu system; that Brahmans will take water from certain castes; that Brahmans of high standing will serve particular castes; that certain castes, though not served by the best Brahmans, have nevertheless got Brahmans of their own, whose rank varies according to circumstances; that certain castes are not served by Brahmans at all, but have priests of their own; that the status of certain castes has been raised by their taking to infant-marriage or abandoning the remarriage of widows; that the status of some castes has been lowered by their living in a particular locality; that the status of others has been modified by their pursuing some occupation in a special or peculiar way; that some can claim the services of the village barber, the village palanquin-bearer, the village midwife, etc., while others cannot; that some castes may not enter the courtyards of certain temples; that some castes are subject to special taboos, such as that they must not use the village well, or may draw water only with their own vessels, that they must live outside the village or in a separate quarter, that they must leave the road on the approach of a high-caste man, or must call out to give warning of their approach. In the case of the Animistic tribes it was mentioned that the prevalence of totemism and the degree of adoption of Hindu usage would serve as ready tests. All Superintendents, except three who were either defeated by the complexity of the facts or were afraid of hurting people's feelings, readily grasped the main idea of the scheme, and their patient industry, supplemented by the intelligent assistance readily given by the highest native authorities, has added very greatly to our knowledge of an obscure and intricate subject.

The best evidence of the general success of the experiment, and incidentally of the remarkable vitality of caste at the present day, is to be found in the great number of petitions and memorials to which it gave rise, the bulk of which were submitted in English and emanated from the educated classes who are sometimes alleged to be anxious to free themselves from the trammels of the caste system. If the principle on which the classification was based had not appealed to the usages and traditions of the great mass of Hindus, it is inconceivable that so many people should have taken much trouble and incurred substantial expenditure with the object of securing its application in a particular way. Of these memorials the most elaborate was that received from the Khatris of the Punjab and the United Provinces, who felt themselves aggrieved by the Superintendent of Census in the latter Province having provisionally classified them as Vaisyas, whereas in the specimen table circulated by me they had been placed in the same group as the Rajputs. A meeting of protest was held at Bareilly, and a great array of authorities was marshalled to prove that the Khatris are lineally descended from the Kshatriyas of Hindu mythology, much as if the modern Greeks were to claim direct descent from Achilles and were to cite the Catalogue of the Ships in the second book of the Iliad in support of their pretensions. In passing orders on their memorial I pointed out that they were

Its practical working.

mistaken in supposing that this was the first census in which any attempt had been made to classify castes on a definite principle, or that the selection of social precedence as a basis was an entirely new departure. As a matter of fact the scheme of classification adopted in 1891 purported to arrange the groups more or less in accordance with the position generally assigned to each in the social scale, as had been suggested by Sir Denzil Ibbetson in his Report on the Punjab Census of 1881. The result, in the case of the Khatris, was to include them as number 13 in "Group XV—Traders" immediately after the Aroras of the Punjab, ten places lower than the Agarwāls, and several places below the Kāndus and Kasarwānis of the United Provinces and the Subarnabaniks of Bengal. The Rajputs, on the other hand, ranked first in the entire scheme as number I of "Group I—Military and Dominant." In the Bengal Census Report of 1891 the Rajputs were placed among "the patrician class," while the Khatris were grouped with the Baniyas between the Baidyas and Kāyasthas in a group described as "the Vaisyas Proper or Plebeian

Middle Class." It was obviously improbable that the Khatris desired this classification to be maintained, and the evidence laid before me not only brought out the conspicuous part played by them in the authentic history of the Punjab in modern times, but seemed to make it clear that in British India at any rate they are generally believed to be the modern representatives of the Kshatriyas of Hindu tradition. For census purposes the fact that most people do hold this belief was sufficient in itself, and it would have been irrelevant to enquire into the grounds upon which the opinion was based. Superintendents of census were accordingly instructed to include the Khatris under the heading Kshatriya in their classification of castes. The decision gave general satisfaction and served to illustrate the practical working of the principle that the sole test of social precedence prescribed was Indian public opinion, and that this test was to be applied with due consideration for the susceptibilities of the persons concerned. The other memorials were disposed of by the Provincial Superintendents on similar lines.

As no stereotyped scheme of classification was drawn up, but every Province was left to adopt its own system in consultation with its own experts and representative men, it was clearly impossible to draw up any general scheme for the whole of India. One might as well have tried to construct a table of social precedence for Europe, which should bring together on the same list Spanish grandees, Swiss hotel-keepers, Turkish Pashas, and Stock Exchange millionaires, and should indicate the precise degree of relative distinction attaching to each. The problem, in fact, is essentially a local one. Every man has honour in his own country, and India is no more one country than Europe—indeed very much less. The Provincial schemes of classification are summarised in Appendix II. Although they cannot be reduced to common terms, they exhibit points of resemblance and difference which deserve some further examination. The first thing to observe is the predominance throughout India of the influence of the traditional system of four original castes. In every scheme of grouping the Brahman heads the list. Then come the castes whom popular opinion accepts as the modern representatives of the Kshatriyas, and these are followed by the mercantile groups, supposed to be akin to the Vaisyas. When we leave the higher circles of the twice-born, the difficulty of finding a uniform basis of classification becomes apparent. The ancient designation Sudra finds no great favour in

Its general results.

modern times, and we can point to no group that is generally recognized as representing it. The term is used in Bombay, Madras, and Bengal to denote a considerable number of castes of moderate respectability, the higher of whom are considered 'clean' Sudras, while the precise status of the lower is a question which lends itself to endless controversy. At this stage of the grouping a sharp distinction may be noticed between Upper India and Bombay and Madras. In Rajputana, the Punjab, the United Provinces, the Central Provinces, Bengal, and Assam the grade next below twice-born rank is occupied by a number of castes from whose hands Brahmans and members of the higher castes will take water and certain kinds of sweetmeats. Below these again is a rather indeterminate group from whom water is taken by some of the higher castes but not by others. Further down, where the test of water no longer applies, the status of a caste depends on the nature of its occupation and its habits in respect of diet. There are castes whose touch defiles the twice-born, but who refrain from the crowning enormity of eating beef; while below these again, in the social system of Upper India, are people like Chamārs and Doms who eat beef and various sorts of miscellaneous vermin. In Western and Southern India the idea that the social status of a caste depends on whether Brahmans will take water and sweetmeats from its members is unknown, for the higher castes will, as a rule, take water only from persons of their own caste and sub-caste. In Madras especially the idea of ceremonial pollution by the proximity of a member of an unclean caste has been developed with much elaboration. Thus the table of social precedence attached to the Cochin report shows that while a Nāyar can pollute a man of a higher caste only by touching him, people of the Kammālan group, including masons, blacksmiths, carpenters, and workers in leather, pollute at a distance of twenty-four feet, toddy-drawers (Iluvan or Tiyan) at thirty-six feet, Pulāyan or Cheruman cultivators at forty-eight feet, while in the case of the Paraiyan (Pariahs) who eat beef, the range of pollution is stated to be no less than sixty-four feet. Where these fantastic notions prevail and the authority of the Brahman is unquestioned, it follows as a necessary consequence that the unhappy people who diffuse an atmosphere of impurity wherever they go are forbidden to enter the high caste quarter of the village, and are compelled either to leave the road when they see a Brahman coming or to announce their own approach by a special cry like the lepers of

Europe in the Middle Ages. Such is the logic of intolerance in parts of Southern India.

The subject of classification is examined fully in some of the Provincial Census Reports, to which the reader is referred for further particulars. No attempt was made to grade every caste. Large classes were formed, and the various groups included in these were arranged in alphabetical order, so as to escape the necessity of settling the more delicate questions of precedence. As an illustration of the method of procedure I may refer to the table of precedence for Bengal Proper, which was compiled by me some years ago and has been adopted by Mr. Gait for the purpose of the Bengal Census Report after careful examination by local committees of Indian gentlemen appointed for the purpose.

The entire Hindu population of this tract, numbering twenty millions, has been divided into seven classes. The first class is reserved for the Brahmans, of whom there are more than a million, forming six per cent of the Hindus of Bengal. As everyone knows, there are Brahmans and Brahmans, of status varying from the Rārhi, who claim to have been imported by Adisura from Kanauj, to the Barna Brahmans who serve the lower castes and from whose hands pure Brahmans will not take water. No attempt has been made to deal with these multifarious distinctions in the table. It would be a thankless task to try to determine the precise degree of

Social precedence of Hindus in Bengal.

social merit or demerit that attaches to the Pirāli Brahmans, who are supposed to have been forced, some four centuries ago, to smell or, as some say, to eat the beefsteaks that had been cooked for the renegade Brahman Pir Ali, the dewān of the Muhammadan ruler of Jessore; to the Vyasokta Brahmans who serve the Chāsi Kaibartta caste and rank so low that even their own clients will not touch food in their houses; to the Agradāni who preside at funeral ceremonies and take the offerings of the dead; to the Achārji fortune-teller, palmist, and maker of horoscopes; and to the Bhāt Brahman, a tawdry parody of the bard and genealogist of heroic times, whose rapacity and shamelessness are proverbial.

Next in order, at the top of the second class, come the Rajputs, who disown any connexion with Bengal, and base their claims to precedence on their supposed descent from the pure Rajputs of the distant Indo-Aryan tract. Their number (113,405) must include a large number of families belonging to local castes who acquired land

and assumed the title of Rajput on the strength of their territorial position. Then follow the Baidyas, by tradition physicians, and the writer caste of Kāyasth. The former pose as the modern representatives of the *Ambastha* of Manu and assert their superiority to the Kāyasthas on the ground that the latter have been pronounced by the High Court of Calcutta to be Sudras, a Kāyasth judge concurring, and that their funeral usages confirm this finding; that the Sanskrit College, when first opened, admitted only Brahmans and Baidyas as students; that the Kāyasths were originally the domestic servants of the two higher castes, and when poor take service still; and that native social usage concedes higher rank to the Baidyas at certain ceremonies to which members of the respectable castes are invited. The Kāyasths, on the other hand, claim to be Kshatriyas, who took to clerical work; deny the identity of the Baidyas with the Ambasthas; and describe them as a local caste, unknown in the great centres of Hinduism, who were Sudras till about a century ago, when they took to wearing the sacred thread, and bribed the Brahmans to acquiesce in their pretensions. The alphabetical arrangement observed in the table leaves the question an open one.

The third class, numbering three millions, comprises the functional castes originally known as Navasākha, the nine 'branches' or 'arrows,' and other clean Sudras, from whose hands the higher castes take water, and who are served by high-class Brahmans. Confectioners, perfume vendors, betel growers, pressers and sellers of oil, gardeners, potters, and barbers figure in this group, the constitution of which appears to have been largely determined by considerations of practical convenience. The preparation of a Hindu meal is a very elaborate performance, involving lengthy ablutions and a variety of ritualistic observances which cannot be performed on a journey, and it is essential to the comfort of the orthodox traveller that he should be able to procure sweetmeats of various kinds without being troubled by misgivings as to the ceremonial cleanliness of the people from whom he buys them. In matters of food and drink caste rules are wisely elastic. It has, I believe, been held that neither ice nor soda-water count as water for the purpose of conveying pollution; there are special exemptions in favour of biscuits and patent medicines, for the last of which the Bengali has an insatiable appetite; and in an outlying district where the only palanquin-bearers available were Dravidian Bhuiyas, I have known them to be given brevet rank as a water-giving (*jalācharaniya*) caste in order that the twice-born traveller might be able to get a drink without quitting his palanquin.

The fourth class includes only two castes—the Chāsi Kaibartta and the Goāla—from whom water is taken by the high castes, but whose Brahmans are held to be degraded. About the former group I wrote in 1891 : "It seems likely, as time goes on, that this sub-caste will rise in social estimation, and will altogether sink the Kaibartta, so that eventually it is possible that they may succeed in securing a place with the Navasākha." The forecast has to this extent been fulfilled that at the recent Census the Chāsi Kaibartta called themselves Māhisya, the name of the offspring of a legendary cross between Kshatriyas and Vaisya, and posed as a separate caste. In Nadia, according to Mr. Gait, "the new idea gained such ground that many Chāsi Kaibarttas in domestic service under other castes threw up their work, saying it was beneath their dignity. Finding, however, that no other means of livelihood were available they were soon fain to return and beg their employers' forgiveness." The higher castes, moreover, expressed their disapproval of a movement which upset their domestic arrangements by a concerted refusal to take water from the hands of a Chāsi. Notwithstanding these discouragements I have little doubt that by the next Census the Māhisya will have succeeded in establishing their claim. Their case is of interest for the light that it throws on the evolution of a caste.

The fifth class contains a rather miscellaneous assortment of castes, including the Baishtam, the Sunri, and the Subarnabanik, from whom the higher castes do not usually take water. Their precedence is also defined by the fact that although the village barber will shave them he will not cut their toe-nails nor will he take part in their marriage ceremonies. Here again quaint problems of status arise. The Baishtams are a group formed by the conversion to Vaishnavism of members of many different castes, who have embraced the tenets of different Vaishnava sects. In theory inter-marriage between these sects is prohibited, but if a man of one sect wishes to marry a woman of another, he has only to convert her by a simple ritual to his own sect, and the obstacles to their union are removed. The social standing of the caste is necessarily low, as it is recruited from among all classes of society, and large numbers of prostitutes and people who have got into trouble in consequence of sexual irregularities are found among its ranks. Within the caste, however, many of them retain their old social distinctions, and a Baishtam of Kāyasth origin would not ordinarily take water from the hands of one whose ancestors were Chandāls. Outsiders also recognize these differences and take water from Baishtams who are known to have belonged to one of the clean castes. Where the origin of a Baishtam is unknown, water which he has touched can only be used for washing.

The Subarnabaniks are a mercantile caste peculiar to Bengal Proper, who claim to be the modern representatives of the ancient Vaisya. In spite of their wealth and influence, their high-bred appearance, and the notorious beauty of the women of the caste, their claim to this distinguished ancestry has failed to obtain general recognition. They are excluded from the ranks of the Navasākha, or nine clean Sudra castes, and none but Vaidik Brahmans will take water from their hands. To account for the comparatively low status assigned to them, the Subarnabaniks cite a variety of traditions, some of which, however unsupported by historical evidence, deserve to be briefly mentioned here as illustrations of the kind of stories which tend to grow up wherever the business talents and practical ability of a particular community have advanced it in the eyes of the world conspicuously beyond its rank in the theoretical order of castes. These people, for example, say that their ancestors came to Bengal from Oudh during the reign of Adisura, who was struck by their financial ability and conferred on them the title of Subarnabanik, or trader in gold, as a mark of his favour. They then wore the Brahmanical thread, studied the Vedas and were generally recognized as Vaisyas of high rank. The stories of their degradation all centre round the name of Ballāl Sen, who was Raja of Eastern Bengal in 1070 A.D. His intrigue with a beautiful Pātni girl is said to have been ridiculed on the stage by some young Subarnabaniks, while the entire body refused to be present at the penance whereby the king affected to purify himself from the sin of intercourse with a maiden of low caste. Another cause of offence is said to have been the refusal of a leading Subarnabanik to lend Ballāl large sums of money to carry on a war with Manipur. Authorities differ concerning the method by which the Raja obtained his revenge. Some say that in the course of the penance already referred to, a number of small golden calves had been distributed to the attendant Brahmans. One of these Brahmans was suborned by Ballāl Sen to fill the hollow inside of a calf with lac-dye, and to take the figure to a Subarnabanik for sale. In testing the gold the Subarnabanik let out the lac-dye, which was at once pronounced to be blood. Having thus fastened upon the caste the inexpiable guilt of killing a cow, Ballāl Sen publicly declared them and their Brahmans to be degraded, deprived them of the right to wear the sacred thread, and threatened with similar degradation any one who should eat or associate with them.

In default of independent testimony to the accuracy of this tradition we can hardly accept it as a narrative of historical events. It is no doubt conceivable that a despotic monarch might order the social degradation of a particular class of his subjects provided that it were not too numerous or too influential; and it is generally believed that Ballāl Sen did effect some changes of this kind in the relative status of certain families of Brahmans. Notwithstanding this, the story of the depression of an entire caste from a very high to a comparatively low rank in the social system makes a large demand on our belief, and inclines one to suspect that it may have been evolved in recent times to account for the position actually occupied by the caste being lower than that to which their riches and ability would entitle them to lay claim. From this point of view, the conjecture that the Subarnabaniks are Hindustani Baniyas, who lost status by residing in Bengal and marrying Bengali women, seems to deserve some consideration.

The sixth class includes a long list of castes, numbering nearly eight millions, who abstain from eating beef, pork, and fowls, but from whom the higher castes will not take water. They are served by degraded Brahmans; the regular barbers refuse to shave them; and some of them have special barbers of their own. Most of them, however, can get their clothes washed by the village washerman. The typical members of the group are the Bāgdi (1,032,004), Dravidian cultivators and labourers, the Jeliya or fishing Kaibartta (447,237), the Namasudra or Chandāl (1,860,914), the Pod (464,921), fishermen and cultivators, and the Rājbansi-Koch (2,065,982), nearly all of whom are small cultivators.

The seventh class represents the lowest grade of the Bengal system, castes who eat all manner of unclean food, whose touch pollutes, whom no Brahman, however degraded, will serve, and for whom neither barber nor washerman will work. It comprises the scavenging Doms and Hāris, the leather-working Chamārs and Mochis, and the Bauris who eat rats and revere the dog as their totem because, as they told Colonel Dalton, it is the right thing to have a sacred animal of some kind, and dogs are useful while alive and not very nice to eat when dead.

Islam, whether regarded as a religious system or as a theory of things, is in every respect the antithesis of Hinduism. Its ideal is strenuous action rather than hypnotic contemplation ; it allots to man a single life and bids him live it and make the best of it ; its practical spirit knows nothing of a series of lives, of transmigration, of *karma*, of the weariness of existence which weighs upon the Indian mind. For the dream of absorption into an impersonal *Weltgeist* it substitutes a very personal Paradise made up of joys such as all Orientals understand. On its social side the religion of Muhammad is equally opposed to the Hindu scheme of a hierarchy of castes, an elaborate stratification of society based upon subtle distinctions of food, drink, dress, marriage, and ceremonial usage. In the sight of God and of his prophet all followers of Islam are equal. In India, however, caste is in the air ; its contagion has spread even to the Muhammadans ; and we find its evolution proceeding on characteristically Hindu lines. In both communities foreign descent forms the highest claim to social distinction ; in both promotion cometh from the West. As the twice-born Aryan is to the mass of Hindus, so is the Muhammadan of alleged Arab, Persian, Afghan or Moghal origin to the rank and file of his co-religionists. And just as in the traditional Hindu system men of the higher groups could marry women of the lower while the converse process was vigorously condemned, so within the higher ranks of the Muhammadans a Saiyad will marry a Shekh's daughter but will not give his daughter in return, and inter-marriage between the upper circle of *soi-disant* foreigners and the main body of Indian Muhammadans is generally reprobated, except in parts of the country where the aristocratic element is small and must arrange its marriages as best it can. Even there, however, it is only under the stress of great poverty that a member of the *Ashrāf* or 'noble' class will give his daughter to one of the *Ajlāf* or 'low people,' as converts of indigenous origin are called in Bengal. Of course, the limits of the various groups are not defined as sharply as they are with the Hindus. The well-known proverb, which occurs in various forms in different parts of Northern India—"Last year I was a Jolāha ; now I am a Shekh ; next year if prices rise, I shall become a Saiyad"—marks the difference, though analogous changes of status are not unknown among Hindus, and, as Mr. Gait observes, 'promotion is not so rapid in reality as it is in the proverb.' But speaking generally, it

Social precedence among Muhammadans.

may be said that the social cadre of the higher ranks of Muhammadans is based on hypergamy with a tendency in the direction of endogamy, while the lower functional groups are strictly endogamous, and are organized on the model of regular castes with councils and officers who enforce the observance of caste rules by the time-honoured sanction of boycotting.

According to Mr. Gait the Bengal Muhammadans "recognize two main social divisions: (1) Ashrāf or Sharif and (2) Ajlāf, which in Bengali has been corrupted to Atrāp. The first, which means 'noble' or 'persons of high extraction,' includes all undoubted descendants of foreigners and converts from the higher castes of Hindus.* All other Muhammadans, including the functional groups to be presently mentioned, and all converts of lower rank are collectively known by the contemptuous term Ajlāf, 'wretches' or 'mean people;' they are also called Kamina or Itar, 'base' or 'Razil,' a corruption of Rizal, 'worthless.' This category includes the various classes of converts who are known as Nāo Muslim in Bihar and Nasya in North Bengal, but who in East Bengal, where their numbers are greatest, have usually succeeded in establishing their claim to be called Shekh. It also includes various functional groups such as that of the Jolāha or weaver, Dhunia or cotton-carder, Kulu or oil-presser, Kunjra or vegetable-seller, Hajjām or barber, Darzi or tailor, and the like. Of these divisions, the Ashrāf takes no count. To him all alike are Ajlāf. This distinction, which is primarily one between the Muhammadans of foreign birth and those of local origin, corresponds very closely to the Hindu division of the community into Dwijas or castes of twice-born rank, comprising the various classes of the Aryan invaders, and the Sudras or aborigines whom they subdued. Like the higher Hindu castes, the Ashrāf consider it degrading to accept menial service or to handle the plough. The traditional occupation of the Saiyads is the priesthood, while the Moghals and Pathāns correspond to the Kshatriyas of the Hindu regime.

In some places a third class, called Arzāl or 'lowest of all,' is added. It consists of the very lowest castes, such as the Halālkhor, Lālbegi, Abdāl, and Bediya, with whom no other Muhammadan would associate, and who are forbidden to enter the mosque or to use the public burial ground."

I have described the Bengal scheme of social precedence at some length, because of the curious beliefs and traditions

* In some places many of the Moghals and Pathāns are regarded as Ajlāf.

which it embodies and by reason of the testimony which it bears to the remarkable stability of the caste instinct in spite of the many modern influences which seem at first sight to be sapping its foundations. The scheme deals, moreover, with conditions with which I am to some extent familiar, and it represents an advanced stage of a process which appears to me to be going on with varying degrees of rapidity in all parts of India where Hindu sentiment and tradition are the dominant factors of social development. The extension of railways which indirectly diffuses Brahmanical influence and at the same time weakens trivial caste restrictions ; the tendency to revive the authority of the Hindu scriptures and to find in them the solution of modern problems ; the advance of vernacular education which increases the demands for popular versions of, and extracts from, these writings, and the spread of English education which encourages sceptical tendencies ;—these are among the causes which, in my opinion, are tending on the one hand to bring about among the population regarded as a whole a more rigid observance of the essential incidents of caste, especially of those connected with marriage, and on the other to introduce greater laxity in respect of the minor injunctions which are concerned with food and drink.

Case of Baluchistan.

On the outskirts of the Empire there are two regions where Hindu standards of social precedence and Hindu notions of caste are neither recognized nor known. In Baluchistan, until less than a generation ago, Hindus were tolerated only as a useful class of menials who carried on the petty trade which the fighting races deemed below their dignity. They adopted the device, not unknown in mediæval Europe, of putting themselves under the protection of their more powerful neighbours, and Mr. Hughes-Buller tells us that even now a Hindu when asked to what caste he belongs 'will often describe himself by the name of the tribal group to whom he holds himself attached. Their position generally was extremely degraded, and may best be gauged by the fact that among Baloch, Brāhui, and Afghans there was an unwritten rule that in the course of raids and counter-raids women, children and Hindus were to be spared.' Among the non-Hindu people of Baluchistan the question of social precedence is intricate and obscure and its details must be studied in Mr. Hughes-Buller's excellent report. Of the three chief races the Afghans rank highest in virtue of their former sovereignty ; then comes the Baloch who also once bore rule, and last the Brāhui who were in power at the time of the British occupation. The relative position of the two latter tribes is indicated by various proverbs, by the attempts of the Brāhui to trace their descent to the Baloch, and by the fact that "no self-respecting Baloch will give his daughter to a Brāhui." The test of marriage, however, appears not to apply to the Afghan, who regards the question as a matter of business and will sell his daughter to any man who can pay her price. Below these races come the Jats, a term which seems to be loosely used to denote all sorts of menial classes, including professional musicians (Langahs), blacksmiths (Loris), and leather-workers (Mochis). But even here there is no hard and fast prohibition of intermarriage, and both Baloch and Brāhui will take wives from among the Jats. Within the circle of each tribe a condition of theoretical equality appears to prevail, tempered by personal considerations arising from capacity to lead, religious sanctity, age and kinship with a ruling family.

In Burma caste is so little known that the Burmese language possesses no word for it, while one of the difficulties of conducting the Census of the numerous Indian immigrants is the impossibility of making the average Burman enumerator understand the meaning of the Indian term *zāt* or *jāt*. Differences of religion he can grasp in a vague sort of way, he has a notion of what is meant by race, but caste remains to him an insoluble mystery—a thing with which his democratic spirit, regardless of social distinctions, has no sympathy whatever. Mr. Lowis assures us that there are not and never have been any true castes in Burma, though a class of landed proprietors in Minbu known as the Thugaungs appear to be endogamous, and thirty-six professional groups with hereditary occupations are said to have existed among the Chins.

Distribution of social groups.

No attempt can be made here to analyse and explain the distribution of the 2,300 castes and tribes which have been enumerated in the Census. The mere bulk of the undertaking would in any case ensure its failure; the mass of detail would be tedious and bewildering; while the causes which have determined the settlement and diffusion of particular groups belong more properly to local history and are, in any case, largely a matter of conjecture. In order, however, to give some idea of the facts and to provide a statistical basis for further researches, I have selected thirty-six of the principal tribes and castes and have shown their distribution by Provinces and States in the series of small maps annexed to this volume. The maps are constructed on the principle of graphic representation recommended by M. Bertillon. The strength of the caste to which a map relates is depicted in each province by a rectangle, of which the base indicates the total population of the province, while the height denotes the proportion which the numbers of the caste bear to the total population ; thus the area of the rectangle gives the actual strength of the caste. Most of the names have also been entered in the large map showing the physical types.

Diffused groups.

A glance at the maps will show that some castes are diffused over the whole of India, while others are localised in particular provinces or tracts of country. The typical instance of a widely diffused caste is furnished by the Brahmans, who number nearly fifteen millions, and represent a proportion of the total population ranging from ten per cent in the United Provinces, Central India, and Rajputana to three per cent in Madras, the Central Provinces and Bengal, and two per cent in Assam and Chutia Nagpur. The distribution accords fairly well with the history and traditions of the caste. They are strongest in their original centre, numbering nearly five millions in the United Provinces, and weakest in the outlying tracts, peopled mainly by non-Aryan races, which their influence has even now only imperfectly reached. There can, however, be little doubt that many of the Brahmans of the more remote tracts have been manufactured on the spot by the simple process of conferring the title of Brahman on the tribal priests of the local deities. The so-called Barna Brahmans who serve the lower castes of Bengal probably obtained sacerdotal rank in this fashion. That the priestly caste is not of altogether unmixed descent is attested by the numerous legends of Rajas, who, having sworn a rash oath to feed a stated number of Brahmans, usually a lakh and a quarter, found the supply run out and were obliged to make them up for the occasion out of any materials that were at hand. A similar conclusion may perhaps be drawn from the well-known distich—

Karia Brahman, gora Chamār,
Inke sāth na utariye pār.
If the Brahman be black,
Or the Chamār be fair ;
At the ford of the river
Let the wise man beware !

As with the Brahmans so in the chief functional groups the tendency is towards wide diffusion, and their racial composition probably varies materially in different provinces. Owing to differences of language the maps fail to bring out the complete facts in relation to the whole of India. Thus the leather workers (Chamār and Muchi) of Upper India, numbering over eleven millions and forming twelve per cent of the population of the United Provinces, correspond with the Chakkiliyan (486,884) and Madiga (755,316) of Madras, but the map does not include these. The large pastoral group (Ahir and Goāla) numbering nearly ten millions in Upper India and forming eight per cent of the population of the United Provinces appears in the South of India under the names Gola (855,221) and Idaiyan (694,829), neither of which are taken account of in the map. The same may be said of the potters (Kumhār) and the oilmen (Teli, and Tili) both widely diffused functional groups whose distribution is imperfectly exhibited in the maps. In each province such groups form, of course, distinct castes which have probably been evolved independently.

Localised groups.

Of the localised groups a large number are admittedly tribes. The Bhil, Gond, Koli, and Santāl come within this category and are still outside the Hindu social system. The Doms, Dosādhs, Gujars, Jāts, Kaibarttas, Nāmasudras (Chandāls), Pods, Nayars, Pallis, Paraiyans (Pariahs), and Rājbansi-Koch represent tribes which have been transformed into castes at a comparatively recent date and retain some traces of the tribal stage of development.

Muhammadan groups.

The three Muhammadan maps—Jolāha, Pathān, and Saiyad—are of interest for the light that they throw upon the spread of Islam. The Jolāha weavers number nearly three millions in all, and the solid blocks which they form in the Punjab (695,216), in the United Provinces (923,042), and in Bengal (1,242,049), seem to mark the area in which the lower classes of the community were converted *en masse* to a faith which seemed to hold out to them the prospect of a social status unattainable under the rigid system of caste. The Pathān map denotes a different order of phenomena, and may be taken to indicate roughly the degree of diffusion of the main body of the foreign Musalman element and their descendants. It shows us the sturdy, pugnacious, enterprising Pathān pushing forward from the frontier and establishing himself among the feebler folk of India wherever there was fighting to be done or money to be made. The Saiyad map on the other hand seems to give some clue to the distribution of the upper classes of the immigrant Musalmans.

ABOUT THE EDITOR

Pramod K. Nayar teaches at the Department of English, University of Hyderabad. His works on British India include, *English Writing and India, 1600-1920* (2008), *The Great Uprising* (2007), *Colonial Voices* (2012), *The British Raj: Keywords* (2017) and *Indian Travel Writing in the Age of Empire* (Bloomsbury 2020). He has edited *The Trial of Bahadur Shah Zafar* (2007), *The Penguin 1857 Reader* (2007), *Days of the Raj* (2009), *Women in Colonial India* (5 volumes, 2013), *English Siege and Prison Writings* (2016), *Indian Travel Writing, 1830-1947* (5 volumes, 2016) and *Colonial Education in India* (5 volumes, 2019). Besides these, he has also published extensively on Human Rights and Literature, the graphic novel and celebrity culture.